DOWN THESE MEAN STREETS

DOWN THESE MEAN STREETS

Piri Thomas

VINTAGE BOOKS
A Division of Random House, Inc.
New York

VINTAGE BOOKS EDITION, JANUARY 1991

 Published in the United States by Vintage Books, a division of Random House, Inc., New York, and simultaneously in Canada by Random House of Canada Limited, Toronto.
Originally published in hardcover by Alfred A. Knopf, Inc., in 1967.

Library of Congress Cataloging in Publication Data
Thomas, Piri, 1928–
Down these mean streets.
Autobiographical.
1. Thomas, Piri, 1928– 2. Puerto Ricans in New York (City)—Personal narratives. I. Title.
[F128.9.P85T48 1974] 301.45'16'8729507471 [B]
ISBN 0-679-73238-1 90-50144

Manufactured in the United States of America
10 9 8 7 6 5 4 3

To Daniela, *mi nelin*

AUTHOR'S ACKNOWLEDGMENTS

Richard Leacock, godfather to my book, a man with much heart and a swinging sense of inner beauty.

The Louis M. Rabinowitz Foundation, whose grants gave me the space and time to write my book, *gracias.*

Angus Cameron, editor at Knopf, for his encouragement, patience, and sense of feeling for my feelings.

Oscar Lewis, *gracias con todo mi corazón.* When I most needed assurance as a writer, your letter came.

Harding Lemay, we both have many brothers, *no es así, mi hermano?*

Elaine de Kooning, a real person with a love for all creative people.

Joseph Alvarez, a sensitive man from whom I have learned a great deal.

Isabella, a long-time-ago memory that will live with me forever.

John and Grace Killens. You once told me to keep wailing. I did, baby.

Rev. Rafael Hernandez, Tía Angelina, Pasqualita, Nelo Y Victor, Dr. Efrem Ramirez, Professor Larry Alan Bear, Professor Gordon Jaeck, Reverend Leo Rosado, Roberta Pryor, Dr. Freed, Roy Godes, Marion Godes, Bob Drew, Jim Lipscomb, Pat Jaffee, Bob Jaffee, Peter Powell, Patricia Powell, Wes Pullen, Dave Dugan, Nancy Sens, Jerry Wiseman, Ray Abel, Michael Lawrence, Rev. Norman Eddy, Relia, Carmen, Josie, Henry, Josefa, Pampin.

And many, many others, all my boys, those who made it and those who didn't, in remembrance.

My mother, Lolita; my father, Johnny; and my brothers and my sister.

And most of all, *con todo mi amor,* to Nelin, my wife; my son, Ricardo; and my little girl, San-Dee.

PROLOGUE

YEE-AH!! Wanna know how many times I've stood on a rooftop and yelled out to anybody:
"Hey, World—here I am. Hallo, World—this is Piri. That's me.
"I wanna tell ya I'm here—you bunch of mother-jumpers—
I'm here, and I want recognition, whatever that mudder-fuckin word means."

Man! How many times have I stood on the rooftop of my broken-down building at night and watched the bulb-lit world below.
Like somehow it's different at night, this my Harlem.
There ain't no bright sunlight to reveal the stark naked truth of garbage-lepered streets.
Gone is the drabness and hurt, covered by a friendly night.
It makes clean the dirty-faced kids.

This is a bright *mundo,** my streets, my *barrio de noche,*
With its thousands of lights, hundreds of millions of colors
Mingling with noises, swinging street sounds of cars and curses,
Sounds of joys and sobs that make music.
If anyone listens real close, he can hear its heart beat—

YEE-AH! I feel like part of the shadows that make company for me in this warm *amigo* darkness.

* All Spanish and slang terms in the text are explained in the glossary that begins on page 332.

I am "My Majesty Piri Thomas," with a high on anything and
like a stoned king, I gotta survey my kingdom.
I'm a skinny, dark-face, curly-haired, intense Porty-Ree-can—
Unsatisfied, hoping, and always reaching.

I got a feeling of aloneness and a bitterness that's growing and
growing
Day by day into some kind of hate without *un nombre.*
Yet when I look down at the streets below, I can't help thinking
It's like a great big dirty Christmas tree with lights but no
fuckin presents.
And man, my head starts growing bigger than my body as it gets
crammed full of hate.
And I begin to listen to the sounds inside me.
Get angry, get hating angry, and you won't be scared.
What have you got now? Nothing.
What will you ever have? Nothing
. . . *Unless you cop for yourself!*

CONTENTS

SUBURBIA

DOWN SOUTH

HARLEM

PRISON

NEW YORK TOWN

HARLEM

Pops, how come me and you is always on the outs? Is it something we don't know nothing about? I wonder if it's something I done, or something I am.

1. CUTTING OUT

I had been walking around since 9 p.m. My thoughts were boiling. *Poppa ain't ever gonna hit me again. I'm his kid, too, just like James, José, Paulie, and Sis. But I'm the one that always gets the blame for everything. I'm sorry Momma's gotta worry, but she gotta understand that it wasn't my fault.*

"*Caramba,*" I muttered aloud, "I'm getting hungry."

The streets of Harlem make an unreal scene of frightened silence at 2 a.m. Like everything got a layoff from noise and hassling. Only the rumbling of a stray car passing by or the shy foraging of a cat or dog make the quietness bearable—especially to a twelve-year-old kid whose ability to make noise had got him a whipping from his poppa.

I could see Poppa's face, tired and sleepy, yelling, "Goddammit, can't a man get any sleep around this house? I work my ass off and can't even sleep when I get home. Whatta ya making all that racket for?"

I could feel my mouth making the motions of wanting to say something in my defense. Of how it wasn't my fault that José had almost knocked the toaster off the table, and how I had tried to save it from falling, and in trying had finished knocking it to the floor along with a large jar of black coffee. But I just couldn't get the words out. Poppa just stood there, eyes swollen and hurting from too much work, looking at a river of black coffee. He didn't give me a chance. Even before the first burning slap of his belt awakened tears of pain, I was still trying to get words out that would make everything all right again. The second whap of the belt brought words of pain to my lips, and my blind running retreat was a mixture of tears and "I hate you."

But Park Avenue—Harlem Park Avenue—was scary, specially that dirty stone trestle of the New York Central that ran right down the middle of the avenue making long, gloomy tunnels at each street corner. I watched the moving shadows in the street. I listened to the crazy noises—a fire engine screaming down a side street, the clatter of a garbage-can lid knocked off by a hungry cat, a broad moaning in pain, "Ohhhh, no, please don't." I wondered if it hurt all that much.

The lampposts made a big shadow on the stoops. I couldn't help wishing I'd run away in the daytime. I kept walking. I saw a tall figure coming toward me about a block away. *Poppa,* I thought, and jumped into the nearest hallway and sat down in the darkness and watched the figure pass. I saw the gleam of a badge. *Policía.* I was glad I hadn't been seen.

I had run away from home but not from Harlem. I decided to sleep on the roof of the tenement across the street from my house. The staircase up to the roof creaked under quiet, careful steps. I felt like giving it a whipping for making all that noise. Up on the roof the night air was more friendly. I peeked over the ledge and saw the street below with sleepy eyes and a hungry belly.

I bet Poppa's worried.

All of a sudden a sick feeling of all this being for nothing shot up inside of me. Poppa couldn't be worried, 'cause Poppa was working his night shift and wouldn't know about my running away till he got home from work! I felt my eyes brim with tears. I felt so fucking cheated out of whipping Poppa back with worry. I walked back to the hallway.

"I shoulda waited till he got home from work. Man, what a *bomba!* Well, he'll find out soon enough—"

I heard a noise under the stairs. I froze in the hallway and listened.

"Man, you got that stuff?"

"Yeah. Jesus, I'm burning up like with a *puta*'s fever."

"So work, man. Here, take the *tapita*."

I laid cool. Even my breathing was cool.

"*Coño*, man, cook this shit up."

My mouth began to water. I wondered what they were going to cook. I thought probably these two bums copped some shit out of some garbage can. Man, I was so hungry, I wondered maybe if I asked—but wait a minute, that cat said *tapita* . . .

I saw the light of a match flickering from side to side under the bottle cap. I saw the eyedropper with the shining needle. I watched the junkies' faces, taut, like waiting was the worst thing in the world. The match burned out. Another match popped. The eyedropper sucked up what the junkies had cooked in the bottle cap. One of the cats took his belt off, and this brought a twinge of memory of what Poppa had laid on me earlier. But this belt wasn't for whipping. I saw the belt go around the cat's arm and tugged tight. Another match was lit, and the eyedropper's needle was pushed into the junkie's arm.

"Come on, man, lemme turn on," said the other cat.

"Save the cotton."

"Yeah, man, this is smooth, but we gotta do some better dealing; this five-cent bag ain't enough. Like man, we is strung out."

I heard the change in his voice. The *cura* was taking effect. He was like normal now that the drug was part of him.

I lost interest. I got up, and the scraping of my shoes started a panic. The two junkies jumped up and made it. They thought I was *la hara*—a cop. Their running feet down the stairs made me feel sorry for them. But, Jesus, I was hong-ree.

The bad-o feeling came back. About Poppa not knowing I'd cut out from home, and Momma worrying 'cause she knew. That wasn't fair at all. *Coño*, she wasn't the one that laid that belt on my ass and it wasn't fair that she should get whipped for something she didn't do. So I made up my mind. I made it down the stairs, my feet smashing out loud echoes. I didn't give a shit who heard; I wasn't a runaway any more.

As I came out into the street. I saw the same shining badge. I just kept walking toward him. Man, I was going home. The cop came up to me and passed me without even giving me a second look. After all, a twelve-year-old kid walking the streets at 3 a.m. was a nothing sight in Harlem.

I made it into my building, climbed up two flights of stairs, and knuckled a bold but respectful noise on the door that sounded like a pat instead of a knock.

The door opened and Poppa was there in his undershirt. I looked under his arm and saw Mr. Gonzalez, Mr. Riviera, and Mr. Lopez. There were coffee cups and dominoes on the table, and the radio was playing.

"Well, son, come on in. Don't just stand there," Poppa said, and then he turned and shouted, "Hey, whose turn is it to play?"

"Yours, I think," Mr. Riviera called back.

I slipped under Poppa's arm.

"Go to bed, son," Poppa said, playfully kicking me in the *culo*.

I walked toward my bedroom but Poppa called me back.

"Don't you know how to say hello to guests?" he said.

"*Cómo estás*, Mr. Riviera?"

"*Muy bien*, Piri. *Y tu?*"

"*Muy bien, gracias. Cómo estás*, Mr. Gonzalez?"

"*Bien, gracias. Y tu?*"

"*Bien, gracias. Cómo estás*, Mr. Rod—excuse me—er, Mr. Lopez?"

"Fine, *hijo*. You are up late, eh?"

I pretended not to hear him and looked at Momma, who had been watching me with that "*Dios bendito*, what am I going to do with this boy?" look.

"Are you hon-gree, *hijo?*"

"No, Moms." I felt like crying. All that running away for

nothing. Poppa hadn't even gone to work. He had known about my cutting out and hadn't even worked up a sweat.

I climbed into bed, taking off just my shoes. There was no use getting undressed; I was gonna be up in a couple of hours. I heard Mr. Lopez asking Poppa where I had been.

"What a kid," Poppa answered. "He probably was up some friend's house. I'm gonna talk to him in the daytime. It's too late to make noise now."

Ain't that a bitch, I thought. *Nobody here even knows I cut out from home. I'm getting an ass-whipping for staying over at somebody's house.*

"Whose play is it?" came a voice from the kitchen.

2. PUERTO RICAN PARADISE

Poppa didn't talk to me the next day. Soon he didn't talk much to anyone. He lost his night job—I forget why, and probably it was worth forgetting—and went back on home relief. It was 1941, and the Great Hunger called Depression was still down on Harlem.

But there was still the good old WPA. If a man was poor enough, he could dig a ditch for the government. Now Poppa was poor enough again.

The weather turned cold one more time, and so did our apartment. In the summer the cooped-up apartments in Harlem seem to catch all the heat and improve on it. It's the same in the winter. The cold, plastered walls embrace that cold from outside and make it a part of the apartment, till you don't know whether it's better to freeze out in the snow or by the stove, where four jets, wide open, spout futile, blue-yellow flames. It's hard on the rats, too.

Snow was falling. "My *Cristo*," Momma said, "*qué frío*. Doesn't that landlord have any *corazón*? Why don't he give more heat?" I wondered how Pops was making out working a pick and shovel in that falling snow.

Momma picked up a hammer and began to beat the beat-up radiator that's copped a plea from so many beatings. Poor steam radiator, how could it give out heat when it was freezing itself? The hollow sounds Momma beat out of it brought echoes from other freezing people in the building. Everybody picked up the beat and it seemed a crazy, good idea. If everybody took turns beating on the radiators, everybody could keep warm from the exercise.

We drank hot cocoa and talked about summertime. Momma talked about Puerto Rico and how great it was, and how she'd like to go back one day, and how it was warm all the time there and no matter how poor you were over there, you could always live on green bananas, *bacalao*, and rice and beans. "*Dios mío*," she said, "I don't think I'll ever see my island again."

"Sure you will, Mommie," said Miriam, my kid sister. She was eleven. "Tell us, tell us all about Porto Rico."

"It's not P*or*to Rico, it's P*ue*rto Rico," said Momma.

"Tell us, Moms," said nine-year-old James, "about P*ue*rto Rico."

"Yeah, Mommie," said six-year-old José.

Even the baby, Paulie, smiled.

Moms copped that wet-eyed look and began to dream-talk about her *isla verde*, Moses' land of milk and honey.

"When I was a little girl," she said, "I remember the getting up in the morning and getting the water from the river and getting the wood for the fire and the quiet of the greenlands and the golden color of the morning sky, the grass wet from the *lluvia* . . . *Ai, Dios*, the *coquís* and the *pajaritos* making all the *música* . . ."

"Mommie, were you poor?" asked Miriam.

"*Sí, muy pobre,* but very happy. I remember the hard work and the very little bit we had, but it was a good little bit. It counted very much. Sometimes when you have too much, the good gets lost within and you have to look very hard. But when you have a little, then the good does not have to be looked for so hard."

"Moms," I asked, "did everybody love each other—I mean, like if everybody was worth something, not like if some weren't important because they were poor—you know what I mean?"

"*Bueno hijo*, you have people everywhere who, because they have more, don't remember those who have very little. But in Puerto Rico those around you share *la pobreza* with you and they love you, because only poor people can understand poor people. I like *los Estados Unidos,* but it's sometimes a cold place to live—not because of the winter and the landlord not giving heat but because of the snow in the hearts of the people."

"Moms, didn't our people have any money or land?" I leaned forward, hoping to hear that my ancestors were noble princes born in Spain.

"Your grandmother and grandfather had a lot of land, but they lost that."

"How come, Moms?"

"Well, in those days there was nothing of what you call *contratos,* and when you bought or sold something, it was on your word and a handshake, and that's the way your *abuelos* bought their land and then lost it."

"Is that why we ain't got nuttin' now?" James asked pointedly.

"Oh, it—"

The door opened and put an end to the kitchen yak. It was Poppa coming home from work. He came into the kitchen and brought all the cold with him. Poor Poppa, he looked so lost in the clothes he had on. A jacket and coat, sweaters on top of sweaters, two pairs of long johns, two pairs of pants, two pairs of socks, and a woolen cap. And under all that he was cold. His eyes were cold; his ears were red with pain. He took off his gloves and his fingers were stiff with cold.

"*Cómo está?*" said Momma. "I will make you coffee."

Poppa said nothing. His eyes were running hot frozen tears. He worked his fingers and rubbed his ears, and the pain made him make faces. "Get me some snow, Piri," he said finally.

I ran to the window, opened it, and scraped all the snow on the sill into one big snowball and brought it to him. We all watched in frozen wonder as Poppa took that snow and rubbed it on his ears and hands.

"Gee, Pops, don't it hurt?" I asked.

"*Sí*, but it's good for it. It hurts a little first, but it's good for the frozen parts."

I wondered why.

"How was it today?" Momma asked.

"Cold. My God, ice cold."

Gee, I thought, *I'm sorry for you, Pops. You gotta suffer like this.*

"It was not always like this," my father said to the cold walls. "It's all the fault of the damn depression."

"Don't say 'damn,' " Momma said.

"Lola, I say 'damn' because that's what it is—*damn*."

And Momma kept quiet. She knew it was "damn."

My father kept talking to the walls. Some of the words came out loud, others stayed inside. I caught the inside ones—the damn WPA, the damn depression, the damn home relief, the damn poorness, the damn cold, the damn crummy apartments, the damn look on his damn kids, living so damn damned and his not being able to do a damn thing about it.

And Momma looked at Poppa and at us and thought about her Puerto Rico and maybe being there where you didn't have to wear a lot of extra clothes and feel so full of damns, and how when she was a little girl all the green was wet from the *lluvias*.

And Poppa looking at Momma and us, thinking how did he get trapped and why did he love us so much that he dug in damn snow to give us a piece of chance? And why couldn't he make it from home, maybe, and keep running?

And Miriam, James, José, Paulie, and me just looking and thinking about snowballs and Puerto Rico and summertime in the street and whether we were gonna live like this forever and not know enough to be sorry for ourselves.

The kitchen all of a sudden felt warmer to me, like being all together made it like we wanted it to be. Poppa made it into the toilet and we could hear everything he did, and when he finished, the horsey gurgling of the flushed toilet told us he'd soon be out. I looked at the clock and it was time for "Jack Armstrong, the All-American Boy."

José, James, and I got some blankets and, like Indians, huddled around the radio digging the All-American Jack and his adventures, while Poppa ate dinner quietly. Poppa was funny about eating—like when he ate, nobody better bother him. When Poppa finished, he came into the living room and stood there looking at us. We smiled at him, and he stood there looking at us.

All of a sudden he yelled, "How many wanna play 'Major Bowes' Amateur Hour'?"

"Hoo-ray! Yeah, we wanna play," said José.

"Okay, first I'll make some taffy outta molasses, and the one who wins first prize gets first choice at the biggest piece, okay?"

"Yeah, hoo-ray, *chevere*."

Gee, Pops, you're great, I thought, *you're the swellest, the bestest Pops in the whole world, even though you don't understand us too good.*

When the candy was all ready, everybody went into the living room. Poppa came in with a broom and put an empty can over the stick. It became a microphone, just like on the radio.

"Pops, can I be Major Bowes?" I asked.

"Sure, Piri," and the floor was mine.

"Ladies and gentlemen," I announced, "tonight we present 'Major Bowes' Amateur Hour,' and for our first number—"

"Wait a minute, son, let me get my ukelele," said Poppa. 'We need music."

Everybody clapped their hands and Pops came back with his ukelele.

"The first con-tes-tant we got is Miss Miriam Thomas."

"Oh no, not me first, somebody else goes first," said Miriam, and she hid behind Momma.

"Let me! Let me!" said José.

Everybody clapped.

"What are you gonna sing, sir?" I asked.

"Tell the people his name," said Poppa.

"Oh yeah. Presenting Mr. José Thomas. And what are you gonna sing, sir?"

I handed José the broom with the can on top and sat back. He sang well and everybody clapped.

Everyone took a turn, and we all agreed that two-year-old Paulie's "gurgle, gurgle" was the best song, and Paulie got first choice at the candy. Everybody got candy and eats and thought how good it was to be together, and Moms thought that it was wonderful to have such a good time even if she wasn't in Puerto Rico where the grass was wet with *lluvia*. Poppa thought about how cold it was gonna be tomorrow, but then he remembered tomorrow was Sunday and he wouldn't have to work, and he said so and Momma said "*Sí*," and the talk got around to Christmas and how maybe things would get better.

The next day the Japanese bombed Pearl Harbor.

"My God," said Poppa. "We're at war."

"*Dios mío*," said Momma.

I turned to James. "Can you beat that." I said.

"Yeah," he nodded. "What's it mean?"

"What's it mean?" I said. "You gotta ask, dopey? It means a rumble is on, and a big one, too."

I wondered if the war was gonna make things worse than they were for us. But it didn't. A few weeks later Poppa got a job in an airplane factory. "How about that?" he said happily. "Things are looking up for us."

Things *were* looking up for us, but it had taken a damn war to do it. A lousy rumble had to get called so we could start to live better. I thought, *How do you figure this crap out?*

I couldn't figure it out, and after a while I stopped thinking about it. Life in the streets didn't change much. The bitter cold was followed by the sticky heat; I played stickball, marbles, and Johnny-on-the-Pony, copped girls' drawers and blew pot. War or peace—what difference did it really make?

3. PLAYING IT SMOOTH

Hanging around on the block is a sort of science. You have a lot to do and a lot of nothing to do. In the winter there's dancing, pad combing, movies, and the like. But summer is really the kick. All the blocks are alive, like many-legged cats crawling with fleas. People are all over the place. Stoops are occupied like bleacher sections at a game, and beer flows like there's nothing else to drink. The block musicians pound out gone beats on tin cans and conga drums and bongos. And kids are playing all over the place—on fire escapes, under cars, over cars, in alleys, back yards, hallways.

We rolled marbles along the gutter edge, trying to crack them against the enemy marbles, betting five and ten marbles on being able to span the rolled distance between your marbles and the other guy's. We stretched to the limit skinny fingers with dirty gutter water caked between them, completely oblivious to the islands of dog filth, people filth, and street filth that lined the gutter.

That gutter was more dangerous than we knew. There was a kid we called Dopey, a lopsided-looking kid who was always drooling at the mouth. Poor Dopey would do anything you'd tell him, and one day somebody told him to drink dirty street water. He got sick, and the ambulance from City Hospital came and took him away. The next time we saw Dopey, he was in a coffin box in his house. He didn't look dopey at all; he looked like any of us, except he was stone dead.

All of us went to Dopey's funeral. We were sweeter to him in death than we ever had been in life. I thought about death, that bogeyman we all knew as kids, which came only to the other guy, never to you. You would live forever. There in front of Dopey's very small, very cheap coffin I promised myself to live forever; that no matter what, I'd never die.

For a few days after Dopey's funeral we talked about how Dopey now was in a big hole in the ground till his bones grew rotten and how none of us was afraid of death or dying. I even described how I'd die and breathe my last. I did the whole bit, acting out every detail. I had a kid hold my head in his lap while I spoke about leaving for the last roundup in the ranch house up yonder, an idea I got from a Johnny Mack Brown cowboy flicker. It was swell acting. I ended with a long, shuddering expelling of breath, a rolling of the eyeballs, whites showing carefully, and jaws falling slack amidst cries of "Holy Jesus" and "Man, what a fuckin' actor that guy is!" Then I arose from my flat sidewalk slab of death, dusted myself off, looked around and said, "Hey, man, let's play Johnny-on-the-Pony, one-two-three."

At thirteen or fourteen we played a new game—copping girls' drawers. It became part of our street living—and sometimes a messy part. Getting yourself a chick was a rep builder. But I felt that bragging to other fellas about how many cherries I'd cracked or how many panties came down on rooftops or back yards was nobody's business but my own, and besides, I was afraid my old lady would find out and I'd get my behind wasted. And anyway it was better to play mysterious with the guys at bullshit sessions, just play it cool as to who and how you copped.

It was all part of becoming *hombre,* of wanting to have a

beard to shave, a driver's license, a draft card, a "stoneness" which enabled you to go into a bar like a man. Nobody really digs a kid. But a man—cool. Nobody can tell you what to do—and nobody better. You'd smack him down like Whiplash does in the cowboy flick or really light him up like Scarface in that gangster picture—swoon, crack, bang, bang, bang—short-nose, snub-nose pistol, and a machine gun, and a poor fuckin' loud-mouth is laid out.

That was the way I felt. And sometimes what I did, although it was real enough, was only a pale shadow of what I felt. Like playing stickball . . .

I stood at the side of the sewer that made home plate in the middle of the street, waiting impatiently for the Spalding ball to be bounced my way, my broomstick bat swinging back and forth.

"Come on, man, pitch the ball!" I shouted.

"Take it easy, buddy," the pitcher said.

I was burning, making all kinds of promises to send that rubber ball smashing into his teeth whenever he decided to let it go.

"Come on, Piri, lose that ball—smack it clear over to Lexington Avenue."

"Yeah, yeah, watch me."

The ball finally left that hoarder's hand. It came in on one bounce, like it was supposed to, and slightly breaking into a curve. It was all mine.

"Waste it, *panín*," shouted my boy Waneko.

I gritted my teeth and ran in to meet the ball. I felt the broomstick bat make connection and the ball climb and climb like it was never coming back. It had "home run" all over it. One runner came in and I was right behind him. My boys pushed out their hands to congratulate me. We had twelve *bolos* (dollars) on the game. I slapped skin with them, playing it cool all the way. Man, that was the way to be.

It was hot, and I walked over to El Viejo's candy store for a cold soda.

"Hey, Piri," someone called.

I looked around. It was Carlito, little Carlito, who was always trying to hang around with us big guys.

"Where ya going, Piri?"

"To the candy store, shorty. Wanna soda?"

"*Chevere*, thanks."

Carlito was a good kid. Someday he was gonna go through hell. Carlito was gonna be a junkie, like most of us would be—but that was in the future.

I wiped the sweat from two Coke bottles and gave one to Carlito. I gulped down the coldness—so cold it hurt my throat clear around to the back of my neck. But it was stone good. I whipped off the handkerchief tied around my forehead. I wore this Apache style to keep the sweat from running into my eyes and because it was a kick—it made you feel a little different from the guy who didn't wear it.

Zero, our second baseman, popped his head into the doorway. "Come on, man, take the field," he yelled.

"Okay, okay, I'm coming," I said. I grabbed hold of a glove the other team's outfielder tossed to me and ran down the middle of the street, dodging a car that screeched to a stop a couple of inches from me.

"Hey, you goddamn kid, why don't you watch where the hell you're running?"

"Cool it, man," I said and grinned a screw-you-*amigo* smile. "I was here before you. This is my block, you're just riding through and we're nice enough to let you, *amigo*."

"What did you say, you little—?"

The door of his car swung open—and closed just as fast as both teams suddenly stopped playing ball and everybody all of a sudden had a stickball bat in his hands.

"Hey, *amigo*," I shouted as the car pulled away. "What you say?"

He didn't say anything, and everybody fell out with a laugh kick.

"Come on, *chicos*," I said. "Let's get this game going."

Later, walking home, everybody had some kind of excuse for losing.

"Damn Sam," said Waneko. "We should've won that game."

"Yeah," said Zero. "Everybody played like an old *puta.*"

"Aw, next time we'll waste them chumps."

But we couldn't shake off the gloom of losing twelve *bolos.* My God, do you know what it took to hustle twelve *bolos* between us? Every damn bottle we could steal from one grocery store to sell to another. All our movie money. And all the change we could beat out of our girl-debs.

"Man," I said. "What a ball we could've had with all that loot."

"Aw, fuck it," said Little Louie. "Why crap over split milk?"

"You mean *spilled* milk, *stúpido,*" said Waneko.

"Split, spilled, what's the difference? We lost."

I got to my stoop, and made it into the dark gloomy hallway. I cut up the stairs and pushed the door on Apartment 3 and slammed it shut behind me with a blast.

"Hey, what's the matter with you?" my mother called from the kitchen. She came to see for herself. "*Qué muchacho!* You would think you never learned how to shut a door. Listen, go outside and come in again like people."

"Aw, Moms, everything bothers you."

"You heard me."

"Okay, okay, Moms."

I walked out the door, stood outside for a moment, and then opened the door. I looked at fat little Moms standing there with a very serious look on her face. I turned and very deliberately, an inch at a time, slowly closed the door, my face all screwed up with gentle effort and my fingers curled around the doorknob. I took a long few minutes to get the door turned around and sweet Momma was shaking all over with laughter. "What a funny *morenito,*" she said.

I joined her and we just laughed and laughed. I kissed her

and went into the back room feeling her full-of-love words floating after me.

"Hey, Moms," I called out from the back room. "How come you're so pretty, eh? How come, huh?"

"*Ai, qué negrito.*"

I felt happy. I could hear her softly laughing to herself.

"*Qué bueno* to have a Moms like my Moms . . . umm, *qué eso?* What's smelling so great?"

I walked out in my shorts and came into the kitchen, my face screwed up in a funny face, my nose twitching like a rabbit sniffing. I made like I was floating in the air toward the pots. Ah, I lifted the cover and rolled my eyeballs. I looked out of the corner of my eyes to dig Momma. She was holding her sides, my fat little Momma, tears rolling out of her eyes. *Caramba,* it was great to see Momma happy. I'd go through the rest of my life making like funnies if I was sure Momma would be happy. I stuck my finger in that sweet-smelling pot.

"*Vete! Vete!* Get away from that food with your dirty hands. *Dios mio,* you smell bad, all full of sweat and—"

"Gimme a kiss, Moms; come on, *vente*—a big *jalumbo* kiss."

"Get away, you smell bad, all full of sweat. Go, get in that bathtub and let the water and soap make you soft so the dirt has a chance to come off."

"Aw, Moms, you love me any way I am, clean or dirty, white or black, pretty or ugly."

"*Sí,* you're right, and, my son, I have to love you because only your mother could love you, *un negrito* and ugly. And to make it badder, you're dirty and smelly from your sweat!"

"Aw, look at her." I made a look of disbelief. "Trying to make like I'm not your big love. Ain't I your firstborn, the oldest, the biggest, the strongest?"

"*Sí, sí,*" Momma came back at me, "and the baddest. "*Vete,* soak for a long time or no dinner."

The water in the bathtub was hot and I looked at my fourteen-year-old frame, naked. I was pretty skinny. I should get fatter. Maybe weightlifting would help, like that ad in the funny book about a 97-pound weakling before and after. Man, the water felt good. I ducked under and held my breath as long as I could. It seemed like hours. I was already bursting my lungs when somebody grabbed my hair and pulled me up.

"Hey, whatta ya think you're doing?" I shouted. I could make out my brother James's face through the water in my eyes.

"Whatta ya think, mopey? I thought you were drowning."

I threw some water at him. "Ah, ha," he said. "So you wanna play, eh?" He ducked and turned on the cold water in the sink, filling the glass we used for gargling.

"Cool, cool, James, I was only kidding. Hold that water, man; I can catch a cold. Be nice, James." He held the freezing water over my head. "Come on, man," I added. "Don't play around. Hey, Moms, tell James to stop farting around."

A little drop of cold water hit my back. I crawled under the water and the rest of the cold water came down. Brrr, I almost left the bathtub in one jump.

"James, I'm gonna punch you in the mouth."

"Sez who?"

"Sez me, you little runt." James filled the glass again. "Whatta ya gonna do?" he said. I couldn't help laughing.

"Nothing, brother dear, I ain't gonna do nothing."

"You cop out?"

"Yeah, I cop out."

"You cop a plea?"

"Yeah, man, I cop a plea. Now will you get the fuck outta here?"

"Moms, Piri's cursing again."

"Why, you stoolpigeon," I said hurt-like, "you Puerto Rican squealer."

"Piri," said Momma from the kitchen, "this is a Christian home. I don't want no bad things said inside a house that belongs to God."

"Moms, I didn't say nothing to James."

"You did so say a curse," she said.

"You heard wrong. I said *buck*, get the *buck* outta here."

"You didn't," James piped in. "I heard you say 'Will you get the *fuck* outta here.' "

"Hey, Moms," I yelled out, "did you hear James, huh? Did you hear him? Go on, stoolpigeon," I said to James. "Whatta ya got to say now, huh? Look in the mirror! Hey Moms," I shouted. "Ain't you gonna holler at him too?"

"What for?"

"What *for*, Moms? Didn't you hear him?"

"I didn't hear nothing."

"Moms, you're deaf. James said, 'Will you get the fuck outta here.' "

"Piri, if you going to keep cursing, when your father comes home you're going to get a strap across your skinny behind."

"My God, there ain't no justice!"

I started to climb out of the bathtub to belt my brother. He didn't back away an inch. He held that damn cold glass of water, and we just looked at each other and burst out laughing.

"Okay, man, we call it a draw," I said, and I eased back into the tub. James started to wash his face and hands. "Say, James," I said half-minded.

"Yeah," came a soap-flubbed answer.

"Did you ever notice how when you're in the bathtub and you lay a fart, little bubbles come up and, *blueeee*, they burst and, man, what a stink? Look, look, there's one, two, three, four, five of them coming up."

"Mowoo, whew, Piri, you're rotten, what a stinking smell, let me outta here."

I said nothing. I just looked at his retreat and smiled an I-got-even-anyhow smile. Then I heard all the kids running to meet Poppa at the door. I wanted to run to meet him too, but I couldn't somehow, and it wasn't because I was in the tub. Even when I did run to meet him, I was like a stranger, outta place, like I wasn't supposed to share in the "Poppy, Poppy" routine.

"Piri, have you finished yet?" Momma called. "Your *padre*'s home and he has to take a bath."

Pops, I wondered, *how come me and you is always on the outs? Is it something we don't know nothing about? I wonder if it's something I done, or something I am. Why do I feel so left outta things with you—like Moms is both of you to me, like if you and me was just an accident around here? I dig when you holler at the other kids for doing something wrong. How come it sounds so different when you holler at me? Why does it sound harder and meaner? Maybe I'm wrong, Pops. I know we all get the same food and clothes, anything and everything —except there's this feeling between you and me. Like it's not the same for me. How come when we all play with you, I can't really enjoy it like the rest? How come when we all get hit for doing something wrong, I feel it the hardest? Maybe 'cause I'm the biggest, huh? Or maybe it's 'cause I'm the darkest in this family. Pops, you ain't like Herby's father, are you? I mean, you love us all the same, right?*

My mind kept up the reverie; my fingers absent-mindedly pulling my floating pee-pee into a long string, like a toy balloon when it's empty, and let it snap back.

Pops, you're the best and greatest Pops in the whole world. It's just that I don't dig why I feel this way. Like I can't get next to you. Jesus, wouldn't it be a bitch if Poppa really didn't love me, I thought. But I doubted it. I mean, you didn't have to dig each other to love each other. Maybe that was it. We didn't dig each other so it made me think he didn't love me. But how come he called Miriam "honey" and the rest of those sweet names and me hardly ever? *Miriam gets treated like a princess. I'd like to punch her in her straight nose. I don't care if Pops don't love me a lot. It just don't mean a thing . . .*

The door opened and Poppa walked in. I looked at him and he smiled at me and swooped down and scooped a handful of water into my face.

Jesus, Pops, you really love me like all the rest, eh? Don't you? Poppa pulled the chain as he took a long, long leak.

"Look, Pops, I can stay under water a long, long time. Watch," I said. And under I went. I held my breath as long as I could. I felt my lungs bursting, like they were on fire, but I hadda show Poppa. I couldn't hold out much longer, but I hadda show Poppa. The lights in my head started to spin and I couldn't stay under any more. I exploded up out of the water, sputtering but happy.

"You see me, Pops?" I gasped, screwing the water out of my eyes. "Did you see me, Pops? I musta stayed under five minutes." I looked up happily, but there was no one there. The bathroom was empty. I felt like I lost something, something more, and I couldn't tell the salty tears from the bath water.

I dried myself off, put on my clean clothes, and walked out into the kitchen. Poppa was standing by the icebox. I didn't look at him as I walked toward the back room. If I wasn't there for him, he wasn't there for me.

"Hey, son," he called. I stopped and my back stayed toward him. "I heard you when you exploded out of that water, you sure got a lot of lung power. I bet you could be a great swimmer."

"You mean it, Pops?" I lit up like a bomb. Poppa *had* noticed my show. "You really think so, huh, Pops? I mean I got good lungs. I'm a little skinny but I'm going to lift weights."

Pops was turning away, losing interest, but who cared? I mean, he had a right to be tired; he needed some rest after working for a wife and kids. I couldn't expect him to be mushy over me all the time. Sure, it was all right for the other kids; they were small and they needed more kisses and stuff. But I was the oldest, the firstborn, and besides, I was *hombre*.

4. ALIEN TURF

Sometimes you don't fit in. Like if you're a Puerto Rican on an Italian block. After my new baby brother, Ricardo, died of some kind of germs, Poppa moved us from 111th Street to Italian turf on 114th Street between Second and Third Avenue. I guess Poppa wanted to get Momma away from the hard memories of the old pad.

I sure missed 111th Street, where everybody acted, walked, and talked like me. But on 114th Street everything went all right for a while. There were a few dirty looks from the spaghetti-an'-sauce cats, but no big sweat. Till that one day I was on my way home from school and almost had reached my stoop when someone called: "Hey, you dirty fuckin' spic."

The words hit my ears and almost made me curse Poppa at the same time. I turned around real slow and found my face pushing in the finger of an Italian kid about my age. He had five or six of his friends with him.

"Hey, you," he said. "What nationality are ya?"

I looked at him and wondered which nationality to pick. And one of his friends said, "Ah, Rocky, he's black enuff to be a nigger. Ain't that what you is, kid?"

My voice was almost shy in its anger. "I'm Puerto Rican," I said. "I was born here." I wanted to shout it, but it came out like a whisper.

"Right here inna street?" Rocky sneered. "Ya mean right here inna middle of da street?"

They all laughed.

I hated them. I shook my head slowly from side to side. "Uh-uh," I said softly. "I was born inna hospital—inna bed."

"Umm, *paisan*—born inna bed," Rocky said.

I didn't like Rocky Italiano's voice. "Inna hospital," I whispered, and all the time my eyes were trying to cut down the long distance from this trouble to my stoop. But it was no good; I was hemmed in by Rocky's friends. I couldn't help thinking about kids getting wasted for moving into a block belonging to other people.

"What hospital, *paisan*?" Bad Rocky pushed.

"Harlem Hospital," I answered, wishing like all hell that it was 5 o'clock instead of just 3 o'clock, 'cause Poppa came home at 5. I looked around for some friendly faces belonging to grown-up people, but the elders were all busy yakking away in Italian. I couldn't help thinking how much like Spanish it sounded. Shit, that should make us something like relatives.

"Harlem Hospital?" said a voice. "I knew he was a nigger."

"Yeah," said another voice from an expert on color. "That's the hospital where all them black bastards get born at."

I dug three Italian elders looking at us from across the street, and I felt saved. But that went out the window when they just smiled and went on talking. I couldn't decide whether they had smiled because this new whatever-he-was was gonna get his ass kicked or because they were pleased that their kids were welcoming a new kid to their country. An older man nodded his head at Rocky, who smiled back. I wondered if that was a signal for my funeral to begin.

"Ain't that right, kid?" Rocky pressed. "Ain't that where all black people get born?"

I dug some of Rocky's boys grinding and pushing and punching closed fists against open hands. I figured they were looking to shake me up, so I straightened up my humble voice and made like proud. "There's all kinds of people born there.

Colored people, Puerto Ricans like me, an'—even spaghetti-benders like you."

"That's a dirty fuckin' lie"—*bash,* I felt Rocky's fist smack into my mouth—"you dirty fuckin' spic."

I got dizzy and then more dizzy when fists started to fly from everywhere and only toward me. I swung back, *splat, bish*—my fist hit some face and I wished I hadn't, 'cause then I started getting kicked.

I heard people yelling in Italian and English and I wondered if maybe it was 'cause I hadn't fought fair in having hit that one guy. But it wasn't. The voices were trying to help me.

"Whas'sa matta, you no-good kids, leeva da kid alone," a man said. I looked through a swelling eye and dug some Italians pushing their kids off me with slaps. One even kicked a kid in the ass. I could have loved them if I didn't hate them so fuckin' much.

"You all right, kiddo?" asked the man.

"Where you live, boy?" said another one.

"Is the *bambino* hurt?" asked a woman.

I didn't look at any of them. I felt dizzy. I didn't want to open my mouth to talk, 'cause I was fighting to keep from puking up. I just hoped my face was cool-looking. I walked away from that group of strangers. I reached my stoop and started to climb the steps.

"Hey, spic," came a shout from across the street. I started to turn to the voice and changed my mind. "Spic" wasn't my name. I knew that voice, though. It was Rocky's. "We'll see ya again, spic," he said.

I wanted to do something tough, like spitting in their direction. But you gotta have spit in your mouth in order to spit, and my mouth was hurt dry. I just stood there with my back to them.

"Hey, your old man just better be the janitor in that fuckin' building."

Another voice added, "Hey, you got any pretty sisters? We might let ya stay onna block."

Another voice mocked, "Aw, fer Chrissake, where ya ever hear of one of them black broads being pretty?"

I heard the laughter. I turned around and looked at them. Rocky made some kind of dirty sign by putting his left hand in the crook of his right arm while twisting his closed fist in the air.

Another voice said, "Fuck it, we'll just cover the bitch's face with the flag an' fuck er for old glory."

All I could think of was how I'd like to kill each of them two or three times. I found some spit in my mouth and splattered it in their direction and went inside.

Momma was cooking, and the smell of rice and beans was beating the smell of Parmesan cheese from the other apartments. I let myself into our new pad. I tried to walk fast past Momma so I could wash up, but she saw me.

"My God, Piri, what happened?" she cried.

"Just a little fight in school, Momma. You know how it is, Momma, I'm new in school an' . . ." I made myself laugh. Then I made myself say, "But Moms, I whipped the living —— outta two guys, an' one was bigger'n me."

"*Bendito*, Piri, I raise this family in Christian way. Not to fight. Christ says to turn the other cheek."

"Sure, Momma." I smiled and went and showered, feeling sore at Poppa for bringing us into spaghetti country. I felt my face with easy fingers and thought about all the running back and forth from school that was in store for me.

I sat down to dinner and listened to Momma talk about Christian living without really hearing her. All I could think of was that I hadda go out in that street again. I made up my mind to go out right after I finished eating. I had to, shook up or not; cats like me had to show heart.

"Be back, Moms," I said after dinner, "I'm going out on the stoop." I got halfway to the stoop and turned and went back to our apartment. I knocked.

"Who is it?" Momma asked.

"Me, Momma."

She opened the door. "*Qué pasa?*" she asked.

"Nothing, Momma, I just forgot something," I said. I went into the bedroom and fiddled around and finally copped a funny book and walked out the door again. But this time I made sure the switch on the lock was open, just in case I had to get back real quick. I walked out on that stoop as cool as could be, feeling braver with the lock open.

There was no sign of Rocky and his killers. After awhile I saw Poppa coming down the street. He walked like beat tired. Poppa hated his pick-and-shovel job with the WPA. He couldn't even hear the name WPA without getting a fever. *Funny,* I thought, *Poppa's the same like me, a stone Puerto Rican, and nobody in this block even pays him a mind. Maybe older people get along better'n us kids.*

Poppa was climbing the stoop. "Hi, Poppa," I said.

"How's it going, son? Hey, you sure look a little lumped up. What happened?"

I looked at Poppa and started to talk it outta me all at once and stopped, 'cause I heard my voice start to sound scared, and that was no good.

"Slow down, son," Poppa said. "Take it easy." He sat down on the stoop and made a motion for me to do the same. He listened and I talked. I gained confidence. I went from a tone of being shook up by the Italians to a tone of being a better fighter than Joe Louis and Pedro Montanez lumped together, with Kid Chocolate thrown in for extra.

"So that's what happened," I concluded. "And it looks like only the beginning. Man, I ain't scared, Poppa, but like there's nothin' but Italianos on this block and there's no me's like me except me an' our family."

Poppa looked tight. He shook his head from side to side and mumbled something about another Puerto Rican family that lived a coupla doors down from us.

I thought, *What good would that do me, unless they prayed over my dead body in Spanish?* But I said, "Man! That's great.

Before ya know it, there'll be a whole bunch of us moving in, huh?"

Poppa grunted something and got up. "Staying out here, son?"

"Yeah, Poppa, for a little while longer."

From that day on I grew eyes all over my head. Anytime I hit that street for anything, I looked straight ahead, behind me and from side to side all at the same time. Sometimes I ran into Rocky and his boys—that cat was never without his boys—but they never made a move to snag me. They just grinned at me like a bunch of hungry alley cats that could get to their mouse anytime they wanted. That's what they made me feel like—a mouse. Not like a smart house mouse but like a white house pet that ain't got no business in the middle of cat country but don't know better 'cause he grew up thinking he was a cat—which wasn't far from wrong 'cause he'd end up as part of the inside of some cat.

Rocky and his fellas got to playing a way-out game with me called "One-finger-across-the-neck-inna-slicing-motion," followed by such gentle words as "It won't be long, spico." I just looked at them blank and made it to wherever I was going.

I kept wishing those cats went to the same school I went to, a school that was on the border between their country and mine, and I had *amigos* there—and there I could count on them. But I couldn't ask two or three *amigos* to break into Rocky's block and help me mess up his boys. I knew 'cause I had asked them already. They had turned me down fast, and I couldn't blame them. It would have been murder, and I guess they figured one murder would be better than four.

I got through the days trying to play it cool and walk on by Rocky and his boys like they weren't there. One day I passed them and nothing was said. I started to let out my breath. I felt great; I hadn't been seen. Then someone yelled in a high, girlish voice, "Yoo-hoo . . . Hey, *paisan* . . . we see yoo . . ." And right behind that voice came a can of evaporated milk—

whoosh, clatter. I walked cool for ten steps then started running like mad.

This crap kept up for a month. They tried to shake me up. Every time they threw something at me, it was just to see me jump. I decided that the next fucking time they threw something at me I was gonna play bad-o and not run. That next time came about a week later. Momma sent me off the stoop to the Italian market on 115th Street and First Avenue, deep in Italian country. Man, that was stompin' territory. But I went, walking in the style which I had copped from the colored cats I had seen, a swinging and stepping down hard at every step. Those cats were so down and cool that just walking made a way-out sound.

Ten minutes later I was on my way back with Momma's stuff. I got to the corner of First Avenue and 114th Street and crushed myself right into Rocky and his fellas.

"Well-l, fellas," Rocky said. "Lookee who's here."

I didn't like the sounds coming out of Rocky's fat mouth. And I didn't like the sameness of the shitty grins spreading all over the boys' faces. But I thought, *No more! No more! I ain't gonna run no more.* Even so, I looked around, like for some kind of Jesus miracle to happen. I was always looking for miracles to happen.

"Say, *paisan*," one guy said, "you even buying from us *paisans*, eh? Man, you must wantta be Italian."

Before I could bite that dopey tongue of mine, I said, "I wouldn't be a guinea on a motherfucking bet."

"Wha-at?" said Rocky, really surprised. I didn't blame him; I was surprised myself. His finger began digging a hole in his ear, like he hadn't heard me right. "Wha-at? Say that again?"

I could feel a thin hot wetness cutting itself down my leg. I had been so ashamed of being so damned scared that I had peed on myself. And then I wasn't scared any more; I felt a fuck-it-all attitude. I looked real bad at Rocky and said, "Ya heard me. I wouldn't be a guinea on a bet."

"Ya little sonavabitch, we'll kick the shit outta ya," said one guy, Tony, who had made a habit of asking me if I had any sen-your-ritas for sisters.

"Kick the shit outta me yourself if you got any heart, you motherfuckin' fucker," I screamed at him. I felt kind of happy, the kind of feeling that you get only when you got heart.

Big-mouth Tony just swung out, and I swung back and heard all of Momma's stuff plopping all over the street. My fist hit Tony smack dead in the mouth. He was so mad he threw a fist at me from about three feet away. I faked and jabbed and did fancy dance steps. Big-mouth put a stop to all that with a punch in my mouth. I heard the home cheers of "Yea, yea, bust that spic wide open!" Then I bloodied Tony's nose. He blinked and sniffed without putting his hands to his nose, and I remembered Poppa telling me, "Son, if you're ever fighting somebody an' you punch him in the nose, and he just blinks an' sniffs without holding his nose, you can do one of two things: fight like hell or run like hell—'cause that cat's a fighter."

Big-mouth came at me and we grabbed each other and pushed and pulled and shoved. *Poppa,* I thought, *I ain't gonna cop out. I'm a fighter, too.* I pulled away from Tony and blew my fist into his belly. He puffed and butted my nose with his head. I sniffed back. *Poppa, I didn't put my hands to my nose.* I hit Tony again in that same weak spot. He bent over in the middle and went down to his knees.

Big-mouth got up as fast as he could, and I was thinking how much heart he had. But I ran toward him like my life depended on it; I wanted to cool him. Too late, I saw his hand grab a fistful of ground asphalt which had been piled nearby to fix a pothole in the street. I tried to duck; I should have closed my eyes instead. The shitty-gritty stuff hit my face, and I felt the scrappy pain make itself a part of my eyes. I screamed and grabbed for two eyes with one hand, while the other I beat some kind of helpless tune on air that just couldn't be hurt. I heard Rocky's voice shouting, "Ya scum bag, ya didn't have to fight the spic dirty; you could've fucked him up fair and square!" I couldn't see. I heard a fist hit a face, then Big-mouth's voice: "Whatta ya hittin' me for?" and then Rocky's voice: "*Putana!* I ought ta knock all your fuckin' teeth out."

I felt hands grabbing at me between my screams. I punched out. *I'm gonna get killed,* I thought. Then I heard many voices: "Hold it, kid." "We ain't gonna hurt ya." "Je-*sus*, don't rub your eyes." "Ooooohhhh, shit, his eyes is fulla that shit."

You're fuckin' right, I thought, *and it hurts like* coño.

I heard a woman's voice now: "Take him to a hospital." And an old man asked: "How did it happen?"

"Momma, Momma," I cried.

"Comon, kid," Rocky said, taking my hand. "Lemme take ya home." I fought for the right to rub my eyes. "Grab his other hand, Vincent," Rocky said. I tried to rub my eyes with my eye-lids. I could feel hurt tears cutting down my cheeks. "Come on, kid, we ain't gonna hurt ya," Rocky tried to assure me. "Swear to our mudders. We just wanna take ya home."

I made myself believe him, and trying not to make pain noises, I let myself be led home. I wondered if I was gonna be blind like Mr. Silva, who went around from door to door selling dish towels and brooms, his son leading him around.

"You okay, kid?" Rocky asked.

"Yeah," what was left of me said.

"A-huh," mumbled Big-mouth.

"He got much heart for a nigger," somebody else said.

A *spic*, I thought.

"For anybody," Rocky said. "Here we are, kid," he added. "Watch your step."

I was like carried up the steps. "What's your apartment num-ber?" Rocky asked.

"One-B—inna back—ground floor," I said, and I was led there. Somebody knocked on Momma's door. Then I heard running feet and Rocky's voice yelling back, "Don't rat, huh, kid?" And I was alone.

I heard the door open and Momma say, "*Bueno*, Piri, come in." I didn't move. I couldn't. There was a long pause; I could hear Momma's fright. "My God," she said finally. "What's happened?" Then she took a closer look. "Ai-eeee," she screamed. "*Dios mío!*"

"I was playing with some kids, Momma," I said, "an' I got some dirt in my eyes." I tried to make my voice come out without the pain, like a man.

"*Dios eterno*—your eyes!"

"What's the matter? What's the matter?" Poppa called from the bedroom.

"*Está ciego!*" Momma screamed. "He is blind!"

I heard Poppa knocking things over as he came running. Sis began to cry. Blind, hurting tears were jumping out of my eyes. "Whattya mean, he's blind?" Poppa said as he stormed into the kitchen. "What happened?" Poppa's voice was both scared and mad.

"Playing, Poppa."

"Whatta ya mean, 'playing'?" Poppa's English sounded different when he got warm.

"Just playing, Poppa."

"Playing? Playing got all that dirt in your eyes? I bet my ass. Them damn Ee-ta-liano kids ganged up on you again." Poppa squeezed my head between the fingers of one hand. "That settles it—we're moving outta this damn section, outta this damn block, outta this damn shit."

Shit, I thought, *Poppa's sure cursin' up a storm.* I could hear him slapping the side of his leg, like he always did when he got real mad.

"Son," he said, "you're gonna point them out to me."

"Point who out, Poppa? I was playin' an'—"

"Stop talkin' to him and take him to the hospital!" Momma screamed.

"*Pobrecito*, poor Piri," cooed my little sister.

"You sure, son?" Poppa asked. "You was only playing?"

"Shit, Poppa, I said I was."

Smack—Poppa was so scared and mad, he let it out in a slap to the side of my face.

"*Bestia!* Ani-*mul!*" Momma cried. "He's blind, and you hit him!"

"I'm sorry, son, I'm sorry," Poppa said in a voice like almost-crying. I heard him running back into the bedroom, yelling, "Where's my pants?"

Momma grabbed away fingers that were trying to wipe away the hurt in my eyes. "*Caramba,* no rub, no rub," she said, kissing me. She told Sis to get a rag and wet it with cold water.

Poppa came running back into the kitchen. "Let's go, son, let's go. Jesus! I didn't mean to smack ya, I really didn't," he said, his big hand rubbing and grabbing my hair gently.

"Here's the rag, Momma," said Sis.

"What's that for?" asked Poppa.

"To put on his eyes," Momma said.

I heard the smack of a wet rag, *blapt,* against the kitchen wall. "We can't put nothing on his eyes. It might make them worse. Come on, son," Poppa said nervously, lifting me up in his big arms. I felt like a little baby, like I didn't hurt so bad. I wanted to stay there, but I said, "Let me down, Poppa, I ain't no kid."

"Shut up," Poppa said softly. "I know you ain't, but it's faster this way."

"Which hospeetal are you taking him to?" Momma asked.

"Nearest one," Poppa answered as we went out the door. He carried me through the hall and out into the street, where the bright sunlight made a red hurting color through the crap in my eyes. I heard voices on the stoop and on the sidewalk: "Is that the boy?"

"A-huh. He's probably blinded."

"We'll get a cab, son," Poppa said. His voice loved me. I heard Rocky yelling from across the street, "We're pulling for ya, kid. Remember what we . . ." The rest was lost to Poppa's long legs running down to the corner of Third Avenue. He hailed a taxi and we zoomed off toward Harlem Hospital. I felt the cab make all kinds of sudden stops and turns.

"How do you feel, *hijo?*" Poppa asked.

"It burns like hell."

"You'll be okay," he said, and as an afterthought added, "Don't curse, son."

I heard cars honking and the Third Avenue el roaring above us. I knew we were in Puerto Rican turf, 'cause I could hear our language.

"Son."

"Yeah, Poppa."

"Don't rub your eyes, fer Christ sake." He held my skinny wrists in his one hand, and everything got quiet between us.

The cab got to Harlem Hospital. I heard change being handled and the door opening and Poppa thanking the cabbie for getting here fast. "Hope the kid'll be okay," the driver said.

I will be, I thought. *I ain't gonna be like Mr. Silva.*

Poppa took me in his arms again and started running. "Where's emergency, mister?" he asked someone.

"To your left and straight away," said a voice.

"Thanks a lot," Poppa said, and we were running again. "Emergency?" Poppa said when we stopped.

"Yes, sir," said a girl's voice. "What's the matter?"

"My boy's got his eyes full of ground-up tar an'—"

"What's the matter?" said a man's voice.

"Youngster with ground tar in his eyes, doctor."

"We'll take him, mister. You just put him down here and go with the nurse. She'll take down the information. Uh, you the father?"

"That's right, doctor."

"Okay, just put him down here."

"Poppa, don't leave me," I cried.

"Sh, son, I ain't leaving you. I'm just going to fill out some papers, an' I'll be right back."

I nodded my head up and down and was wheeled away. When the rolling stretcher stopped, somebody stuck a needle in me and I got sleepy and started thinking about Rocky and his boys, and Poppa's slap, and how great Poppa was, and how my eyes didn't hurt no more . . .

I woke up in a room blind with darkness. The only lights were the ones inside my head. I put my fingers to my eyes and felt bandages. "Let them be, sonny," said a woman's voice.

I wanted to ask the voice if they had taken my eyes out, but I didn't. I was afraid the voice would say yes.

"Let them be, sonny," the nurse said, pulling my hand away from the bandages. "You're all right. The doctor put the bandages on to keep the light out. They'll be off real soon. Don't you worry none, sonny."

I wished she would stop calling me sonny. "Where's Poppa?" I asked cool-like.

"He's outside, sonny. Would you like me to send him in?"

I nodded, "Yeah." I heard walking-away shoes, a door opening, a whisper, and shoes walking back toward me. "How do you feel, *hijo?*" Poppa asked.

"It hurts like shit, Poppa."

"It's just for awhile, son, and then off come the bandages. Everything's gonna be all right."

I thought, *Poppa didn't tell me to stop cursing.*

"And son, I thought I told you to stop cursing," he added.

I smiled. Poppa hadn't forgotten. Suddenly I realized that all I had on was a hospital gown. "Poppa, where's my clothes?" I asked.

"I got them. I'm taking them home an'—"

"Whatta ya mean, Poppa?" I said, like scared. "You ain't leavin' me here? I'll be damned if I stay." I was already sitting up and feeling my way outta bed. Poppa grabbed me and pushed me back. His voice wasn't mad or scared any more. It was happy and soft, like Momma's.

"Hey," he said, "get your ass back in bed or they'll have to put a bandage there too."

"Poppa," I pleaded. "I don't care, wallop me as much as you want, just take me home."

"Hey, I thought you said you wasn't no kid. Hell, you ain't scared of being alone?"

Inside my head there was a running of *Yeah, yeah, yeah,* but I answered, "Naw, Poppa, it's just that Momma's gonna worry and she'll get sick an' everything, and—"

"Won't work, son," Poppa broke in with a laugh.

I kept quiet.

"It's only for a couple days. We'll come and see you an' everybody'll bring you things."

I got interested but played it smooth. "What kinda things, Poppa?"

Poppa shrugged his shoulders and spread his big arms apart and answered me like he was surprised that I should ask. "Uh . . . fruits and . . . candy and ice cream. And Momma will probably bring you chicken soup."

I shook my head sadly. "Poppa, you know I don't like chicken soup."

"So we won't bring chicken soup. We'll bring what you like. Goddammit, whatta ya like?"

"I'd like the first things you talked about, Poppa," I said softly. "But instead of soup I'd like"—I held my breath back, then shot it out—"some roller skates!"

Poppa let out a whistle. Roller skates were about $1.50, and that was rice and beans for more than a few days. Then he said, "All right, son, soon as you get home, you got 'em."

But he had agreed too quickly. I shook my head from side to side. Shit, I was gonna push all the way for the roller skates. It wasn't every day you'd get hurt bad enough to ask for something so little like a pair of roller skates. I wanted them right away.

"Fer Christ sakes," Poppa protested, "you can't use 'em in here. Why, some kid will probably steal 'em on you." But Poppa's voice died out slowly in a "you win" tone as I just kept shaking my head from side to side. "Bring 'em tomorrow," he finally mumbled, "but that's it."

"Thanks, Poppa."

"Don't ask for no more."

My eyes were starting to hurt like mad again. The fun was starting to go outta the game between Poppa and me. I made a face.

"Does it hurt, son?"

"Naw, Poppa. I can take it." I thought how I was like a cat in a movie about Indians, taking it like a champ, tied to a stake and getting like burned toast.

Poppa sounded relieved. "Yeah, it's only at first it hurts." His hand touched my foot. "Well, I'll be going now . . ." Poppa rubbed my foot gently and then slapped me the same gentle way on the side of my leg. "Be good, son," he said and walked away. I heard the door open and the nurse telling him about how they were gonna move me to the ward 'cause I was out of danger. "Son," Poppa called back, "you're *un hombre*."

I felt proud as hell.

"Poppa."

"Yeah, son?"

"You won't forget to bring the roller skates, huh?"

Poppa laughed. "Yeah, son."

I heard the door close.

5. HOME RELIEF

In two days I was home, sitting on the stoop with my roller skates. I wasn't blind, and I hadn't ratted on Rocky. I was in like a mother. I could walk that mean street and not get hurt; I was king shit and bottle washer.

As I took my roller skates off, Rocky came over. "How ya doin', kid?" he said. "Wanna go steal some clams on Second?"

"Later, Rocky," I said. I watched his back leave me, and it wasn't too hard to like him. But I still wanted Poppa to move outta this block. I flung my skates over my shoulder and walked up the stoop, thinking Italianos wouldn't be so bad if they spoke Spanish. In the dark hallway I thought how nasty "spic" sounded hand in hand with "guinea." I looked at the roller skates, and I felt a little bad about how I had held Poppa up for them.

I pushed my door open and heard the noises of anger: "Goddammit, woman, goddammit to hell! I can't stand no more of this shit. For Christ sake, can't you understand? I'm just like any other man, one hunk of shit hung up." I was home again. I walked into the apartment. *Jesus, Poppa,* I thought, *you talk like I feel.* I held the thought close; Poppa was slapping the side of his leg.

"Hon-nee," Momma said, and I saw Poppa's look turn to gentle anger.

"Can't you see," he said, "I'm plastered in between Home Relief and the WPA? I'm tired, woman, tired. I'm so goddamned tired of making believe all this shit ain't happening."

Momma looked as always, like she only understood a little of what Poppa was saying in English.

"Poppa, Poppa," my name for my creator came shouting from inside of me. In the other room my sister was crying.

"Goddammit, goddammit, goddammit, goddammit . . ." Poppa hung on to all his "goddammits" like it was the only record in the world.

"Poppa, Poppa," I cried. The shouting had sunk into a copped-out plea of less understanding and more fright. *How can gods like Momma and Poppa receive and give anger that should only belong to strangers?* I wondered.

"I can't take it any more!" Momma screamed. "I can't take it any more!"

Why are you fighting each other from in between your love that is also for us?

"I'm leaving," Poppa shouted.

Damn, Poppa, don't say that.

"Go to hell if you want to," Momma screamed.

Poppa started to walk toward the door, but Momma's fat little body ran by him and spread itself across the lock. "No go," she said in a tone that sounded like love.

Poppa, I thought, *don't you love Momma any more?*

Poppa turned away from the door and ran into the back room, almost knocking me down. I smiled for both of us. Poppa slammed his fist against the wall. The flaky, time-worn wall shook under the pressure of the angry blow. I could almost hear the dust burst from the hundred-year-old wall of paint and plaster.

The rest of us waited in the kitchen, listening to the sounds of Poppa pacing the floor. Then we heard the sound of Poppa opening the back window; he was climbing out on the fire escape. Momma began screaming, "I'm going! I'm going!"

Don't go, Poppa, I thought. *Don't go, Momma.*

Sis began to cry, and I heard my little brother mumble something about wanting a pacifier. *Shit!* I thought. *All this shit going on an' he's buggin' for a fuckin' pacifier.*

"I'm going! I'm going!" Momma screamed. She stomped out of the kitchen.

Damn, Momma, you're wearin' the needle out.

I heard the door open. "Momma, don't go," I called. "Hey, Moms, don't go. Momma!"

The door closed and Momma walked out. I ran to the back room and leaned out the open window to the fire escape. "Poppa! Poppa! Momma's going," I shouted. But the fire escape was empty.

I walked back into the kitchen and put a smile on my face. My sister and brothers smiled back at me. *Oh, you shitty world, why do you have to smell so bad?* I thought. *Why do you make me choose sides?*

About an hour later Momma and Poppa came back. They didn't talk much to each other. Momma made supper for us kids and put us to bed. After lying awake for a while trying to think out some of the confusion of Momma and Poppa fighting again, I went to sleep. Some time later I awoke to the noise of my little brother's crying. Momma came into the room and made some cooing sounds, and the noises stopped. I heard her go back to her room. The bedsprings squeaked as she got into bed, and there was a long silence. After a while I heard her and Poppa talking. It was something about Poppa having lost his job with the WPA. Poppa was saying that foreman or no foreman, he wasn't gonna take crap from nobody. I fell asleep again.

The next morning Momma said to me, "*Hijo,* today you no go to school. I want you to go to the Home Relief Office and help me explain about your father losing his job with WPA."

An hour later we got off the trolley and walked into the ugly brown Home Relief building. We climbed up to the second floor and walked into a room that looked as big as Madison Square Garden and was just as packed with people. Most of the people were Puerto Ricans and Negroes; a few were Italians. It seemed that every mother had brought a kid to interpret for her.

Momma and I walked over to a desk titled INFORMATION. A thin woman sat behind it. Momma pulled her yellow Home Relief membership card out and handed it to the thin woman, who plucked it from Momma's hand without even looking up. She handed Momma a card with a number on it and made a motion with a thin finger where Momma was supposed to sit and wait for the investigator to call her number. Momma smiled at the thin woman; she didn't smile back—one smile wasted. I stuck my tongue out at her; she didn't see it—one stuck-out tongue wasted.

We sat down and started a long wait. I tried to bring my patience to the long-waiting point. I listened to all the murmuring around me—the sounds of pleading, of defense, of anger—and in my mind I broke the sounds into separate conversations:

"But you don't understand, Mr. King," said a woman to a most understanding investigator. "It's not that my husband don't wanna work—it's just that he can't. He's been sick an' he—"

"Mrs. Romero, I understand, but we've asked him to submit himself to a medical examination, and he's constantly refused—"

"He's so proud—my God, he's so proud that even when he should be in bed he just gets up and staggers all over the place. He does not like the sickness to knock him down. When he is well, no man can stand up to him. But now even I can take him back to bed. Mr. King, I do not ask for him, only for the kids and myself. I do not ask for him—he hates you all. He screams, 'I'm gonna get me a gun—I ain't been born to beg—no goddam man was born to beg. I'm gonna get me a gun and take whatever I can get to live on.' "

"Hush-sh," Mr. King said nervously. "He says things like that because he's just overwrought."

I wondered what "overwrought" meant. It sounded like a word you'd use when somebody had split his wig.

"Please, please," the woman said, "my husband is sick. He's sick and proud; don't drive him to death. Why can't you trust him—trust us? We don't want something for nothing. We don't want to be ashamed of being poor. Don't make us. Don't make us."

"I'll see what can be done."

"Aghh," the woman said disgustedly, then quickly added, "No-o, I didn't mean that, Mr. King. Yes, please—try to do the best you can. Try to . . ."

I turned my attention elsewhere. Her pleading was too close to my people's: taking with outstretched hands and resenting it in the same breath.

"What you-all mean, man?" a colored woman asked another investigator. "That Ah'm taking help frum you-all an' hit ain't legal? Ah tole you-all that mah man done split one helluva scene on me an' the kids. Shi-it, iffen that sonavabitch evah showed his skinny ass round ouah pad, Ah'd put a foot up his ass so fast his eyebrows would swing."

"Mrs. Powell," the investigator said impatiently, "we happen to know that he's living there. As a matter of fact, the last time I was at your house, I heard him climbing out on the fire escape while you were opening the door."

"Deah gawd, how can you-all say that? How come you-all can be so suspicious?"

"Very simple, Mrs. Powell. I heard you telling him it was me at the door. I heard him breathing—er, he's a heavy drinker, isn't he?"

"Ah swears to mah mudder, Mr. Rowduski, Ah ain't never seen that man touch so much as a malt beer—leas' not whilst he was livin' wif me. Ah knows he ain't too damn much ta be proud of, but shit, there's a whole lots worstah. 'Sides, he's the only one Ah evah known."

Investigator (not at all convinced): "He's got a car, hasn't he?"

"Caa-ah? Mah gawd, no. Closes' we evah got to a ca-ah was a taxi—an' damn near couldn't pay it. Nah, man; trolleys, buses, an' subway trains are ouah speed. We all mos'ly walks," she added.

Mrs. Powell put up a defense that would have made any trial lawyer proud. But I got tired of listening and started to think of the many times Momma and I had been in Home Relief offices, and all the scenes that had gone down. Like cops dragging screaming parents outta the Home Relief office, and one woman lying down with her three small kids in the middle of the office and saying over and over that if she couldn't get any help, she was gonna live with the investigators until Christ came. (I wondered just how long that would be, 'cause ever since I was a little kid I'd heard He was coming.)

Then I felt Momma pulling at my arm. "*Vente,*" she said, "they just called our number."

I followed Momma to a desk and stood by her side as she sat down at the signal of the investigator's pointed finger. He asked Momma all kinds of questions that meant, "What was the problem?" I broke down his words into Spanish for Momma, all the time thinking about the stiff, cardboard Home Relief checks and how they brought life to many. Then Momma told me, "*Déle que tu padre perdió su trabajo, porque el boss le tenía antipatía.*"

I moved closer to the investigator's desk. Swersh-swersh-swersh went my corduroy knicker pants as one knee brushed against the other. "My mother says that Poppa lost his job 'cause the boss got not to like him," I said.

"I gathered that, son," the investigator replied. "My Spanish is not that great, but I catch a little here and there. Er, ask your mother why your father didn't come with you."

I asked Momma. Momma looked like she was hung up tight, then said something.

"My mother says that Poppa is out looking for a job that don't belong to the WPA."

"I see," said the investigator, and he started to read a stack of papers that had all our personal life put down in good English for all to dig. After a while he said, "Tell your mother that if your father finds a job to let us know."

I told Momma. She shook her head up and down.

"What was it you needed again, señora?" he asked.

Momma said, *"Piri, déle sábanas, frizas, un matre, zapatos para los nene, abrigos y unos pantalones para ti."*

Damn, I thought, *don't beg that* maricón, *don't get on your knees no more, Momma.* But I said: "My mother says she needs sheets, blankets, a mattress, shoes for the kids, coats and a pair of pants for me." Then I bent down and whispered into Momma's ear, "Can I tell him I need some gloves too?" She nodded "yes," and I added the gloves to the list.

The investigator wrote very fast what we needed. I wondered if we'd get it just as fast. When he stopped writing, he smiled gently at us and handed Momma her yellow Home Relief card. "*No se apure, señora,*" he whispered, reaching for somebody else's number.

Momma thanked him and got up slowly, like she was old and wasted (although she was only something like thirty). We went down the stairs and left that ugly brown building. We caught the trolley and watched Third Avenue go by. As we passed Joe's Pet Shop I began thinking about all the business he and I did. Joe gave me a pigeon for every three cans of Home Relief corned beef I brought in. I picked up cans of corned beef that had been chucked into empty lots and garbage cans by members of the welfare rolls who had copped a corned-beef complex and just couldn't think of other ways to cook the stuff. Sometimes I ended up with fifteen cans of the stuff and came home with five pigeons. But even that wore off, after eating pigeon soup, fried pigeon, pigeon and rice, rice and pigeon, and pigeon and pigeon and pigeon.

We passed the secondhand-clothing store, and I thought of all the business that Poppa gave it and all the others like it. It was fun going with Poppa to buy secondhand clothes. When it came to buying clothes, no dealer living could take Poppa.

He knew everything about material, and he knew the prices in all the stores in Harlem. He always got his price, 'cause he promised to send more customers if he got a good deal—and to keep them from coming if he didn't. When the dealers saw Poppa coming, they turned their backs on him.

The trolley stopped on 114th Street and we got off; Momma wanted to go to *La Marketa*. The Market ran from 110th to 116th Street on Park Avenue. It splat out on both sides of the street and all the way up the middle, and there wasn't anything you couldn't buy there. It was always packed with a mess of people selling or buying, and talking different languages. Most of the vendors were Jewish, but they spoke Spanish like Puerto Ricans.

Momma and I walked into the Market. The *vendedores* were shouting that their stuff was better and cheaper than anybody else's, and the suspicious looks on the customers' faces said, "Ya fulla crap." Momma felt some tomatoes, and the vendor said, nasty-like, "Lady, you vant to buy or you vant to squeezing?" Momma kept on squeezing, and every one she squeezed, she bought. Momma never argued.

It was more fun to go with Poppa to the Market. He fought down to the last penny and sometimes came out winning. The vendors seemed to enjoy the hassling. In a bag of apples they would put four good apples on top of a pile of soon-to-rot ones. Poppa called this selling irregular goods at first-class prices. He fought to get first-class goods at the price of irregulars.

Poppa discounted the vendors' friendly "*Cómo estás?*" He said that "How are you?" were the first Spanish words the vendors learned so they could win the people's confidence and gyp them in their own language. I wondered if Poppa didn't like Jews the way I didn't like Italians.

6. IF YOU AIN'T GOT HEART, YOU AIN'T GOT NADA

We were moving—our new pad was back in Spanish Harlem—to 104th Street between Lex and Park Avenue.

Moving into a new block is a big jump for a Harlem kid. You're torn up from your hard-won turf and brought into an "I don't know you" block where every kid is some kind of enemy. Even when the block belongs to your own people, you are still an outsider who has to prove himself a down stud with heart.

As the moving van rolled to a stop in front of our new building, number 109, we were all standing there, waiting for it—Momma, Poppa, Sis, Paulie, James, José, and myself. I made out like I didn't notice the cats looking us over, especially me—I was gang age. I read their faces and found no trust, plenty of suspicion, and a glint of rising hate. I said to myself, *These cats don't mean nothin'. They're just nosy.* But I remembered what had happened to me in my old block, and that it had ended with me in the hospital.

This was a tough-looking block. That was good, that was cool; but my old turf had been tough, too. *I'm tough,* a voice within said. *I hope I'm tough enough. I am tough enough. I've got* mucho corazón, *I'm king wherever I go. I'm a killer to my heart. I not only* can *live, I* will *live, no punk out, no die out, walk bad; be down, cool breeze, smooth.* My mind raced, and thoughts crashed against each other, trying to reassemble themselves into a pattern of rep. I turned slowly and with eyelids half-closed I looked at the rulers of this new world and with a cool shrug of my shoulders I followed the movers into the hallway of number 109 and dismissed the coming war from my mind.

The next morning I went to my new school, called Patrick Henry, and strange, mean eyes followed me.

"Say, pops," said a voice belonging to a guy I later came to know as Waneko, "where's your territory?"

In the same tone of voice Waneko had used, I answered, "I'm on it, dad, what's shaking?"

"Bad, huh?" He half-smiled.

"No, not all the way. Good when I'm cool breeze and bad when I'm down."

"What's your name, kid?"

"That depends. 'Piri' when I'm smooth and 'Johnny Gringo' when stomping time's around."

"What's your name now?" he pushed.

"You name me, man," I answered, playing my role like a champ.

He looked around, and with no kind of words, his boys cruised in. Guys I would come to know, to fight, to hate, to love, to take care of. Little Red, Waneko, Little Louie, Indio, Carlito, Alfredo, Crip, and plenty more. I stiffened and said to myself, *Stomping time, Piri boy, go with heart.*

I fingered the garbage-can handle in my pocket—my homemade brass knuckles. They were great for breaking down large odds into small, chopped-up ones.

Waneko, secure in his grandstand, said, "We'll name you later, *panín*."

I didn't answer. Scared, yeah, but wooden-faced to the end, I thought, *Chevere, panín.*

It wasn't long in coming. Three days later, at about 6 p.m., Waneko and his boys were sitting around the stoop at number 115. I was cut off from my number 109. For an instant I thought, *Make a break for it down the basement steps and through the back yards—get away in one piece!* Then I thought, *Caramba! Live punk, dead hero. I'm no punk kid. I'm not copping any pleas.* I kept walking, hell's a-burning, hell's a-churning, rolling with cheer. *Walk on, baby man, roll on without fear. What's he going to call?*

"Whatta ya say, Mr. Johnny Gringo?" drawled Waneko.

Think, man, I told myself, *think your way out of a stomping. Make it good.* "I hear you 104th Street coolies are supposed to have heart," I said. "I don't know this for sure. You know there's a lot of streets where a whole 'click' is made out of punks who can't fight one guy unless they all jump him for the stomp." I hoped this would push Waneko into giving me a fair one. His expression didn't change.

"Maybe we don't look at it that way."

Crazy, man. I cheer inwardly, the cabrón *is falling into my setup. We'll see who gets messed up first, baby!* "I wasn't talking to you," I said. "Where I come from, the pres is president 'cause he got heart when it comes to dealing."

Waneko was starting to look uneasy. He had bit on my worm and felt like a sucker fish. His boys were now light on me. They were no longer so much interested in stomping me as in seeing the outcome between Waneko and me. "Yeah," was his reply.

I smiled at him. "You trying to dig where I'm at and now you got me interested in you. I'd like to see where you're at."

Waneko hesitated a tiny little second before replying, "Yeah."

I knew I'd won. Sure, I'd have to fight; but one guy, not ten or fifteen. If I lost I might still get stomped, and if I won I might get stomped. I took care of this with my next sentence. "I don't know you or your boys," I said, "but they look cool to me. They don't feature as punks."

I had left him out purposely when I said "they." Now his boys were in a separate class. I had cut him off. He would have to fight me on his own, to prove his heart to himself, to his boys, and most important, to his turf. He got away from the stoop and asked, "Fair one, Gringo?"

"Uh-uh," I said, "roll all the way—anything goes." I thought, *I've got to beat him bad and yet not bad enough to take his prestige all away*. He had *corazón*. He came on me. *Let him draw first blood*, I thought, *it's his block*. Smish, my nose began to bleed. His boys cheered, his heart cheered, his turf cheered. "Waste this chump," somebody shouted.

Okay, baby, now it's my turn. He swung. I grabbed innocently, and my forehead smashed into his nose. His eyes crossed. His fingernails went for my eye and landed in my mouth—crunch, I bit hard. I punched him in the mouth as he pulled away from me, and he slammed his foot into my chest.

We broke, my nose running red, my chest throbbing, his finger—well, that was his worry. I tied him up with body punching and slugging. We rolled onto the street. I wrestled for acceptance, he for rejection or, worse yet, acceptance on his terms. It was time to start peace talks. I smiled at him. "You got heart, baby," I said.

He answered with a punch to my head. I grunted and hit back, harder now. I had to back up my overtures of peace with strength. I hit him in the ribs, I rubbed my knuckles in his ear as we clinched. I tried again. "You deal good," I said.

"You too," he muttered, pressuring out. And just like that, the fight was over. No more words. We just separated, hands half up, half down. My heart pumped out, *You've established your rep. Move over, 104th Street. Lift your wings, I'm one of your baby chicks now.*

Five seconds later my spurs were given to me in the form of

introductions to streetdom's elite. There were no looks of blankness now; I was accepted by heart.

"What's your other name, Johnny Gringo?"

"Piri."

"Okay, Pete, you wanna join my fellows?"

"Sure, why not?"

But I knew I had first joined their gang when I cool-looked them on moving day. *I was cool, man,* I thought. I *could've wasted Waneko any time. I'm good, I'm damned good, pure* corazón. *Viva me!* Shit, I had been scared, but that was over. I was in; it was *my* block now.

Not that I could relax. In Harlem you always lived on the edge of losing rep. All it takes is a one-time loss of heart.

Sometimes, the shit ran smooth until something just had to happen. Then we busted out. Like the time I was leaning against the banister of my stoop, together with Little Louie, Waneko, Indio, and the rest of the guys, and little Crip, small, dark and crippled from birth, came tearing down the block. Crip never ran if he could walk, so we knew there was some kind of trouble. We had been bragging about our greatness in rumbles and love, half truths, half lies. We stopped short and waited cool-like for little Crip to set us straight on what was happening.

"Oh, them lousy motherfuckers, they almost keeled me," he whined.

"Cool it, man," Waneko said, "what happened?"

"I wasn't doin' nothing, just walking through the fuckin' Jolly Rogers' territory," Crip said. "I met a couple of their broads, so friendly-like, I felt one's *culo* and asked, 'How about a lay?' Imagine, just for that she started yelling for her boys." Crip acted out his narrow escape. We nodded in unimpressed sympathy because there wasn't a mark on him. A stomping don't leave you in walking condition, much less able to run. But he was one of our boys and hadda be backed up. We all looked to Waneko, who was our president. "How about it, war counselor?" he asked me.

We were ready to fight. "We're down," I said softly, "an' the shit's on."

That night we set a meet with the Jolly Rogers. We put on our jackets with our club name, "TNT's." Waneko and I met Picao, Macho, and Cuchee of the Jolly Rogers under the Park Avenue bridge at 104th Street. This was the line between their block and ours. They were Puerto Ricans just like we were, but this didn't mean shit, under our need to keep our reps.

"How's it going to be?" I asked Macho.

Picao, who I dug as no heart, squawked out, "Sticks, shanks, zips—you call it."

I looked at him shittily and said, "Yeah, like I figured, you ain't got no heart for dealing on fists alone."

Macho, their president, jumped stink and said, "Time man, we got heart, we deal with our *manos*. Wanna meet here at ten tomorrow night?"

"Ten guys each is okay?"

"That's cool," Macho said and turned away with his boys.
The next night we got our boys together. They were all there with one exception—Crip. He sent word that he couldn't make our little 10 p.m. get-together. His sister, skinny Lena, was having a birthday party. We took turns sounding his mother for giving birth to a *maricón* like him.

Our strategy was simple. We'd meet in the Park Avenue tunnel and each gang would fight with its back to its own block to kill any chance of getting sapped from behind. Our debs sat on the stoops watching for the fuzz or for any wrong shit from the Jolly Rogers.

It got to 10 p.m. and we dug the Jolly Rogers coming under the Park Avenue tunnel. We walked that way too. Macho had heart; he didn't wait for us in the tunnel; he came with his boys right into our block. My guts got tight, as always before a rumble, and I felt my breath come in short spurts. I had wrapped handkerchiefs around each hand to keep my knuckles from getting cut on any Jolly Roger's teeth. We began to pair off. I saw Giant, a big, ugly Jolly Roger, looking me over.

"Deal, motherfucker," I screamed at him.

He was willing like mad. I felt his fist fuck up my shoulder. I was glad 'cause it cooled away my tight guts. I side-slipped and banged my fist in his guts and missed getting my jaw busted by an inch. I came back with two shots to his guts and got shook up by a blast on the side of my head that set my eyeballs afire. I closed on him and held on, hearing the noise of pains and punches. Some sounded like slaps, others hurt dully. I pushed my head into Giant's jaw. He blinked and swung hard, catching my nose. I felt it running. I didn't have a cold, so it had to be blood. I sniffed back hard and drove rights and lefts and busted Giant's lip open. Now he was bleeding too. *Chevere.*

Everybody was dealing hard. Somebody got in between me and Giant. It was Waneko, and he began dealing with Giant. I took over with the Jolly Roger he'd been punching it out with. It was Picao. He had been fighting all along—not too hard, I suspected. I got most happy. I'd been aching to chill that *maricón.* He didn't back down and we just stood there and threw punches at each other. I felt hurt a couple of times, but I wanted to put him out so bad, I didn't give a fuck about getting hurt. And then it happened—I caught Picao on his chin with an uppercut and he went sliding on his ass and just lay there.

I felt king-shit high and I wanted to fight anybody. I had the fever. I started for Giant, who was getting wasted by Waneko, when one of our debs opened up her mouth like an air-raid siren. "Look out, ya gonna get japped," she shouted.

We saw more Rogers coming from Madison Avenue. They were yelling their asses off and waving stickball bats.

"Make it," Waneko shouted. "Them *cabrones* wanna make a massacre!"

Everybody stopped fighting and both gangs looked at that wasting party tearing up the street toward us. We started cutting out and some of the Rogers tried grabbing on to some of us. Waneko pulled out a blade and started slashing out at any

J.R. he could get to. I tore my hand into my back pocket and came out with my garbage-can-handle brass knucks and hit out at a cat who was holding on to one of my boys. He grabbed at a broken nose and went wailing through the tunnel.

We split, everybody making it up some building. I felt bad those *cabrones* had made us split, but I kept running. I made it to number 109 and loped up the stairs. "*Adiós,* motherfuckers," I yelled over my shoulder. "You *cabrones* ain't got no heart!" I crashed through my apartment door with thanks that Momma had left it open, 'cause two or three Jolly Rogers were beating the air inches behind me with stickball bats.

"*Qué pasa?*" yelled Momma.

The Jolly Rogers outside were beating their stickball bats on the door for me to come out if I had any heart. I hollered to them, "I'm coming out right now, you motherfuckers, with my fucking piece!" I didn't have one, but I felt good-o satisfaction at hearing the cattle stampede down the stairs.

"What happened, *muchacho?*" Momma asked, in a shook-up voice.

I laughed. "Nothing, Moms, we was just playing ring-a-livio."

"What about your nose, it got blood on it," said Sis.

I looked bad at her. "Bumped it," I said, then turning to Momma, I asked, "Say, Moms, what's for dinner? Je-sus, I'm starvin'."

The next day I was back on the stoop, slinging sound with my boys, yakking about everything we knew about and also what we didn't, placing ideas on the common altar, splitting the successes and failures of all. That was the part of belonging, the good and bad; it was for all of you.

The talk turned way out, on faggots and their asses which, swinging from side to side, could make a girl look ridiculous, like she wasn't moving. There were some improbable stories of exploits with faggots. Then one stud, Alfredo, said, "Say, man, let's make it up to the faggots' pad and cop some bread."

We all looked at him. He was a little older—not much, but enough to have lived the extra days it takes to learn the needed angles.

"Whatta you cats think?" he said. "Oh, shit, don't tell me you ain't down."

Eyes shifted, feet scratched gravel, fingers poked big holes in noses—all waiting to see who would be the first to say, "Yeah, man, let's make it."

The stud snapped his fingers, as if to say, "Motherfuckers, who's a punk?" Nobody, man. Without a word we jumped off the stoop and, grinning, shuffled toward the faggots' building.

The apartment was on the fifth floor, facing the street. My hand hit the tin-covered walls of the hallway—pam-pa-pa-pam-pa-pa-pam-pa-pa. I was scared, but I wasn't gonna show it. *You know what going down is. You've heard about the acts put on with faggots.* Mother, I had heard that some of them fags had bigger joints than the guy that was screwing. *Oh shit, I ain't gonna screw no motherfuckin' fag. Agh—I'm not gonna get shit all over my peter, not for all the fuckin' coins in the world.*

"Yeah, man, you get a blow job," someone said.

"*Sarito*, ain't those faggots the sickest motherfuckers yet?" I said, but I was thinking, *I don't wanna go! I don't wanna go! Shit, imagine getting your peter pulled like a motherfuckin' straw. I don't wanna go—but I gotta, or else I'm out, I don't belong in. And I wanna belong in! Put* cara palo *on, like it don't move you.*

All the guys felt like I did. Not one of them looked happy. So why were we making it up to the *maricones'* pad? Cause we wanted to belong, and belonging meant doing whatever had to be done.

There was forced happy talk of pot, sneaky pete, smooth music on the record machine, and all the coins we were going to hustle—but no talk about the down payment that had to be made by all of us. I wondered how the fuck I was gonna react. I hoped that somebody would punk out before me so I could slide out too, but I wasn't gonna punk out first.

The pad drew nearer. I climbed the steps to the fifth floor and wondered if hell wasn't up instead of down. We got to the fifth floor and we all walked like backward toward the apartment facing the street. Alfredo put the back of his hand to the door and made a sound. "*Quién es?*" said a woman's voice.

"It's me, Antonia—open up."

"Who ees eet, Antonia?" said another woman's voice from behind the closed door.

"Eet ees Alfredo," said the first voice.

"*Bueno*, let heem in," the voice said.

The door opened and I saw that the women's voices belonged to men.

"Come on, fellas," Alfredo said, leading the way.

The apartment smelled sweet with the stink of women's perfume and powder. I dug the place. It was clean, spotless—like any home-lovin' woman would keep a pad.

"Who are you, frien's of Alfredo?" Antonia asked.

"Fellas, this is Antonia, an' this is Concha, an' the one on the bed is called La Vieja." The first two faggots were boys in their twenties; La Vieja—"the old Lady"—was maybe thirty or forty.

"My name is Waneko."

"My name is Louie."

"Indio."

"Piri."

Antonia smiled and made a sly gesture for us to follow him into the living room. It was a pretty cool living room. There was a record player, a pretty red sofa, and a bar with shiny bottles of high-proof stuff. The lights were red and blue and green.

"Sit down," said Concha.

All us young cats obediently sat down, looking at each other with the swingingest world-wise grins. Antonia put some records on the machine and turned it on. The needle made sharp, scratchy noises as it failed to take hold in the grooves. "Oh, sheet," said Antonia. "Thees needle is for the birds."

Concha made a girl's smile and said, "When needle is no more good, get a sharp one." Antonia giggled. I didn't get it, until Antonia wiggled and said, "The sharper, the better; the longer, the wetter."

Disgust was on all our faces, except for Alfredo's. He tore himself up laughing.

"Anybody wan' drinks?" asked La Vieja from the bed. He was stretched out like a movie queen. All of us nodded, yeah. There's one thing about whalin' on booze—it kills all kinds of bad taste.

The scene continued like it wasn't for real. Time rolled on and so did the drinks. I was gettin' stoned—but I was still there. I listened to the conversations.

"He was like an animal," Antonia was telling Concha. "I tell heem to take eet easy, but that sonavabitch, he pooshed eet in until I think I was gonna die. I trus' him so moch an' I was leetle an' there was nobody else in the house. He was a beeg man. I could not walk for long time without feelin' pain. An' then, after that, every time we was alone, he do eet to me an' teach me to do udder things too. He like for me to put hees thing in my mouth. Thees go on for long time an' then he go away an' I miss what he do to me, so I look for somebody else. I let the janitor do eet to me. He give me mon-nee so I go to his room in the cellar every day."

"You teenk tha's sometheeng?" Concha protested. "I get rape by four boys one night an'—"

"Don't make eet sound so *importante*, beetch," said Antonia. "You can take feefty time that over."

"You no unnerstan'," Concha insisted in a hurt tone, "I haf my period an' eet ees all right for some womans to make love like that, but I no one of them. For me eet ees not comfortable."

If I had had my eyes closed, I would have sworn these were real broads talking.

The whiskey buzz was now in my head and the rest of the insane sounds became blurred without becoming unclear. I closed my eyes and listened to sweet refrains in an unnaturalness without restraint. I smelled sweetness mixed with acridity hanging in the air, the unmistakable, most inhalable smell of all—pot: green dark-dry leaves that have been freed of their seeds. Its pungent, burning smell sticks on you and yours even after you've left it.

"You wan' some?" I heard a voice near me say.

I opened my eye a little. I saw a hand, and between its fingers was a stick of pot. I didn't look up at the face. I just plucked the stick from the fingers. I heard the feminine voice saying, "You gonna like thees pot. Eet's good stuff."

I felt its size. It was king-sized, a bomber. I put it to my lips and began to hiss my reserve away. It was going, going, going. I was gonna get a gone high. I inhaled. I held my nose, stopped up my mouth. I was gonna get a gone high . . . a gone high . . . a gone high . . . and then the stick was gone, burnt to a little bit of a roach.

I got to thinking way-out thoughts on a way-out kick. The words went wasting each other in a mad race inside my head. *Hey world, do you know these mean streets is like a clip machine? It takes, an' keeps on taking, till it makes a cat feel like every day is something that's gotta be forgotten. But there's good things, too, man. Like standing together with your boys, and feeling like king. Like being down for anything, even though you're scared sweat will stand out all over you and your brave heart wants to crawl out through your pores.*

Man! You meet your boys and make it to a jump, where you can break night dancing. You walk down them streets and you feel tall and tough. You dig people watching you an' walk a little more boppy. You let your tailormade hang cool between tight lips, unlit, and when you talk, your voice is soft and deep. Your shoulders brush against your boys. Music pours out of candy stores, restaurants and open windows and you feel good-o at the greatness of the sounds. You see the five-story crumbling building where the dance is happening. You flick your eyeballs around from force of habit, to see if any of the Jolly Rogers are around. The shit's on. But nobody like that's around, so you all make it up the stairs, and the sounds of shoes beating them long, dead wooden steps make it sound like a young army going to war. It's only nine guys, but each is a down stud. You think about how many boys you got an' it's more than you need.

The set is on the fifth floor and the floor is creaking an' groaning under the weight of all the coolies that are swinging. You dig the open door of the roof and smell burning pot. It smells like burned leaves. You and your boys dig each other for the same idea and, like one, make it up to the roof. Joints are pulled out of the brims of hats and soon there's no noise except the music and the steady hiss of cats blasting away on kick-sticks.

Then it comes—the tight feeling, like a rubber band being squeezed around your forehead. You feel your Adam's apple doing an up-an'-down act—gulp, gulp, gulp—and you feel great —great, dammit! So fine,so smooth. You like this feeling of being air-light, with your head tight. You like the sharpness of your ears as they dig the mambo music coming up the stairs. You hear every note clear. You have the power to pick out one instrument from another. Bongos, congas, flute, piano, maracas, marimba. You keep in time with your whole body and swinging soul, and all of a sudden you're in the middle, hung up with a chick; and the music is soft and she's softer, and you make the most of grinding against her warmth. Viva, viva, viva!

Then the Jolly Rogers walk in and everybody starts dealing. Your boys are fighting and you fall in with them. Bottles are hitting everything but the walls. You feel somebody put his damn fist square in your damn mouth and split your damn lip and you taste your own sweet blood—and all of a sudden you're really glad you came. You're glad you smoked pot, you're glad somebody punched you in the mouth; you're glad for another chance to prove how much heart you got. You scream mad and your mouth is full of "motherfuckers!" and you swing out hard. Ah, chevere! *That broke his fuckin' nose.*

Everybody's screaming; there's sounds of feet kicking fallen bad men; there's sounds of chicks screaming "Po-leece" outta open windows. Then the police siren is heard. It sounds like a stepped-on bitch. A blank is put on the rumble and everybody puts the law into effect. The fight stops and everybody makes it outta the place like it had caught fire. We still hate each other, but we hate the cops worse.

Everybody splits and beats it over hills and over dales—and over rooftops. You feel so good that when the cops make it up them five flights, they ain't gonna find nothing but a sad Puerto Rican record playing a sad bolero called "Adiós, *motherfuckers."*

Yeah. But the best is the walk back to the block, with the talk about the heart shown in the rumble, the questions put down and the answers given. The look of pride and the warmth of hurts received and given. And each cat makes it to his pad to cop a nod and have his dreams sweetened by his show of corazón.*Yeah, man, we sure messed them Jolly Rogers up . . . swoommmmm-swoommm . . .*

I came back to my present.

I was still in the faggots' apartment; the red and blue and green lights were still burning. I dug the sounds of Charlie Christian guitar playing. Alfredo was dancing with Antonia. Indio pushed another stick in my hand. I wasted it down to nothing, closed my eyes, and fell asleep.

I awoke because somebody was touching me where only me or a girl should touch. I came back, but my body was still relaxed. I felt my pants zipper being pulled open and cold fingers take my pee-pee out and begin to pull it up and down. I opened my eyes to a shadowy scene of smoke and haze and looked at the owner of the cold fingers. It was Concha.

I tried to make me get up and move away from those squeezing fingers, but no good; I was like paralyzed. I pushed away at the fingers, but they just held on tighter. I tried to stop my pee-pee's growth, but it grew independently. If I didn't like the scene, my pee-pee did. I couldn't move.

I dug the lie before me. Antonia was blowin' Waneko and Indio at the same time. Alfredo was screwing La Vieja. The springs on the bed were squeaking like a million mice. Waneko's eyes were closed and he was breathing hard. Indio's face was white and scared and expectant, but his body was moving in time with Antonia's outrage. I tightened my own body. It was doing the same as Indio's. It was too late. I sucked my belly in and felt the hot wetness of heat. I looked down in time to see my pee-pee disappear into Concha's mouth. I felt the roughness of his tongue as it both scared and pleased me. *I like broads, I like* muchachas, *I like girls,* I chanted inside me. I felt funny, like getting dizzy and weak and lazy. I felt myself lurching and straining. I felt like I wanted to yell. Then I heard slurping sounds and it was all over.

Concha was gone. I was left alone, weak and confused. "Here, babee," somebody said, holding out a stick of pot. I took the pot and got up. I smelled the odor of shit and heard Alfredo say, "Ya dirty *maricón,* ya shitted all over me."

"I'm sor-ree," said La Vieja, "I no could help eet."

"Ya stinkin' faggot—"

I floated toward the door. I had to get air inside me. I heard the last sounds of Alfredo's anger beating out against La Vieja —blap, blap, blap—and the faggot's wail, "Ayeeeee, no heet me, no heet—"

I walked up on the roof and breathed in as hard as I could. I wanted to wash my nose out from all the stink. I felt both good and bad. I felt strong and drained. I hadn't liked the scene, but if a guy gotta live, he gotta do it from the bottom of his heart; he has to want it, to feel it. It's no easy shake to hold off the pressure with one hand while you hold up your sagging pants with the other. But the game is made up as you go along, and you got to pick up what you have or dive out the top-floor window.

I lit the stick of pot. Damn, that whole scene was a blip. I looked over the roof ledge and dropped imaginary bombs on the people below. I felt nice an' high, sailing.

I decided to take a long walk down Fifth Avenue, downtown to the streets of big rich buildings with cool doormen and even cooler rich men. What a smooth idea, I thought, to live right across from Central Park. I tried not to be too jealous. After all, like people said, money wasn't everything—just 99 per cent of living and one per cent of dying. Your insurance took care of the last.

I crossed Fifth Avenue and walked into the wide-open country of Central Park. What a great feeling. I struck out for the hills and picked a cool-looking tree with grass underneath it and lay down under it and chewed up the blue sky through the thick leaves. The afternoon was fading. I felt around without looking, trying to find a nice piece of twig or a blade of country Central Park grass to chew on, just like they do in the movies.

Isn't this boss, I thought, *just lying here, like this was my whole world? Someday I'm gonna buy this here country Central Park—and anybody can come in, but only if they promise not to chew more than one twig or a blade of country Central Park grass. On second thought, not everybody can come in, only people like me. Along with the "No Dogs Allowed" signs, I'll have "Only People Like Me Allowed." I'll tear down the "Keep off the Grass" signs. And while I'm doing this, I might as well tear down the "No Dogs Allowed" and the "Curb Your Dogs" signs also. Maybe I'll put up "Curb Your People" signs. Man, if this is gonna be my country Central Park, I might as well do it up right. Let's see, "No Bopping Allowed" signs, or better yet:*

BOPPING ALLOWED FROM
9 P.M. to 1 A.M.—MON. TO FRI.
1 A.M. to 6 P.M.—SAT.
NO BOPPING ON SUN.
LORD'S DAY

7. LITTLE RED SCHOOLHOUSE

When you're a kid, everything has some kind of special meaning. I always could find something to do, even if it was doing nothing. But going to school was something else. School stunk. I hated school and all its teachers. I hated the crispy look of the teachers and the draggy-long hours they took out of my life from nine to three-thirty. I dug being outside no matter what kind of weather. Only chumps worked and studied.

Every day began with a fight to get me out of bed for school. Momma played the same record over an' over every day: "Piri, get up, it's time to go to school." And I played mine: "Aw, Moms, I don't feel so good. I think I got a fever or something."

Always it ended up the same old way: I got up and went to school. But I didn't always stay there. Sometimes, I reported for class, let my teacher see me and then began the game of sneaking out of the room. It was like escaping from some kind of prison. I waited for the teacher to turn her back, then I slipped out of my seat and, hugging the floor, crawled on my belly toward the door. The other kids knew what I was doing; they were trying not to burst out laughing. Sometimes a wise guy near me made a noise to bring the teacher's attention my way. When this happened, I lay still between the row of desks until the teacher returned to whatever he or she had been doing.

I sneaked my way to the door, eased it open and—swoom! —I was on my way. It was a great-o game, slipping past the other classes and ducking the other teachers or monitors.

One class I didn't dig at all was the so-called "Open Air Class" for skinny, "underweight" kids. We had to sleep a couple of half hours every day, and we got extra milk and jelly and peanut butter on brown bread. The teacher, Miss Shepard, was like a dried-up grape. One day I raised my hand to go to the toilet, but she paid me no mind. After a while, the pain was getting bad, so I called out, "Miss Shepard, may I leave the room?"

She looked up and just shook her head, no.

"But I gotta go, Miss Shepard."

"You just went a little while ago," she said.

"I know, Miss Shepard, but I gotta go again."

"I think it's sheer nonsense," said the old bitch. "You just want an excuse to play around in the hallways."

"No, ma'am, I just wanna take a piss."

"Well, you can't go."

I had to go so badly that I felt the tears forming in the corners of my eyes to match the drops that were already making a wet scene down my leg. "I'm goin' anyway," I said, and started toward the door.

Miss Shepard got up and screamed at me to get back to my seat. I ignored her.

"Get back to your seat, young man," she screamed. "Do you hear me? Get right back—"

"Fuck you," I mumbled. I reached the door and felt her hands grab out at me and her fingers hook on to the back of my shirt collar. My clean, washed-a-million-times shirt came apart in her hand.

I couldn't see her face clearly when I turned around. All I

could think about was my torn shirt and how this left me with only two others. All I could see was her being the cause of the dampness of my pants and hot pee running down my leg. All I could hear was the kids making laughing sounds and the anger of my being ashamed. I didn't think of her as a woman, but as something that had to be hit. I hit it.

"Ohhhhhh, you *struck* me," she cried, in surprise as much as pain.

I thought, *I did not, you fuckin' liar. I just hit you.*

"You struck me! You *struck* me! Oh, help, help!" she cried.

I cut out. Man, I ran like hell into the hallway, and she came right after me, yelling, "Help, help!" I was scared now and all I could think about was getting back to my Moms, my home, my block, where no one could hurt me. I ran toward the stairway and found it blocked off by a man, the principal. I cut back toward the back stairs.

"Stop him! Stop him!" dear Miss Shepard yelled, pointing her finger at me. "He struck me, he struck me."

I looked over my shoulder and saw the principal talk to her for a hot second and then take off after me, yelling: "Stop! Stop!" I hit the stairs and went swooming down like it was all one big step. The principal was fast and I could hear him swearing right behind me. I slammed through the main-floor door that led to the lunchroom and jumped over benches and tables, trying like hell to make the principal trip and break a leg. Then I heard a muted cry of pain as a bench caught him in the shin. I looked over my shoulder and I dug his face. The look said that he was gonna hit me; that he wasn't gonna listen to my side of the story; that I had no side. I figured I better not get caught.

I busted my legs running toward the door that led to the outside and freedom, and with both hands out in front of me I hit the brass bar that opens the door. Behind me I heard a thump as the principal smacked into it. I ran down the block, sneaking a look behind me. The principal was right behind me, his face redder and meaner. People were looking at the uneven contest.

I tore into my hallway, screaming as loud as I could for help. The apartment doors opened up, one right after another. Heads of all colors popped out. "*Qué pasa?*" asked a Puerto Rican woman. "Wha's happenin'?" said a colored lady.

"They wanna beat me up in school and that's one of them," I puffed, pointing at the principal, who was just coming into view.

"Hooo, ain't nobody gonna hurt you, sonny," said the colored lady, whose name was Miss Washington. She gently pushed me behind her with one hand and with the other held it out toward the principal roaring down at us.

The principal, blocked by Miss Washington's 280 pounds and a look of "Don't you touch that boy," stopped short and puffed out, "That—that—kid—he—punched a teacher and—he's got to be chastised for it. After all, school disci—"

"Now hol' on, white man," Miss Washington interrupted. "There ain't nobody gonna chaz—whatever it is—this boy. I knows him an' he's a good boy—at least good for what comes outta this heah trashy neighborhood—an' you ain't gonna do nuttin' to him, unless you-all wan's to walk over me."

Miss Washington was talking real bad-like. I peeked out from behind that great behind.

"Madam, I assure you," the principal said, "I didn't mean harming him in a bodily manner. And if you knew the whole issue, you would agree with me that he deserves being chastised. As principal of his school, I have his best interest at heart. Ha, ha, ha," he added, "you know the old saying, madam, 'A stitch in time saves nine.' Ha, ha, ha—*ahurmph.*"

I could see him putting that stitch in my head.

"I assure you, madam," he continued, smilingly pretty, "we have no intention of doing him bodily harm."

Once again I peeked out from behind Miss Washington's behind. "Yeah, that's what you say," I said. "How about alla time you take kids down to your office for some crap and ya start poking 'em with that big finger of yours until they can't take it any more?"

There were a lot of people in the hall by this time. They were all listening, and I knew it. "Yeah, ask any of the kids," I added. "They'll tell ya." I looked sorry-like at the crowd of people, who were now murmuring mean-like and looking at the principal like he didn't have long on this earth.

Smelling a Harlem lynch party in the making, I said, "An'—you—ain't—gonna—do—it—to—me. I'll get me a forty-five an'—"

"Hush you mouth, boy," Miss Washington said; "don't be talkin' like that. We grownups will get this all straightened out. An' nobody's gonna poke no finger in your chest"—she looked dead at the principal—"is they?"

The principal smiled the weakest smile in this smiling world. "I—I—I—er, assure you, madam, this young man is gifted with the most wonderful talent for prevarication I've ever seen."

"What's that mean?" Miss Washington asked suspiciously.

"Er, it means a good imagination, madam. A-ha-ha—yes, *a-hurmph.*"

"That's a lie, Miss Washington," I said. "He's always telling the kids that. We asked Mrs. Wagner, the history teacher, and she said it means to lie. Like he means I'm a liar."

The look in the principal's eye said, "Oh, you smarty pants bastard," but he just smiled and said nothing.

Miss Washington said, "Iffen thar's any pokin' ta be done, we all heah is gonna do it," and she looked hard at the principal. The crowd looked hard at the principal. Hard sounds were taking forms, like, "So this is the way they treat our kids in school?" and "What you-all expect? These heah white people doan give a damn," and "If they evah treats mah boy like that, I'd . . ."

The principal, smiling softly, began backing up.

I heard Momma's voice: "Piri, Piri, *qué pasa?*"

"Everything all right, Mis' Thomas," Miss Washington

assured her. "This heah man was tryin' to hit your son, but ain't, 'cause I'll break his damn head wide open." Miss Washington shifted her weight forward. "Damn, Ah got a good mind to do it right now," she added.

The principal, remembering the bit about discretion being the better part of valor, split.

Everyone tried to calm Moms down. I felt like everybody there was my family. I let Momma lead me upstairs to our apartment. Everyone patted me on the head as we went by.

"You're going to school with your *padre* in the morning," Momma said.

"Uh-uh, Moms," I said. "That principal will stomp my chest in with that finger of his."

"No he won't, *muchacho*. Your father will go with you an' everything will be fixed up."

I just nodded my head and thought how great it would be if Miss Washington could go with me.

8. IN BUSINESS

Living in number 109 was snap breeze. I knew practically everybody on the block and, if I didn't, they knew me. When I went to the barbershop, José the barber would ask me, "Shape up or trim?" He liked to trim because in three hot minutes he could earn fifty cents. But I always gave him a hard way to shovel and said, "Give me the works with a square back." "*Ay coño,*" he groaned and started to cut hair and breathe bad breath on me, on spite, while I ignored him on spite.

Just being a kid, nothing different from all the other kids, was good. Even when you slept over at some other kid's house, it was almost like being in your own house. They all had kids, rats, and roaches in common. And life was full of happy moments—spitting out of tenement windows at unsuspecting people below, popping off with sling shots, or even better, with Red Ryder BB rifles, watching the neighbors fight through their open windows or make love under half-drawn shades.

The good kick in the hot summer was to sleep on the fire escape. Sometimes I lay awake all night and thought about all the things I would do when I grew up, about the nice duds I'd have like a champ uptown and come back around the block and treat all the kids to *cuchifritos* and pour tons of nickels into the jukebox and help anybody that was in trouble, from a junkie to a priest. I dreamed big; it didn't cost anything.

In the morning I stood on Lexington Avenue in Spanish Harlem, one finger poked through my pants pocket, scratching myself, while I droned, "Shine, mister—good shine, only fifteen cents. Shine, mister . . ." It was hard to shine shoes and harder to keep my corner from getting copped by an early-rising shine boy. I had to be prepared to mess a guy up; that corner spot wasn't mine alone. I had to earn it every time I shined shoes there.

When I got a customer, we both played our roles. The customer, tall and aloof, smiled, "Gimme a shine, kid," and I replied, "*Sí, señor,* sir, I'll give you one that you'll have to put sunglasses on to eat the bright down."

My knees grinding against the gritty sidewalk, I adopted a serious, businesslike air. Carefully, but confidently, I snaked out my rags, polish, and brushes. I gave my cool breeze customer the treatment. I rolled his pants cuff up—"That'll keep shoe polish off"—straightened his socks, patted his shoe, assured him he was in good hands, and loosened and retied his shoes. Then I wiped my nose with a delicate finger, picked up my shoe brush, and scrunched away the first hard crust of dirt. I opened my bottle of black shoe cleaner—dab, rub in, wipe off, pat the shoe down. Then I opened my can of polish—dab on with three fingers, pat-a-pid, pat-a-pid. He's not looking—spit on the shoe, more polish, let it dry, tap the bottom of his sole, smile up at Mr. Big Tip (you hope), "Next, sir."

I repeated the process on the other shoe, then picked up my brush and rubbed the bristles very hard against the palm of my hand, scientific-like, to warm the brush hairs up so they would melt the black shoe wax and give a cool unlumpy shine. I peeked out of the corner of my eye to see if Mr. Big Tip was watching my modern shoeshine methods. The bum *was* looking. I hadn't touched his shoe, forcing him to look.

The shoe began to gleam dully—more spit, more polish, more brush, little more spit, little more polish, and a lotta rag. I repeated on the other shoe. As Mr. Big Tip started digging in his pocket, I prepared for the climax of my performance.

Just as he finished saying, "Damn nice shine, kid," I said, "Oh, I ain't finished, sir. I got a special service," and I plunged my wax-covered fingers into a dark corner of my shoe box and brought out a bottle of "Special shoe lanolin cream for better preservation of leather."

I applied a dab, a tiny dab, pausing long enough to say very confidently, "You can't put on too much or it'll spoil the shine. It gotta be just right." Then I grabbed the shoe rag firmly, like a maestro with a baton, and hummed a rhythm with it, slapping out a happy beat on the shoes. A final swish here and there, and *mira!*—finished. Sweating from the effort of my creation, I slowly rose from my knees, bent from the strain, my hand casually extended, palm flat up, and murmured, "Fifteen cents, sir," with a look that said, "But it's worth much more, don't you think?" Mr. Big Tip dropped a quarter and a nickel into the offering plate, and I said, "Thanks a mil, sir," thinking, *Take it cool,* as I cast a watchful eye at his retreating back.

But wasn't it great to work for a living? I calculated how long it would take to make my first million shining shoes. Too long. I would be something like 987 years old. Maybe I could steal it faster.

In Harlem stealing was like natural—and usually a partnership deal. Some of the scores came off like to meet conditions. Like the lemonade syndicate which we started one hot summer day. All of Harlem was melting under the fire of the sun. The stoops and fire escapes groaned under the weight of sweat-drenched humans looking for a way out of their ovenlike pads. We were sitting on the stoop of number 109 reading comic books when Little Louie said, "Hey, dig what it says in the funny book about these kids setting up lemonade stands and—"

"Making money?" I asked.

"Yeah."

"Come on, let's go."

"Where to, Piri?"

"Make money."

"How?"

"You dope, like in the funny book. Let's sell lemonade."

"We ain't got no dough to buy the stuff with."

"Okay, how much we got between us?"

Eight guys searched themselves and came up with fourteen cents between them.

"Aw, we can't make it," said Little Louie.

"Oh yeah we can. Dig, we all go over to the A & P."

"Yeah, and what?"

"Well, it's self-service, ain't it, so we buy a pound of sugar, and cop all the Kool-ade and lemons on the side. Man! You know how much Kool-ade and lemons eight cats can cop?"

"Yeah, but . . ."

"But what?"

"But a poundo' sugar ain't gonna be enough."

"Okay, okay, so we buy two bags of kool-ade and cop as much sugar as we can, along with the resto' the stuff. But let's make it up to our pads and put on some jackets, 'cause five pound bags of sugar sure are gonna show under our tee shirts."

A few minutes later eight guys sweating under their jackets with the club name "TNT's" shining on them walked into the A & P one at a time. We all quickly gained weight in the shape of five-pound bags of sugar and packages of Kool-ade hidden under our jackets. "Come on, *panins*," I said, "Let's make it."

"Hey," Crip asked, "ain't you gonna pay for them bags of Kool-ade?"

"Naw, if we cop a steal, we might as well go all the way."

Everything was going great, until Little Louie, his pockets bulging with Kool-ade packs and lemons and a five-pound bag of sugar, decided to cop a glass pitcher.

"Hey you, kid! Drop that!" the manager yelled.

All us kids stopped dead. Then we saw the manager bearing down on Little Louie.

"Cut out, fellas!" I shouted, and everybody was on his own. Some of the guys lost their sugar, and packs of Kool-ade were strewn all over the store, but nobody got snagged. Back on the block, we made it to the back yard and counted what we had copped.

"How much stuff we got, Piri?"

"Well, let's see . . . fourteen, seventeen, twenty-four, twenty-seven—twenty-seven packs of Kool-ade, fourteen lemons, and five bags of sugar, five pounds each."

"And one glass pitcher," added Little Louie.

"Yeah," I said, "we almost blew the jewels behind your copping that." But we all smiled, and Little Louie felt great. Why not? He was the only one that copped a glass pitcher, besides the other stuff, so he was one up on us. It was like doing something above and beyond the call of duty, just like in the war flicks.

"Okay, let's go," I said. "We're in business."

An hour later, there were four lemonade stands spread throughout the block with two cats to each stand, and we made business. So much so that, at five cents a large glass, we soon sold out. We got together and counted our gold.

"Man! It sure looks like a lot."

"Yeah, we got $4.75, $5.25, $8—man! we got $8.35, $8.37!"

"$8.37? How come it came out $8.37?" Crip asked. "We were selling at a nickel a glass."

"Oh, that was me," said Little Louie. "My girl only had two cents, so I sold her half a glass."

"Well, don't let it happen again," I said. "A nickel or nuttin'."

"Man, but that was my girl—"

"Okay, just our girls, and we can give them a whole glass for two cents, okay?"

"Yeah," says everybody, "that's *chevere.*"

"Okay, what's next?"

"Well, we're outta Kool-ade and stuff," I said, "so we better get some more."

"Yeah," said Waneko. "We can afford to buy the stuff now."

"Do what!" I said. "Man, you getting low or something? That'll eat up the profits."

"Yeah, ain't they got another A & P uptown some place?" Little Louie said pointedly, and within minutes eight young businessmen sneaked under the turnstile of the subway at 103rd Street and Lexington Avenue, on the uptown side.

But the lemonade syndicate, like copping milk bottles, was nickel and dime. We dreamed of bigger scores. One day I was in the grocery with Little Louie and Crip. I was buying something for Momma—on credit, as usual. I saw the groceryman quickly shove a paper bag down into a big burlap bag of rice. He didn't think anybody saw him.

The *bodega* was a drop-off for the *bolita* runners, and I figured the day's bread was in that bag. That was a lot of *dinero*. I nudged Louie, "Hey, man, dig that?" I whispered. He had seen it, too; we both played it cool.

Outside we made plans to cop that bag. This would be a real score—Coney Island, movies, food, girls—man, the works. Around one a.m. the next day we pried a couple of bars off the window in the back of the store. Three of us went in for the bread; Crip stayed behind to play chicky.

Once inside the store we decided we may as well make the whole scene—cigarettes, candy, the cash register, everything.

"Hurry up, man," Crip called from outside. "The fuzz may be coming around any minute."

"Cool it, man, we're almost finished," I whispered back. We found $40 in the cash register. *Now let's look in that bag of rice,* I thought. "Hey, Louie," I whispered as I dug into a hundred-pound bag of rice and beans, "plenty of rice and beans for the Marine Tigers."

"*Coño,* hurry up!" Crip called.

Jesus! I thought, *he's scared to death. I wonder why the fuck he came in the first place. If anything brings the fuzz, it's gonna be his knocking knees.*

"Hey, is the back window open?" Louie asked.

"Yeah," I answered.

"Groovy," came the reply.

"Hey, *panitas!*" came the urgent cry from Crip, "here comes the fuzz. I'm making it." And he was gone.

"*Caramba!*" I choked out, "those cops are bound to see him running and put one and one together. Let's get out of here!"

We scrambled out through the back window, slid down the drainpipe, and cut out. Louie had dropped the cigarettes, and I had left the cash drawer open. How many clues could three fifteen-year-old burglars leave? As we ran out, I thought, *We can't lose ourselves in no crowds at two in the morning, and we're two blocks from home.* I could imagine the fuzz shining their flashlights through that store door, and digging the smokes all over the floor and the cash drawers open. I could see them making it to the back window, digging the pried-out bars. Right about now they'd be cruising the area looking for suspicious-looking cats like us.

We caught up to Crip.

"Stay in the shadows, man," I whispered to Louie and Crip, "and don't make no loud walking noises."

But Louie had steel taps on his shoes, and every step he took made a click-clack, click-clack.

"For God's sake, Louie," I said, "take off those shoes."

Crip froze. "There they are!" he said, pointing to a police car coming up the street.

We melted into a dark alley with a high fence and watched the pretty red light on top of the car as it went around and around. I felt hypnotized, like in the flicks at the movie house. Like in the jungle pictures, where the big snake's head moves around and around, and whoever he's diggin' gets froze.

"Whatta we gonna do?" Crip said. "Man, whatta we do?"

"Hey!" yelled one of the fuzzes, "there's somebody in that alley!"

"Shine the light."

"Yeah, just a minute."

I scraped my eyesight through that black alley and measured

that fence, almost twice as high as me. *I'll try it,* I thought. *I got my sneakers and I'm good. I can run, jump, split better than most. And if I can make that fence, they'll be looking for their mothers all night.*

"Let's try for that fence, *panitas,*" I said.

"I can't make it," said Louie. "I'm gonna try it out the front. Once I'm out there, only a fuckin' bullet is gonna catch me."

"Jesus, I'm scared as hell," Crip said.

"Punk," I said; but I was scared too.

"Okay," Crip said, "I'm down, Piri, I'll go for the fence, too."

The light from the patrol car shone in the alley. It was like the world was all day. Louie split it down the street, putting down shoe leather and picking up gravel.

"There goes one!" yelled the fuzz.

"Now," I whispered, and swoom! I ran at that fence like I was going right through it, like Superman. I scrambled up the side and, thank God, my fingers found the top and I hoisted myself over. I heard a shot and I thought, *Hey, cops, you're supposed to say, "Halt in the name of the law." You ain't playing fair, fuckos.*

I dropped to the other side and I listened for Crip. I heard the cops yelling and Crip's running feet, then the crash of garbage cans. I peeked through a hole. Crip had tripped over a garbage can. The fuzzes were coming into the alley. Crip got up to make another try. *Fly, Crip, oh sweet shit! fly, Crip*—but he didn't have enough running space. Crip's feet left the ground, and I felt the smashing of his body as he crunched against the fence, falling short of the top.

I felt him lying on the ground, and I heard him breathing hard. He was crying. Not because he was afraid, but because he didn't know how to fly.

"Don't move, kid," the fuzz told him.

I started to run. "Crip," I yelled, "don't talk. You're a minor, dig it? You're a minor!"

"I got the other one," said a cop's voice. "That makes two."

I ran through dark yards and over rooftops and climbed fences and fire escapes, all the time crying. I felt the wet tears making salt in my mouth. I felt like I was in a war and I had lost my two best buddies. "The bastard fuzz," I said aloud. "I should've stayed there with Crip and Louie. I should've thrown rocks at them *maricones haras.*" *I should've, I should've . . .*

I climbed up to my pad and sneaked into bed. I was sweated up, and I smelled shook up. I tried to go to sleep, waiting for the knock on my door that would tell me my boys had squealed on me. *I should've stayed there . . . Our Father who art . . . I hope them cats don't squeal on me . . .* "Naw, they won't, naw . . ."

Man! They better not!

SUBURBIA

This Long Island ain't nuttin' like Harlem, and with all your green trees it ain't nuttin' like your Puerto Rico.

9. BABYLON FOR THE BABYLONIANS

In 1944 we moved to Long Island. Poppa was making good money at the airplane factory, and he had saved enough bread for a down payment on a small house.

As we got our belongings ready for the moving van, I stood by watching all the hustling with a mean feeling. My hands weren't with it; my fingers played with the top of a cardboard box full of dishes. My face tried hard not to show resentment at Poppa's decision to leave my streets forever. I felt that I belonged in Harlem; it was my kind of kick. I didn't want to move out to Long Island. My friend Crutch had told me there were a lot of paddies out there, and they didn't dig Negroes or Puerto Ricans.

"Piri," Momma said.

"Yeah, Moms." I looked up at Momma. She seemed tired and beat. Still thinking about Paulie all the time and how she took him to the hospital just to get some simple-assed tonsils out. And Paulie died. I remember she used to keep repeating how Paulie kept crying, "Don't leave me, Mommie," and her saying, "Don't worry, *nene*, it's just for a day." Paulie—I pushed his name out of my mind.

"*Dios mío*, help a little, *hijo*," Momma said.

"Moms, why do we gotta move outta Harlem? We don't know any other place better'n this."

"*Caramba!* What ideas," Momma said. "What for you talk like that? Your Poppa and I saved enough money. We want you kids to have good opportunities. It is a better life in the country. No like Puerto Rico, but it have trees and grass and nice schools."

"Yeah, Moms. Have they got Puerto Ricans out there?"

"*Sí*, I'm sure. Señora Rodriguez an' her family, an' Otelia—remember her? She lived upstairs."

"I mean a lotta *Latinos*, Moms. Like here in the *Barrio*. And how about *morenos?*"

"*Muchacho*, they got all kind." Momma laughed. "Fat and skinny, big and little. And—"

"Okay, Momma," I said. "You win. Give me a kiss."

So we moved to Babylon, a suburb on the south shore of Long Island. Momma was right about the grass and trees. And the school, too, was nice-looking. The desks were new, not all copped up like the ones in Harlem, and the teachers were kind of friendly and not so tough-looking as those in Patrick Henry.

I made some kind of friends with some paddy boys. I even tried out for the school baseball team. There were a lot of paddy boys and girls watching the tryouts and I felt like I was the only one trying out. I dropped a fly ball in the outfield to cries of "Get a basket," but at bat I shut everybody out of my mind and took a swing at the ball with all I had behind it and hit a home run. I heard the cheers and made believe I hadn't.

I played my role to the most, and the weeks turned into months. I still missed Harlem, but I didn't see it for six months. *Maybe*, I thought, *this squeeze livin' ain't as bad as Crutch said.* I decided to try the lunchtime swing session in the school gym. The Italian paddy, Angelo, had said they had hot music there. I dug the two-cents admission fee out of my pocket and made it up the walk that led to the gym.

"Two cents, please," said a little *muchacha blanca.*

"Here you are."

"Thank you," she smiled.

I returned her smile. Shit, man, Crutch was wrong.

The gym was whaling. The music was on wax, and it was a mambo. I let myself react. It felt good to give in to the natural rhythm. Maybe there were other worlds besides the mean streets, I thought. I looked around the big gym and saw some of the kids I knew a little. Some of them waved; I waved back. I noticed most of the paddy kids were dancing the mambo like stiff. Then I saw a girl I had heard called Marcia or something by the other kids. She was a pretty, well-stacked girl, with black hair and a white softness which set her hair off pretty cool. I walked over to her. "Hi," I said.

"Huh? Oh, hi."

"My first time here."

"But I've seen you before. You got Mrs. Sutton for English."

"Yeah, that's right. I meant this is my first time to the gym dance."

"I also was at the field when you smashed that ball a mile."

"That was *suerte,*" I said.

"What's that?" she asked.

"What?"

"What you said—'swear-tay.' "

I laughed. "Man, that's Spanish."

"Are you Spanish? I didn't know. I mean, you don't look like what I thought a Spaniard looks like."

"I ain't a Spaniard from Spain," I explained. "I'm a Puerto Rican from Harlem."

"Oh—you talk English very well," she said.

"I told you I was born in Harlem. That's why I ain't got no Spanish accent."

"No-o, your accent is more like Jerry's."

What's she tryin' to put down? I wondered. Jerry was the colored kid who recently had moved to Bayshore.

"Did you know Jerry?" she asked. "Probably you didn't get to meet him. I heard he moved away somewhere."

"Yeah, I know Jerry," I said softly. "He moved away because he got some girl in trouble. I know Jerry is colored and I know I got his accent. Most of us in Harlem steal from each other's language or style or stick of living. And it's *suerte*, s-u-e-r-t-e. It means 'luck.'" *Jesus, Crutch, you got my mind messed up a little. I keep thinking this broad's tryin' to tell me something shitty in a nice dirty way. I'm gonna find out.* "Your name is Marcia or something like that, eh?" I added.

"Ahuh."

"Mine's Piri. Wanna dance?"

"Well, this one is almost over."

"Next one?"

"Well, er—I, er—well, the truth is that my boyfriend is sort of jealous and—well, you know how—"

I looked at her and she was smiling. I said, "Jesus, I'm sorry. Sure, I know how it is. Man, I'd feel the same way."

She smiled and shrugged her shoulders pretty-like. I wanted to believe her. I did believe her. I had to believe her. "Some other time, eh?"

She smiled again, cocked her head to one side and crinkled her nose in answer.

"Well, take it easy," I said. "See you around."

She smiled again, and I walked away not liking what I was feeling, and thinking that Crutch was right. I fought against it. I told myself I was still feeling out of place here in the middle of all these strangers, that paddies weren't as bad as we made them out to be. I looked over my shoulder and saw Marcia looking at me funny-like. When she saw me looking, her face changed real fast. She smiled again. I smiled back. I felt like I was plucking a mental daisy:

You're right, Crutch
You're wrong, Crutch

You're right, Crutch
You're wrong, Crutch.

I wanted to get outside and cop some sun and I walked toward the door.

"Hi, Piri," Angelo called. "Where you going? It's just starting."

"Aw, it's a little stuffy," I lied. "Figured on making it over to El Viejo's—I mean, over to the soda fountain on Main Street."

"You mean the Greek's?"

"Yeah, that's the place."

"Wait a sec till I take a leak and I'll go over with you."

I nodded okay and followed Angelo to the john. I waited outside for him and watched the kids dancing. My feet tapped out time and I moved closer to the gym and I was almost inside again. Suddenly, over the steady beat of the music, I heard Marcia say, "Imagine the nerve of that black thing."

"Who?" someone asked.

"That new colored boy," said another voice.

They must have been standing just inside the gym. I couldn't see them, but I had that for-sure feeling that it was me they had in their mouths.

"Let's go, Piri," Angelo said. I barely heard him. "Hey fella," he said, "what's the matter?"

"Listen, Angelo. Jus' listen," I said stonily.

". . . do you mean just like that?" one of the kids asked.

"Ahuh," Marcia said. "Just as if I was a black girl. *Well!* He started to talk to me and what could I do except be polite and at the same time not encourage him?"

"Christ, first that Jerry bastard and now him. We're getting invaded by niggers," said a thin voice.

"You said it," said another guy. "They got some nerve. My dad says that you give them an inch them apes want to take a yard."

"He's not so bad," said a shy, timid voice. "He's a polite guy and seems to be a good athlete. And besides, I hear he's a Puerto Rican."

"Ha—he's probably passing for Puerto Rican because he can't make it for white," said the thin voice. "Ha, ha, ha."

I stood there thinking who I should hit first. *Marcia. I think I'll bust her jaw first.*

"Let's go, Piri," Angelo said. "Those creeps are so fuckin' snooty that nobody is good enough for them. Especially that bitch Marcia. Her and her clique think they got gold-plated assholes."

". . . no, *really!*" a girl was saying. "I heard he's a Puerto Rican, and they're not like Neg—"

"There's no difference," said the thin voice. "He's still black."

"Come on, Piri, let's go," Angelo said. "Don't pay no mind to them."

"I guess he thought he was another Jerry," someone said.

"He really asked me to dance with him," Marcia said indignantly. "I told him that my boyfriend . . ."

The rest of the mean sounds faded as I made it out into the sun. I walked faster and faster. I cut across the baseball field, then ran as fast as I could. I wanted to get away from the things running to mind. My lungs were hurting—not from running but from not being able to scream. After a while I sat down and looked up at the sky. How near it seemed. I heard a voice: "Piri! Holy hell, you tore up the ground running." I looked up and saw Angelo. He was huffing and out of wind. "Listen, you shouldn't let them get you down," he said, kneeling next to me. "I know how you feel."

I said to him very nicely and politely, "Do me a favor, you motherfuckin' paddy, get back with your people. I don't know why the fuck you're here, unless it's to ease your—oh, man, just get the fuck outta here. I hate them. I hate you. I hate all you white motherjumps."

"I'm sorry, Piri."

"Yeah, *blanco* boy, I know. You know how I feel, ain't that right? Go on, paddy, make it."

Angelo shook his head and slowly got up. He looked at me for a second, then walked away. I dug the sky again and said to it, "I ain't ever goin' back to that fuckin' school. They can shove it up their asses." I plucked the last mental daisy: *You was right, Crutch.*

10. BUT NOT FOR ME

I really hated Long Island and was makin' the scene in Harlem most often for pot parties, stompings, and chicks. On the train rides to Harlem, I watched the cool frame houses and clean-looking kids roll by and my memory scratched itself and brought back things I didn't like.

This Long Island was a foreign country. It looked so pretty and clean but it spoke a language you couldn't dig. The paddy boys talked about things you couldn't dig, or maybe better, they couldn't dig you. Yeah, that was it; they didn't dig your smooth talk, and you always felt like on the rim of belonging. No matter how much you busted your hump trying to be one of them, you'd never belong, they wouldn't let you. Maybe they couldn't. Maybe they didn't belong themselves.

Momma was having her troubles, too. One day she told me that Poppa had another woman.

"What are you saying, Moms?"

"I said that your father has another woman."

"Naw, Moms, it ain't so. Man! Pops is only for you."

"No, *hijo*, I know. Her name is Ruthie."

I knew it, too, but I'd lie my ass off to make it a lie so that Moms wouldn't have to make it any harder for herself. Moms was dying. I guess she knew it as well as I, but it was different for both of us. I wanted her to live. She didn't want to.

"Naw, Moms, it ain't like that," I lied, and we just looked at each other quietly, both knowing that it was like that.

I got a job, as a kitchen attendant at Pilgrim State Hospital in Brentwood, Long Island. I had the crazy idea that I could save some money and take a pad in Harlem, maybe for Momma, the kids, and me.

The work at the hospital was shitty and the pay was shitty, but it was some kind of independence. There was a cafeteria for employees on the hospital grounds. I went there to eat lunch. As I opened the cafeteria door, a girl was coming out. She was blond and *chevere*-looking. I held the door open for her.

"Thank you," she said, smiling openly.

"You're welcome," I smiled. We looked at each other.

"Er, are you new here?" she asked.

"Yeah, just started today."

"It's a big place, isn't it?"

"You ain't kidding."

"Are you from nearby?"

"Yeah, West Babylon, but originally from the *Barrio*."

"The what?"

"The *Barrio*. Ain't you ever heard of it? Man, girl, it's the coolest place ever. Everybody's always on some kind of kick."

"Is that in New York?" She looked interested.

"Yeah, in Spanish Harlem." I was interested. "How about some coffee," I said, "so I can tell you all about Harlem?"

She smiled and said, "Thank you."

I held the door open, like any gentleman in Harlem would have done, and we sat down at a table. I sensed something. Every eyeball in the cafeteria was pointed our way. But the girl in front of me didn't seem to notice it. I knew what it meant, and she looked at me and I knew she knew. I smiled and said, "Looks like everybody here knows you."

She laughed and said, "Or you."

Her name was Betty. I can't remember her last name. We

went for each other after that. We didn't even mind the looks our way. I took her to Harlem to meet my people. We had a ball; my boys made her feel at ease, at home. Everything went smooth for a while. Then one night we were returning from New York and I heard a steady murmur from two cats seated diagonally across and behind us. It was a while before I dug that they were talking about "some nigger."

"Will you look at that damn nigger with that white girl?" a voice said.

"Sh," said another voice, "he'll hear you."

I looked toward the voice.

"Let him hear me, that black son of a bitch," this cat said, looking straight at me.

I was "that damn nigger" and "that black son of a bitch." I sprang from my seat and through the blur of my rage I heard myself screaming something like "World full of shits!" and "Motherfuckin' supermen!" I wanted to kill, but Betty pulled me back and someone pulled that cat out of our car into another car and off at the next station.

We got off in Babylon and found a field, and I made love to her. In anger, in hate, I took out my madness on her. She understood and kept saying, "I don't care what they think—I love you, I love you."

But inside me I kept saying, *Damn it, I hate you—no, not you, just your damn color. My God, why am I in the middle?*

When it was over we lay there, real beat. She wanted to talk about us, but that was crazy. I took her home. It was the last time I saw her.

The next morning I told Momma, "Moms, I'm going back to the *Barrio.*"

"But *hijo*, stay here; why do you want to go?"

"No, Moms, I can't. I can't get along with anything, no matter what I do. Nothing falls right. I don't like Long Island and *los blancos*, and this world full of shits. I can't put my hand on it, but there's something wrong with all of us—Pops, José, James, Sis, me, and the whole world. Moms, I think the only ones got the right to be happy is dead." I looked at Moms, and she looked so beat, so tired. She hadn't been the same since Paulie died. "Look, Moms, I'm going back to Harlem and save some money so I can set up an apartment in the *Barrio* and you come live with me, okay?"

My little Moms looked at me sadly and said, "Take care of yourself. *Que Dios te bendiga y te guarde.* God bless you and protect you."

"Thanks, Moms, I'll make some money and we'll all go back to Harlem. Pops too, if he wants to." I hugged Momma close to me. Her smallness made me want to cry inside. I made myself think, *Hard, man, like, you're a big man.* At the door I looked back, " 'Bye, Moms," I said.

"*Adiós. Escribe!*"

"Sure, Moms."

I walked down the path toward the main road. I knew Moms was standing at the door, dressed, as always, like somebody that's secondhand. I wasn't gonna look back, but I did. "Moms," I called back.

"*Sí, hijo?*"

"This Long Island ain't nuttin' like Harlem, and with all your green trees it ain't nuttin' like your Puerto Rico."

"I understand, *hijo.*"

"It'll be okay, Moms. Give me your blessing."

"*Que Dios te bendiga, que Dios te bendiga, que Dios te bendiga.*"

I didn't look back any more.

HARLEM

It wasn't right to be ashamed of what one was. It was like hating Momma for the color she was and Poppa for the color he wasn't.

11. HOW TO BE A NEGRO WITHOUT REALLY TRYING

I had been away from home maybe three months, knocking around, sleeping in cold hallways, hungry a lot of the time. The fucking heart was going out of me. Maybe I should make it down to the Bowery, I thought, and lap up some sneaky pete with the rest of the bums.

No, I decided, one thing still stood out clear; one thing still made sense and counted—me. Nothing else but me—and I hadda pull outta this shit kick.

It was winter, and all I had on was a paper-weight sports jacket. The cold winds were blowing my skin against my chest. I walked into a bar at 103rd Street and Third Avenue, trying to look like I had a pound on me and was warm. In front of the jukebox was a colored guy and a big, chunky broad. The guy was beating out time and the girl was digging. Not all of her moved, just the right parts.

I smiled. "Cold, eh?" I said, and added, "My name is Piri."

"Sure is, kid," he said. "Mine's Pane, and that's my sistuh, Lorry." I followed his finger as he pointed to her.

"It's cold," I mumbled to no one in particular.

"Want a drink, kid?"

I tried not to act too anxious. "Yeah, cool man," I said casually. Pane took a bottle from his back pocket and handed it to me. "How strong can I hit it?" I asked, holding the bottle to my lips.

"Roll," he said, and I put inside me the warmth and affection of my new friends.

After half an hour a new bottle popped out and I got another long taste, and home was with me, I wasn't so lonely. The hours slipped by. I talked and Pane and his sister were one with me. Then the place was gonna close and I knew it was going to get cold again. Pane was high but not plastered. He nudged Lorry and said, "Let's go." I just sat there.

They got up and walked away. As they reached the door I saw Lorry nudge her brother and whisper something. He shook his head and looked back at me. I waved at him, hoping that the look on his face meant what I thought it did.

"Hey, kid, what's your name again?"

"Piri—some guys call me Johnny."

"Have you got a place to sleep?"

"Uh-uh," I said. I made a mental list of the places I had slept since I had left home—friends' pads at the beginning, with relatives until the welcome was overdrawn, then rooftops, under the stairs, basements, stoops, parked cars.

"Well, we ain't got much room, but you're welcome to share it," Pane said. "You gotta sleep on the floor, 'cause all we got is one room for Lorry, her two kids, and me."

"Crazy, man. Thanks a lot," I said. I almost felt my luck was going to change. I tightened up against the cold and hustled down the street. A couple of blocks over, between Park and Madison, we went down the stairs into a basement. I felt the warmth from the furnace greet me and I welcomed it like a two-days-late home-relief check. Pane fumbled with the key and opened the door into a small room. I noticed that the cellar had been partitioned into several rooms and one kitchen for sharing. Lorry smiled at me and said, "Honey, it ain't much, but it beats a blank."

"*Gracias.*" I smiled, and it was for real. "Thanks, Lorry."

She spread a quilt on the floor between the big bed where she and the two kids slept and a couch where Pane slept. I lay down on my back, my hands behind my head. The room was so small I could touch both the bed and the couch. I felt almost safe.

Soon Pane was sleeping hard on his whisky. In the dim darkness I saw Lorry looking down at me. "You asleep, honey?" she asked.

"No, I ain't," I answered.

She slowly made room in her big warm bed, and just like that I climbed in and made love to her—"love" because I was grateful to her, because I wanted her body as much as she wanted mine. It was all natural, all good, all as innocent and pure as anything could be in Home, Sweet Harlem. That was that—she was my woman. No matter that I was sixteen and she was thirty-three. Her caring, her loving were as young or as old as I wanted it to be.

Months passed. I got a job—Lorry inspired that with carfare and lunch. Every week I gave her a few bucks and loved her as much as I could. Still, I had the feeling that I was in a deep nothing and had to get on. Then I lost the lousy job.

I decided I couldn't stay with Lorry any more. I had been playing around with this Puerto Rican girl who lived in one of the basement rooms. She was sure a pretty bitch, with a kid and no husband. I didn't want Lorry to cop a complex, but I couldn't dig her the way she wanted me to. One night I cut out. The Puerto Rican girl had just hustled ten bucks, and she was talking about all the things it would buy for the kid. They needed food and clothes real bad. I saw where she put her pocketbook and waited till she was in the kitchen getting some grits for her kid. Then I went to her room and copped the ten bucks and made it up to the Bronx. I had a hangout up there. I gave a street buddy five bucks and he let me share his pad for a couple of weeks till I could cop a job.

A few days after I'd copped the ten dollars I ran into the girl. She knew it had been me. She made a plea for her bread back, for her kid. I said I didn't take it and brushed past her. I didn't have to look into her eyes to know the hate she bore me. But it was her or me, and as always, it had to be me. Besides, I had bought some pot with the five left over and rolled some good-size bombers that immediately put me in business. I had a good-o thought: soon as I was straight, I'd lay her ten *bolos* back on her.

I looked for work, but not too hard. Then I saw this ad in a newspaper:

YOUNG MEN, 17–30
GREAT OPPORTUNITY
LEARN WHILE WORKING
EARN WHILE TRAINING
Door-to-door salesmen in household wares. Guaranteed by Good Housekeeping. Salary and commission.
603 E. 73 St. 2nd fl.—9 a.m.

"Dig, Louie, this sounds good," I said to my boy. "Let's go over in the morning. Hell, with our gift of *labia* we're a mother-hopping cinch to cop a slave."

"*Chevere*, Piri, man, we got all Harlem and we know plenty people. Bet we can earn a hundred bucks or more on commissions alone."

We went down the next day and walked into the office and a girl handed me and Louie each a paper with a number on it and told us to please have a seat. My number was 16 and Louie's was 17. Man, me and Louie were sparklin'. We had our best togs on; they were pressed like a razor and our shoes shone like a bald head with a pound of grease on it.

"Number 16, please?" the girl called out.

I winked at Louie and he gave me the V-for-victory sign.

"Right this way, sir, through the door on your left," the girl said.

I walked into the office and there was this paddy sitting there. He looked up at me and broke out into the friendliest smile I ever saw, like I was a long-lost relative. "Come in, come right in," he said. "Have a chair—that's right, sit right there. Well, sir, you're here bright and early. That's what our organization likes to see. Yes sir, punctuality is the first commandment in a salesman's bible. So you're interested in selling our household wares—guaranteed, of course, by *Good Housekeeping*. Had any experience selling?"

"Well, not exactly, sir, but—er—when I was a kid—I mean, younger, I used to sell shopping bags in the *Marketa*."

"The what?"

"The *Marketa* on 110th Street and Park Avenue. It, er, runs all the way up to 116th Street."

"Ummm, I see."

"And my mom—er, mother, used to knit fancy things called *tapetes*. I think they're called doilies, and I used to sell them door to door, and I made out pretty good. I know how to talk to people, Mr.—er—"

"Mr. Christian, Mr. Harold Christian. See?" and he pointed a skinny finger at a piece of wood with his name carved on it. "Ha, ha, ha," he added, "just like us followers of our Lord Jesus Christ are called. Are you Christian?"

"Yes, sir."

"A good Catholic, I bet. I never miss a Sunday mass; how about you?"

"No, sir, I try not to." *Whee-eoo!* I thought. *Almost said I was Protestant.*

"Fine, fine, now let's see . . ." Good Catholic Mr. Christian took out some forms. "What's your name?"

"Piri Thomas—P-i-r-i."

"Age?"

"Er, seventeen—born September 30, 1928."

Mr. Christian counted off on the fingers of one hand . . . "twenty-eight, er, thirty-eight, forty-five—ahum, you were just seventeen this September."

"That's right. Paper said from seventeen to thirty."

"Oh, yes—yes, yes, that's correct. Where do you live?"

I couldn't give him the Long Island address; it was too far away. So I said, "109 East 104th Street."

"That's way uptown, isn't it?"

"Yes, sir."

"Isn't that, um, Harlem?"

"Yes, sir, it's split up in different sections, like the Italian section and Irish and Negro and the Puerto Rican section. I live in the Puerto Rican section. It's called the *Barrio*."

"The *Bar-ree-o?*"

I smiled. "Yes, sir, it's Spanish for 'the place'—er—like a community."

"Oh, I see. But you're not Puerto Rican, are you? You speak fairly good English even though once in a while you use some slang—of course, it's sort of picturesque."

"My parents are Puerto Ricans."

"Is Thomas a Puerto Rican name?"

"Er—well, my mother's family name is Montañez," I said, wondering if that would help prove I was a Puerto Rican. "There are a lot of Puerto Ricans with American names. My father told me that after Spain turned Puerto Rico over to the United States at the end of the Spanish-American War, a lot of Americans were stationed there and got married to Puerto Rican girls." *Probably fucked 'em and forgot 'em*, I thought.

"Oh, I—er, see. How about your education? High school diploma?"

"No, sir, I quit in my second year . . ."

"Tsh, tsh, that was very foolish of you. Education is a wonderful thing, Mr. Thomas. It's really the only way for one to get ahead, especially when—er, uh—why did you leave school?"

My mind shouted out, *On account of you funny paddies and*

your funny ideas in this funny world, but I said, very *cara palo*, "Well, sir, we got a big family and—well, I'm the oldest and I had to help out and—well, I quit." Then, in a sincere fast breath, I added, "But I'm going to study nights. I agree with you that education is the only way to get ahead, especially when—"

"Fine, fine. What's your Social Security number?"

I said quickly: "072–20–2800."

"By memory, eh? Good! A good salesman's second commandment should be a good memory. Got a phone?"

"Yes, sir. Lehigh 3–6050, and ask for Mr. Dandy. He's my uncle. He doesn't speak English very well, but you can leave any message for me with him."

"Very, very good, Mr. Thomas. Well, this will be all for now. We will get in touch with you."

"Uh, how soon, about, Mr. Christian? 'Cause I'd like to start work, or rather, training, as soon as possible."

"I can't definitely say, Mr. Thomas, but it will be in the near future. Right now our designated territory is fully capacitated. But we're opening another soon and we'll need good men to work it."

"You can't work the territory you want?" I asked.

"Oh, no! This is scientifically planned," he said.

"I'd like to work in Harlem," I said, "but, uh—I can make it wherever you put me to sell."

"That's the spirit!" Mr. Christian bubbled. "The third commandment of a good salesman is he faces any challenge, wherever it may be."

I took Mr. Christian's friendly outstretched hand and felt the warm, firm grip and thought, *This paddy is gonna be all right to work for*. As I walked out, I turned my head and said, "Thank you very much, sir, for the opportunity."

"Not at all, not at all. We need bright young blood for this growing organization, and those that grow with us will be headed for great things."

"Thank you. So long."

"So long, and don't forget to go to mass."

"No, sir, I sure won't!"

"What church you go to?" he asked suddenly.

"Uh"—I tried to remember the name of the Catholic Church on 106th Street—"Saint Cecilia's!" I finally burst out.

"Oh yes, that's on, er, 106th Street between Park and Lexington. Do you know Father Kresser?"

"Gee, the name sounds sort of familiar," I cooled it. "I can almost place him, but I can't say for sure."

"Well, that's all right. He probably wouldn't remember me, but I was a youngster when he had a parish farther downtown. I used to go there. Well, if you run into him, give him my regards."

"I sure will. So long, and thanks again." I closed the door carefully and walked out to where Louie was still sitting.

"Man, Piri," he said, "you was in there a beau-coup long-ass time."

"Shh, Louie, cool your language."

"Got the job? You were in there long enough for two jobs."

I smiled and made an okay face.

Louie cupped his hand to his mouth and put his head next to mine. "That cat ain't a faggot, is he?" he whispered.

I whispered back with exaggerated disgust, "Man! What a fuckin' dirty mind you got."

"Just asking, man," he said. "Sometimes these guys are *patos* and if you handle them right, you get the best breaks. Well, how'd you make out?"

"In like Flynn, Louie."

"Cool, man, hope I get the same break."

"Number 17," the girl called.

"Here I go," Louie said to me.

"*Suerte*, Louie," I said. I gave him the V-for-victory sign and watched his back disappear and dimly heard Mr. Christian's friendly "Come right in. Have a—" before the door closed behind Louie.

Jesus, I thought. *I hope Louie gets through okay. It'll be great to work in the same job. Maybe we can even work together. He'll cover one side of the street and I'll cover the other. As tight as me and Louie are, we'll pool what we make on commissions and split halfies.*

"Hey Piri," Louie said, "let's go."

"Damn, Louie, you just went in," I said. "You only been in there about five minutes or so. How'd Mr. Christian sound?"

We walked down the stairs.

"Okay, I guess. Real friendly, and he asked me questions, one-two-three."

"And?"

"And I'm in!"

"Cool breeze. What phone did you give?" I asked.

"I ain't got no phone. Hey, there's the bus!"

We started to run. "Fuck running," I said, "let's walk a while and celebrate. Man, you could've gave him Dandy's number like I did. Aw, well, they'll probably send you a telegram or special delivery letter telling you when to start work."

"What for?" Louie asked.

"So's they can tell you when the new territory is opened up and when to come in," I said. " 'Cause the other territory—"

"What new territory?"

I opened my mouth to answer and Louie and I knew what was shakin' at the same fuckin' time. The difference between me and Louie was he was white. "That cat Mr. Christian tell you about calling you when some new territory opens up?" Louie said in a low voice.

I nodded, "Yeah."

"Damn! That motherfucker asked me to come and start that training jazz on Monday. Gave me a whole lotta shit about working in a virgin territory that's so big us future salesmen wouldn't give each other competition or something like that." Louie dug that hate feeling in me. He tried to make me feel good by telling me that maybe they got a different program and Mr. Christian was considering me for a special kinda job.

"Le's go back," I said coldly.

"What for, Piri?"

"You see any colored cats up there?"

"Yeah, *panín*, there's a few. Why?"

"Le's wait here in front of the place."

"*Por qué?*" asked Louie.

I didn't answer. I just watched paddies come down out of that office and make it. "Louie," I said, "ask the next *blanco* that comes down how the job hiring is. There's one now."

Louie walked over to him. "Say, excuse me, Mac," he said. "Are they hiring up there—you know, salesmen?"

"Yes, they are," the guy answered. "I start Monday. Why don't you apply if you're looking for work? It's—"

"Thanks a lot, Mac," Louie said. "I might do that." He came back and started to open his mouth.

"Forget it, *amigo*," I said. "I heard the chump."

We waited some more and a colored cat came down. "Hey, bruh," I called.

"You callin' me?"

"Yeah. I dug the ad in the paper. How's the hiring? Putting guys on?"

"I don't know, man. I mean I got some highly devoted crap about getting in touch with me when a new turf opens up."

"Thanks, man," I said.

"You're welcome. Going up?"

"Naw, I changed my mind." I nodded to Louie, and he came up to me like he was down for whatever I was down for.

"Let's walk," I said. I didn't feel so much angry as I did sick, like throwing-up sick. Later, when I told this story to my buddy, a colored cat, he said, "Hell, Piri, Ah know stuff like that can sure burn a cat up, but a Negro faces that all the time."

"I know that," I said, "but I wasn't a Negro then. I was still only a Puerto Rican."

12. MY MARINE TIGER

Fuck Mr. Christian. I didn't need his job anyway. I was selling pot—and smoking it, too—regularly. A bomber here, a bomber there; it kept me going, inside and out. I even visited at home occasionally. I told Momma I had a job on the docks. But I was swinging in Harlem, my Harlem, next to which Babylon was like cotton candy—white and sticky, and tasteless in the mouth.

In the daytime Harlem looks kinda dirty and the people a little drab and down. But at night, man, it's a swinging place, especially Spanish Harlem. The lights transform everything into life and movement and blend the different colors into a magic cover-all that makes the drabness and garbage, wailing kids and tired people invisible. Shoes and clothes that by day look beat and worn out, at night take on a reflected splendor that the blazing multicolored lights burn on them. Everyone seems to develop a sense of urgent rhythm and you get the impression that you have to walk with a sense of timing.

The daytime pain fades alongside the feeling of belonging and just being in swing with all the humming kicks going on around you. I'd stand on a corner and close my eyes and look at everything through my nose. I'd sniff deep and see the *cuchifritos* and hot dogs, stale sweat and dried urine. I'd smell the worn-out mothers with six or seven kids, and the nonpatient fathers beating the hell out of them. My nose would get a high-pitch tingling from the gritty wailing and bouncing red light of a squad car passing the scene like a bat out of Harlem, going to cool some trouble, or maybe cause some.

I'd walk on Lexington Avenue, where a lot of things were going on, and hear the long, strung-out voice of a junkie, "Hey, man, you got a couple charlies you can lend me?"

"Sorry, man, I wish I did have two bucks, but here's half a man," and I really wouldn't hear the "Thanks, man," as I slid half a dollar into a hand that somehow would convert that change into a fix of heroin that would drive away for a while whatever needed driving away.

The blocks would fall back, and without feeling the distance I would have gone twenty blocks. At Ortiz' Funeral Parlor there would be a wreath of white flowers indicating that death had copped another customer. I'd try not to become involved in all the sorrow sounds that loved ones made for someone that was beyond their loving.

I'd turn and head back to my block, noticing the overflow wash strung out on front fire escapes and thinking about the people who complain that clothes on front-side fire escapes make the block look cheap, that people who do that have no sense of values and destroy the worth of the neighborhood. But I liked it; I thought it gave class to the front fire escapes to be dressed up with underwear, panties, and scrubbed work clothes.

I'd meet my boys, and all the other hearing and seeing suddenly became unimportant. Only my boys were the important kick, and for good reasons—if I had boys, I had respect and no other clique would make me open game. Besides, they gave me a feeling of belonging, of prestige, of accomplishment; I felt *grande* and bad. Sometimes the thoughts would start flapping around inside me about the three worlds I lived in—the world of home, the world of school (no more of that, though), and the world of street. The street was the best damn one. It was like all the guys shouting out, "Hey, man, this is our kick."

The worlds of home and school were made up of rules laid down by adults who had forgotten the feeling of what it means to be a kid but expected a kid to remember to be an adult—something he hadn't gotten to yet. The world of street belonged to the kid alone. There he could earn his own rights, prestige, his good-o stick of living. It was like being a knight of old, like being ten feet tall.

I was kicking these thoughts around one day, sitting in El Viejo's candy store, digging the scene. Suddenly everybody looked younger and less experienced than me. I felt like I was one of the few who had broken up into little bits of world. Then I saw across the street Carlito Diaz, his sister Ava, and their momma walking alongside the prettiest, softest, widest-eyed Puerto Rican girl in the whole world. I got up from the twisted fountain stool and went outside.

I whistled and Carlito looked over. With my shoulders I asked, "Who's she?"

Carlito handed a cardboard-looking suitcase to his sister and crossed the street toward me, in the process letting me know that "she" was his cousin, a year older than he, single, and just arrived from Puerto Rico, and why didn't I come up to the house?

I made a move with my head that said, "Now?" and Carlito shook a head full of yesses and turned away from me to help Ava lift the cardboard-looking suitcase from its sidewalk gravity and into number 109.

Two hours later I knocked at the door and watched it open.

"Come in, Piri," said Ava's momma.

I nodded thanks, and my serious look at Carlito wiped off his shitty grin of knowing that this wasn't no ordinary visit. I followed them right into the kitchen, where "she" was sitting, eating. I looked at her and said, "My name is Piri. What's yours, girl?"

"Trinidad," she answered, smiling shyly.

"Trinidad?"

"Yes, but I like 'Trina' better," she said, cutting out my tongue with her white teeth and red mouth and smile. She started to get up from the table and I thought, *Don't get up, Señorita Trina. Keep eating; finish your plate of rice and beans. Do you know that your lips shine with the oil from your food?*

She got up anyhow and washed a glass with hot water, filled it with cold water, drank a little, then returned to her place at the table. She didn't look at me in all this time, and her shy ignoring of me left me helpless. I stood there like a Central Park statue. I was saved by Mrs. Diaz. "Would you like to eat, Piri?" she said.

I nodded, "Yes," gratefully and sat down at the table right across from Trina. Nothing could be as great as being able to sit close to this girl-woman who had upset my sense of balance. I felt weak in my kneecaps, yet I was able to keep my street face straight. Nothing shook, nothing showed, but my heart said, *Girl, I do dig you.* I wished I could tell it to her, like I was thinking it.

Instead there was a lot of small talk between small mouthfuls, like this meal had to last forever.

"Where are you from, girl?" I asked.

"Rio Piedras, Puerto Rico. And you?"

"Harlem, *Barrio*. Uh—are you here for long?"

"I'm not sure. Maybe long time or *un poco tiempo*."

I looked at her like I didn't really care and thought, *No, no, chica, forever, say forever!*

Eventually dinner ended and some kind of rest mixed with coffee was had in the living room. Then it was time for me to go. I got up and everyone convoyed me to the door.

"I'm glad to have met you, Piri," Trina said.

"Me, too." I grinned, thinking, *Girl, you have set me on a rumble*, but saying, "Well, I'll see you again."

There was no answer, just a shy smile.

I shook her hand and held it too long. I felt like an ass, and finally I let her hand go. The door closed behind me.

Damn, she's fine, I thought, *fine, fine, fine.*

Later I called her my "Marine Tiger," after the ship that brought so many Puerto Ricans to New York. We dug each other, and soon we were going to all the dances together. At Christmas we made a date to go to a party one of her cousins was giving. Man, I felt great. I had some long bread in my pockets 'cause I'd just finished selling some fine pot and had bought some more all rolled up. I had about two hundred sticks. At three for a buck, I'd make about $65. Like Mr. Christian had said, "Our designated territory was fully capacitated."

It was a fine night, cold but not freezing. I was waiting downstairs in front of El Viejo's for Trina. I was togged real sharp, with a fine suit, boss coat, and soft Florsheims, real dancing shoes. Man, what was taking her so long, I wondered, a little peeved, a little impatient to get going to the party. I started to cross the street and give her another yell to hurry up. But I changed my mind and decided to wait inside the candy store, where some of my boys were. Acting real cool, I walked slowly, deliberately back to El Viejo's, pausing long enough to light up a long, slim cigar. Wild, hot mambo music blared from the jukebox inside. Mambo! My feet automatically reacted and I danced the last few steps to the door.

I stood there a second, listening to the music, and opened the door. I saw they were snorting *tecata.* I smoked marijuana, which was just like smoking cigarettes, but I was down on drugs. I had seen the young-old cats that dope had messed up, the poor chumps who would try to hustle a buck or steal anything that would bring the price of a cap, a fix, to drive that mean devil away for a while.

I started turning away, snapping and shaking my head as if I'd forgotten something, when Alfredo called me. Alfredo and I had never been too tight and we never seemed to miss a chance to sound each other. Someday, I thought, we're going to have it out for good. "Say, *panín*," he said, "come and dig."

It was too late; I had to bluff. I cool-walked into El Viejo's and slapped skin all around. "What's shakin'?" I asked, like I didn't know.

"Cool, man," warned Waneko, "we've got some bad stuff, real down and we're going high. Cop some."

I felt something thrust into my hand and saw a cap and a piece of match-book cover folded into a V-shaped scoop.

"Snort, man," Waneko said. "It's H."

How can I make out of this? I was thinking. "Nay, dad, I've been blasting *yerba*. I have a going high and I don't want to mess it up."

"Oh, man," said Alfredo, "I'm digging maybe you're fronting now, cool Piri, making like you're a down stud. Now I ain't signifying, but I never dug you for a punk."

I felt myself stiffen and let my face set into a hard black mask, and in a low, just barely controlled whisper I hissed out, "Daddy-o, I'm going to make like I didn't dig what you just put down." I took the match-book scoop and shook out the stuff.

"Say, man," Crip's voice warned, "that's a big jolt you got heaped in your hand."

"Look," I said bad-like, "I've used this stuff before. But some wise motherfucker don't seem to know that I did and maybe like punks gotta be shown." Looking dead at Alfredo, I inhaled, first through one nostril, then through the other. Then, turning quickly, away I went into the cold street. Almost immediately I felt a burning sensation in my nose, like a sneeze coming. I pulled out my handkerchief and had barely enough time to put it to my nose when the blood came pouring out. *Man,* I thought, *this cap has blown out the insides of my nose.* But in a few seconds the bleeding stopped just as it had started.

Now the night lights seemed to get duller and duller, my awareness of things grew delayed. But the music was clearer and I felt no pain, nothing at all. I seemed sort of detached. I felt a little sick in my belly, but the good-o feeling was even better. I saw Trina coming to meet me, and I crossed the street and walked toward her, walking real light, real dreamy and slow, so she would have to meet me more than halfway. Sometimes I'd make her walk all the way to me, but tonight I felt good.

"Hi, Marine Tiger," I greeted her. She was a beautiful girl—dark, curly hair, large black eyes, red mouth, and a real down figure. Tonight she had a new dress. *Man,* I thought, *she's action come alive.* But when she asked me how she looked, I merely grunted, "*Buena, nena.*"

She told me she felt good to be by my side. *Man, I love you, Trina. I feel good.* I felt my face. It was like touching someone else. A little voice bugged me: *You're on your way, baby, you're walking into junkies' alley.* "Aw, the hell with you," I half blurted out and turned the corner, my arms tightly around Trina.

On the stairs leading up to the pad, I said, "Trina?"

"*Sí,* Piri?"

"Look, baby, I don't want you to drink too much. Like it don't look good and you don't stand much in order to get high. Okay?"

"*Bueno,* but I'm not a little girl," she said.

I laughed. "You sure ain't, but that's how I want it. Okay?"

"*Sí,* okay."

"That's my Marine Tiger."

There were quite a few cats at the party, and I got separated from Trina. Still feeling easy, I danced with a couple of the broads. I was grinding against one when I heard Carlito's voice. "Hey, Piri," he said, "Trina's drinking. She's talking about how you're making out with—" and he pointed a silent finger at the chick in my arms. "She's had beau-coup."

I looked toward the kitchen. Trina was just finishing a drink. I whispered to the broad that was grinding against me, "Later for you," and walked over to the kitchen, "cool" like I was supposed to. "Trina?" I said.

"*Sí?*"

"Look, *niña,* you're drinking too much; better like cool it, eh?"

"*Sí,* I will. It's just my second one and—and it is Christmas."

"Okay, but no more. Come here."

She swayed a little and gave a dirty look to the girl I had been grinding. I smiled at her and we danced. A little later I was dancing with the grinding broad again and I looked toward the kitchen and saw Trina with a drink in her hand, talking with a guy who I knew was always on the make. She looked at me and the glass dropped out of her hand and she ran into the bathroom. The guy who was giving her the drinks started to say something and I cooled him. Then I went over to the bathroom and pounded on the door. "Trina, open up," I shouted.

A small high voice said, "Go away, I can drink if I want to."

I was high enough to break the door down but I cooled my role. No use starting trouble in a family house. I called Ava. "Look, Ava, you better get your cousin out of that shithouse. Get her out and we'll give her some black coffee and some grease from that *lechón* on the stove."

A little later the party broke up, and Trina and I and Ava and Carlito left for home. Trina seemed sobered up, but as soon as the night air hit her, it brought back her high. She started talking trash through her hair. "I can drink anytime I want to," she said. I walked on ahead with Carlito and pretended not to hear her. Ava was walking with Trina and I heard her trying to calm her down. But she was just getting wound up. "After all, I'm free, white, and over the age," she said in Spanish. *Damn,* I thought, *why did she have to be so damned hard on the white part?* I felt my anger coming up, but I still cooled myself and we walked down Park Avenue toward 104th Street and number 109.

Trina kept up the yak. It was the drinks talking and I got warmer and warmer. I was damn mad. When we got to our stoop I said to Ava and Carlito, "Go on, kids, I want to talk to Trina."

"Okay, Piri, we'll see you later," said Carlito.

"Piri, don't be too mad, she's a little high," said Ava.

Trina tried to go with them, but I held her back. "Look, girl, I want to talk to you," I said. I held her two arms. She was standing in front of the door with its plate-glass windows.

"Let me go. Who do you think you are?" she said.

"I just want to talk with you, and—"

"Let me go," she said. "Who the hell do you think you are?" And she pushed me. I was high enough to go off balance, and before I could hold back, my fist was crashing toward her face. Somehow I missed and my fist smashed through the plate-glass window. I took back my hand and we both stood and looked at it, all cut up and blood spurting from one of the knuckles. Trina, her face pale, turned and ran. I just looked at my hand and walked up the stairs after her.

Upstairs, Trina brought me a towel and I wrapped it around my hand and walked out of the apartment and to Mt. Sinai Hospital, from where I was sent to City Hospital in an ambulance.

Man, City Hospital was like a butcher shop. All kinds of cases were coming in—guys with broken heads, broken arms, stab wounds, and bullet holes. There were no more beds, and bloody and busted guys were lying all over the floor. The doctors were working like mad. The ambulance attendants brought a colored man in on a stretcher. His eyes were rolling.

"What've you got there?" said one of the nurses. She was colored, too.

"Stabbin'," an attendant said. "One in the neck, another in the back."

"Oh, oh, oh," moaned the colored guy. "Ain't gonna die, am I, mister? Ah ain't gonna die? Oh sweet Jesus, Ah ain't gonna die?" Blood oozed out red against his sweating dark skin.

The doctor examined him and patted him on the head and laughed. "Boy, you just got a couple of scratches. You could have put a couple of band-aids on them and nothing more said."

"Ya mean Ah gonna be okay?" the colored cat asked.

"A-huh."

"Man, jus' wait till I git outta here. Ah gonna get that black sonovabitch. E-magine that cat shanking me like that."

"Nurse, put some medication on his wounds after he gets a couple of stitches," the doctor said. The nurse nodded and the colored cat looked at her and began smiling. "Hey there, hon-nee," he said, "take care of your man."

"Mind your tongue," said the nurse.

"Now, hon-nee, I may be dying and—"

"Don't put on a brave act with me, home-boy. You were about to crap when you thought you were dying."

"Ah still may die," he said. "But if Ah makes it, will you go out with me? We can make it down to the Baby Grand and do some shuffling."

"Listen, mister, I'm just interested in them two scratches you got. The rest of you don't count."

"Ah, now, baby, don't act like that. If I don't make it you can have my shoes."

"If you don't shut your mouth," she said, "I'll have the doctor sew it up along with them little scratches."

"Okay, okay, baby. And you nurses is suppose to be sweet and gentle-like. You Negroes are all the same."

Two big cops pushed their way into the room and walked over to the colored cat. "Well, fella, what happened?" asked one of the cops.

The colored cat's face got innocent-looking all of a sudden, and his voice sounded small and weak. "Wal, officers, Ah sure don' know 'xactly for sure. I was walking down the street and Ah passed a dark street and somebody jumped me and tried to cop my wallet. I fought back and he shanked me. I didn't even get a good look at him and I couldn't identify him no matter what. Ah sure wish Ah could help you out."

The two cops looked at each other and, without a word, left. The colored cat watched them leave and smiled and said, "What do they care? It's just another nigger gettin' cut up.

Man, when I get aholt of that Scotty who shanked me, I'll take care of him myself."

I looked around and a guy was looking at me. His wrist was all cut up. He looked at my hand with the bandage on it. "Got into a fight?" he asked.

"Naw, no hassle," I said. "I was just swinging out on my old lady and missed. My hand went through a plate-glass window."

He smiled and said, "Me, too, but I put my fist through a window for kicks."

I looked at him and his face said "junkie." I decided to find out.

"I wish I had me some stuff."

"You on, man?"

"Yeah, you?"

"A-huh, yeah," he said, and looked around. "I got some H," he whispered. "Come on over here and we'll turn on." I sat next to him. "I got no works," he said, "but we can snort." He brought out two caps and handed me one. I carefully opened the cap and let a little jolt of H fall on my thumbnail. *Man, who cares about a cut-up hand? This is the stuff that counts. This is the coolness that'll fix everything.* I held one nostril closed and sniffed hard, then the other, until all the cap was empty. Then I just sat back, and all that misery and pain in that hospital ward became unimportant, like my being there was no concern of mine.

"How you feel, man?" the junkie asked me.

"Cool, man. Say, what's your name?"

"Hector; what's yours?"

"Piri."

"Hey, fella," a voice called, "you're next."

I turned to the voice and it was talking to me. It was a Chinese doctor. My mind was nice and warm; my separation from all was complete.

"Okay, son, let's see your hand," he said.

Man, I thought, *he speaks better English than I do*. I held my hand out. He held his out and there was a needle and thread in his fingers. He started to sew up my gashed hand, but it didn't hurt. Nothing at this point could hurt me.

"Can take it, eh?"

"Yeah," I mumbled. "A-huh." I looked extra bored and cool.

"You hooked?" he asked matter-of-factly.

I looked hard at him. "Whatta ya mean, hooked?" I said.

"You know what I mean. I saw you and that other fellow sniffing."

I was thinking fast now, wondering if the Chinese doctor was planning on getting us busted. "What's on your mind, doc?" I asked cautiously.

"Why don't you guys learn? You can't beat junk. It always ends up beating you."

"Aw, I ain't hooked. Besides, it ain't none of your damn business."

"Okay, son, forget it. Take some of these pills and go to your doctor for a change of bandages, and—"

"Thanks," I said, cutting off any song and dance.

The doctor shook his head. "Okay, you there," he called to one of the walking wounded, "you're next."

I went back to my place on the floor, but it bugged me that the Chinese doctor should know I was hooked. Jesus, did it show so much now? A funny line went through my head: *No stuffee, no druggee; no habit, no junkie,* and I wondered if I really was hooked.

For a few days my hand felt pretty bad. Christmas kicks turned into New Year's kicks, and I took Trina to a big set at the Palladium Dance Hall downtown. The hand still throbbed, but I had gotten a small fix and that pain didn't stay anything special.

It was crowded at the Palladium. I looked around and saw a lot of my boys. I looked at Trina. She was really a good-looking blip, stone-smooth. Some of the guys dug my bandaged hand and I played it cool, like it was nothin'.

"Hey man, Piri, what's with your hand, *hombre?*" Louie asked.

"*Nada,* just a little trouble," I said. I left it hanging there so if he wanted to think I had been in a drag-out fight, he could.

My hand started throbbing worse, so I went into the Palladium toilet. It was packed, and the smell of pot sweetened out the smell of piss from the toilet bowls. I didn't shoot up. I just wasted that stuff up my nose. I wondered how some guys could take the chance of cooking up and shooting up in any public place like a shithouse, where anybody can walk in, but when a cat's in need, he's a fool indeed.

I walked back to our table and a guy was asking Trina for a dance. I heard her saying, "I'm sorry, but my *novio* isn't here and I don't dance with anyone unless he says it's okay." I was feeling good now.

"Say, man, is it all right if I dance with your chick?" the guy asked me.

I didn't care too much for the cat, but it was New Year's Eve, so I said, "Sure, man, I expect you're cool, eh?"

"Yeah, I'm cool."

A little while later Louie said, "Hey, Piri, look out on the dance floor."

I looked, and that cat was trying to cool-lay Trina. He was rubbing close against her, and when he threw her out, he slammed her in fast so that her whole body slammed into him. I got so mad that I clenched my fist, and the pain it caused got me madder.

"Let me get the guy," said Louie.

"Naw, I go first," I said. "It's my old lady. If I ain't cool enough to take care of her, I ain't cool enough to have her."

The music was way out and the well-timed beat of hundreds of feet made a *chevere* noise on the wooden floor of the Palladium. I nodded to Louie and made my way through the twisting mambo-mad people. The cat had just swung Trina out again with the intention of slamming her into him again when I stepped in between them and snatched her cool, without losing a dance step, and kept dancing with her. The cat looked like a fool and jumped stink. "Hey, man, whatcha putting down?" he said angrily. "Can't you see I'm dancing with the broad?"

I stopped dancing and didn't even look at the cat. I took Trina by the hand and walked off the dance floor.

"It's not my fault, Piri," she said.

"I know, baby, forget it."

The cat followed us off the floor, still bullshitting. I sat Trina down and turned toward the cat. "Make it, motherfucker," I said.

"What you say?"

"Make it, motherfucker," I repeated, "while you still able."

Two of the cat's boys walked up and stood looking bad. "This guy giving you any trouble, Tony?" one of them said.

The cat looked badder now and said, "Yeah, but I'll take care of him. He figures that on account of he's got one bad hand it's gonna save him."

I looked at him hard. "I got many hands, motherfucker," I said, nodding my head in the direction of my boys. "Enough for you and them two faggots you got with you." Louie and about fifteen of my boys surrounded us, smooth and quiet. "Wanna leave now, cool, or get wasted, motherfucker?" I said.

The motherfucker and his two faggot boys looked, and without another word, left.

What a world! Whether you're right or wrong, as long as you're strong, you're right.

"Let's dance, Trina," I said.

13. HUNG UP BETWEEN TWO STICKS

Not long afterward me and Louie got a little bit of that shit ourselves. Only we didn't get no choice to cut out. We got hung up by a white clique from downtown as we were coming out of the RKO flick on 86th Street. There were about eight paddies. We tried to cut out, but they got us tight inside their circle. Louie quickly punched his way out and made it. It took me a little longer. I caught four belts for every one I could lay on them. Finally I got out and started putting down shoe leather. But the paddies were hot on doing me up real nice. One of them got so close to me I saw his face over my shoulder. I stopped short and he ran right into a slap with all my weight behind it. He went down on his ass and I told him cool-like, "Motherfucker, I punch men and slap punks." His boys were too near for me to play my grandstand to the most, so I started to make it. I heard him scream out from between his split lips: "You dirty, fucking shine! I'll get one of you black bastards."

I screamed back, "Your mammy got fucked by one of us black bastards." *One of us black bastards. Was that me?* I wondered.

It really bugged me when the paddies called us Puerto Ricans the same names they called our colored aces. Yet it didn't bother Louie or the other fellas who were as white as him; it didn't bother Crip, or the others, who were as dark as me or darker. Why did it always bug me? Why couldn't I just laugh it off with that simple-ass kid rhyme:

> Sticks and stones may break my bones,
> But words will never harm me.

I had two colored cats, Crutch and Brew, for tight *amigos*. All the time I heard them talk about Jim Crow and southern paddies' way-out, screwed-up thinking. Crutch told me once that he was sitting on the curb down South where he used to live and some young white boys passed in a car and yelled out to him, "Hey, nigger, git outta that gutter and climb down the sewer where all you black niggers belong."

It really bugged me, like if they had said it to me. I asked Crutch if he knew any colored cats that had been hung. "Not person'ly," he said, "but my daddy knew some." He said it with a touch of sadness hooked together with a vague arrogance.

Crutch was smart and he talked a lot of things that made sense to any Negro. That was what bothered me—it made a lot of sense to me.

"You ain't nevah been down South, eh, Piri?" Crutch had asked me.

"Uh-uh. *Nunca*, man. Just read about it, and I dug that flick *Gone with the Wind*."

"Places like Georgia and Mississippi and Alabama. All them places that end in i's an' e's an' a whole lotta a's. A black man's so important that a drop of Negro blood can make a black man out of a pink-asshole, blue-eyed white man. Powerful stuff, that thar white skin, but it don't mean a shit hill of beans alongside a Negro's blood."

Yeah, that Crutch made sense.

The next day I looked up at the faces of the people passing by my old stoop. I tried to count their different shades and colors, but I gave it up after a while. Anyway, black and white were the most outstanding; all the rest were in between.

I felt the fuzz on my chin and lazily wondered how long it'd be before I'd have one like Poppa. *I look like Poppa,* I thought, *we really favor each other.* I wondered if it was too mean to hate your brothers a little for looking white like Momma. I felt my hair—thick, black, and wiry. Mentally I compared my hair with my brothers' hair. My face screwed up at the memory of the jillion tons of stickum hair oils splashed down in a vain attempt to make it like theirs. I felt my nose. "Shit, it ain't so flat," I said aloud. But mentally I measured it against my brothers', whose noses were sharp, straight, and placed neat-like in the middle of their paddy fair faces.

Why did this have to happen to me? Why couldn't I be born like them? I asked myself. I felt sort of chicken-shit thinking like that. I felt shame creep into me. It wasn't right to be ashamed of what one was. It was like hating Momma for the color she was and Poppa for the color he wasn't.

The noise of the block began to break through to me. I listened for real. I heard the roar of multicolored kids, a street blend of Spanish and English with a strong tone of Negro American.

"Hey, man," a voice called, "what yuh doing thar sitting on your rump? Yuh look like you're thinking up a storm." It was Brew, one of my tightest *amigos.*

"*Un poco,* Brew," I said. "How's it goin' with you?"

"Cool breeze," he said.

I looked at Brew, who was as black as God is supposed to be white. "Man, Brew," I said, "you sure an ugly spook."

Brew smiled. "Dig this Negro calling out 'spook,' " he said.

I smiled and said, "I'm a Porty Rican."

"Ah only sees another Negro in fron' of me," said Brew.

This was the "dozens," a game of insults. The dozens is a dangerous game even among friends, and many a tooth has been lost between fine, ass-tight *amigos.* Now I wanted the game to get serious. I didn't know exactly why. Brew and me had played the dozens plenty and really gotten dirty. But I wanted something to happen. "Smile, pussy, when you come up like that," I said. "I'm a stone Porty Rican, and—"

"And . . ." Brew echoed softly.

I tried to dig myself. I figured I should get it back on a joke level. What the hell was I trying to put down? Was I trying to tell Brew that I'm better than he is 'cause he's only black and I'm a Puerto Rican dark-skin? Like his people copped trees on a white man's whim, and who ever heard of Puerto Ricans getting hung like that?

I looked down at my hands, curling and uncurling, looking for some kinda answer to Brew's cool echo. "Brew," I finally eased out.

"Yeah."

"Let's forget it, Brew."

"Ain't nothin' to forget, baby."

I lit a butt. Brew offered me a whole weed. "Thanks. Nice day out," I said.

"So-kay," he said, and added: "Look, I ain't rehashin' this shit just went down, but—"

"Forget it, Brew. I'm sorry for the sound."

"Ain't nothin' to be sorry about, Piri. Yuh ain't said nothin' that bad. Mos' people got some kinda color complex. Even me."

"Brew, I ain't said what I'm feeling. I was thinking a little while ago that if you could dig the way I feel, you'd see I was hung up between two sticks. I—"

"Look, Piri," interrupted Brew, "everybody got some kinda pain goin' on inside him. I know yuh a li'l fucked up with some kind of hate called 'white.' It's that special kind with the 'no Mr.' in front of it. Dig it, man; say it like it is, out loud—like, you hate all paddies."

"Just their fuckin' color, Brew," I said bitterly. "Just their color—their damn claim that white is the national anthem of the world. You know?"

"Yeah."

"When I was a little kid in school," I said, "I used to go to general assembly all togged out with a white shirt and red tie. Everybody there wore a white shirt and red tie; and when they played the national anthem, I would put my hand over my heart. It made me feel great to blast out:

> My country, 'tis of thee,
> Sweet land of liberty,
> Of thee I sing . . .

And now when I hear it played I can't help feeling that it's only meant for paddies. It's their national anthem, their sweet land of liberty."

"Yeah, I knows, man," Brew said. "Like it says that all men are created equal with certain deniable rights—iffen they's not paddies. We uns thank you-all, Mistuh Lincoln, suh. Us black folks got through dat ole Civil War about fair, but we all havin' one ole helluva time still tryin' to git through the damn Reconstruction."

We both laughed. "That's pretty fuckin' funny if you can laugh," I said. "Let me try some of that creatin'. Be my straight man."

"What they evah do to yuh, Piri? Yuh ain't never been down South."

"No, man, I ain't," I said, remembering that Crutch had said the same thing.

"So yuh ain't never run into that played-out shit of

> "If you white, tha's all right.
> If you black, da's dat."

"Yeah, Brew," I said, "it must be tough on you Negroes."

"Wha' yuh mean, us Negroes? Ain't yuh includin' yourself? Hell, you ain't but a coupla shades lighter'n me, and even if yuh was even lighter'n that, you'd still be a Negro."

I felt my chest get tighter and tighter. I said, "I ain't no damn Negro and I ain't no paddy. I'm Puerto Rican."

"You think that means anything to them James Crow paddies?" Brew said coolly.

"*Coño,*" I mumbled.

"What yuh say, man?"

"I said I'm really startin' to almost hate Negroes, too," I shot back.

Brew walked away from me stiff-legged. His fists were almost closed. Then he came back and looked at me and, like he wasn't mad, said, "Yuh fuckin' yeller-faced bastard! Yuh goddamned Negro with a white man's itch! Yuh think that bein' a Porto Rican lets you off the hook? Tha's the trouble. Too damn many you black Porto Ricans got your eyes closed. Too many goddamned Negroes all over this goddamned world feel like you does. Jus' 'cause you can rattle off some different kinda language don' change your skin one bit. Whatta yuh all think? That the only niggers in the world are in this fucked-up country? They is all over this whole damn world. Man, if there's any black people up on the moon talkin' that moon talk, they is still Negroes. Git it? Negroes!"

"Brew," I said, "I hate the paddy who's trying to keep the black man down. But I'm beginning to hate the black man, too, 'cause I can feel his pain and I don't know that it oughtta be mine. Shit, man, Puerto Ricans got social problems, too. Why the fuck we gotta take on Negroes', too?" I dug Brew's eyes. They looked as if he was thinking that he had two kinda enemies now—paddies and black Puerto Ricans. "Brew," I said, "I'm trying to be a Negro, a colored man, a black man, 'cause that's what I am. But I gotta accept it myself, from inside. Man, do you know what it is to sit across a dinner table looking at your brothers that look exactly like paddy people? True, I ain't never been down South, but the same crap's happening up here. So they don't hang you by your neck. But they slip an invisible rope around your balls and hang you with nice smiles and 'If we need you, we'll call you.' I wanna feel like a 'Mr.' I can't feel like that just yet, and there ain't no amount of cold wine and pot can make my mind accept me being a 'Mr.' part time. So what if I can go to some paddy pool hall or fancy restaurant? So what if I lay some white chick? She still ain't nothin' but a white blur even if my skin does set off her paddy color."

"So yuh gonna put the Negro down jus' 'cause the paddy's puttin' yuh down," Brew said. "Ain't gonna bring nothin' from us exceptin' us putting you down too."

"Like you're putting me down?"

"I ain't put you down, Piri. You jus' got me warm with that 'I'm a Porty Rican' jazz. But I know where yuh at. You jus' gotta work some things out."

Brew shoved his big hand at me. I grabbed it and shook it, adding a slap of skin to bind it. I looked at our different shades of skin and thought, *He's a lot darker than me, but one thing is for sure, neither of us is white.* "Everything cool?" I said.

"Yee-ah. I ain't mad. I said I dig. Jus' got worried that you might turn to be a colored man with a paddy heart."

Like Poppa, I thought, and my eyes followed a fast-moving behind going up the stoop across the street.

"Nice piece of ass," Brew said.

"Naw, Brew, I—"

"You sayin' that ain't a nice piece of ass?"

"That wasn't what I was gonna say, you horny bastard. I meant that what I want out of life is some of the good things the white man's got. Man, what some of them eat for week-day dinner, we eat for our Sunday dinner—"

" 'Tain't only Porty Ricans."

"Yeah, American Negroes, too."

"Thar's a lotta white people got it kinda bad, too," Brew said. "Some even worse."

"What you doing now, man, defendin' the paddies?" I asked.

"Jus' sayin' like it is."

I thought for a long while and finally said, "I'm gonna have everything good they have for living even if I gotta take it. Fuck it, I care about me a whole lot. Even the poor white people you're talking about are down on the Negro—more so than the paddy that got bread, 'cause since the poor paddy ain't got nothin', he gotta feel big some way, so the Negro's supposed to lie down and let the paddy climb up on his chest with his clodhoppers just so's he can feel three or four inches taller standing on another man's ribs."

"Yuh talking all this stuff, and yuh ain't evah been down South," Brew said disdainfully.

"Brew," I said with quiet patience, "you don't have to be from the South to know what's happenin'. There's toilet bowls wherever you go. Besides, I learn from you and Crutch and the others. I learn from what I read—and from the paddies."

"But it ain't exactly like being down South, Piri," Brew insisted solemnly.

"What's the matter, Brew?" I asked sarcastically. "A cat's gotta be hung before he knows what's happenin'?" I began to whistle, "Way Down Upon the Swanee River."

Brew went on like I hadn't said nothing, "So yuh can't appreciate and therefore you can't talk that much."

"That's what you say, Brew. But the same—"

"Yuh gonna jaw about the difference and sameness up here and down there," Brew broke in. "Man, you think these paddies up here are a bitch on wheels. Ha! They ain't shit alongside Mr. Charlie down thar. Down South, if one ain't real careful, he can grow up smilin' his ass off and showin' pearly whites till his gums catch pneumonia or workin' his behind off fo' nothin'."

"Yeah, but—"

"Let me say it like it is, Piri. It ain't as bad now as when my daddy was a kid, but it's bad enough. Though I guess bad is bad, a little or a lot. Now those Indians sure had some kinda hard way to go, but they had heart."

"Whatcha mean, man?" I asked, wondering what the hell Indians had to do with all this.

"My daddy use to say that

> 'The Indian fought the white man and died
> An' us black folk jus' wagged ouah tails,
> "Yas suhses," smiled and multiplied.' "

I cracked a smile and got up and yawned and stretched. "Brew," I said.

"Still here, man."

"Maybe it wasn't a bad idea to take it low when the weight was all on the other side. Dig it, man, the Indian fought the paddy and lost. And the Indian was on his own turf."

"We mighta won," Brew said.

"Yeah, we mighta, Brew," I said hollowly.

"Okay, man," Brew said, smiling.

"You know, Brew?" I said suddenly. "I'm going down South. Wanna come?"

"What fo', man?"

"It might just set me straight on a lotta things. Maybe I can stop being confused and come in on a right stick."

My man's face screwed up like always when he wasn't sure of something. "Ah don't know, Piri," he said. "Down there it ain't like up here. You can do and say more, but down thar in some of them towns yuh jus' blow your cool and yuh liable to find yuhself on some chain gang or pickin' peas on some prison farm—or worse yet, gettin' them peas planted over yuh."

"That's okay, *amigo*, I still wanna make it. How 'bout it?"

"Ah dunno."

"Don't worry, Negro," I said. "I promise not to pull no Jim Crow act on you when we get there. Some of my best *amigos* are Negroes."

"It ain't that," Brew laughed. "It's jus' that bomb on your shoulder. We go down South and you start all that Porty Rican jazz and we's liable to get it from both sides."

"Brew, I'm serious," I said.

"So am I, man, so am I. How yuh figure on goin'?"

"Merchant Marine's the big kick around here now. All we gotta do is make it down to the NMU."

"What's that?"

"The National Maritime Union," I explained. "That's where we can take out some papers or something. Dickie Bishop works down there and we're tight, so no sweat."

"Okay, man," Brew said, "Ah'm with yuh. But only on the condition you cool your role."

"Till somebody starts something?"

"Till somebody else starts, not you. An' if trouble does start, don't go looking for too much police protection down there. Mos' of the fuzzes down there are cops by day and walkin' bed sheets by night."

"I won't look for it, Brew," I said.

"Sometimes yuh don't hafta, Piri. Sometimes you don't hafta. When we gonna make it over to the NMU?"

"*Mañana,* man. First thing in the morning. You can meet me here around eight. Better yet, stay over my house tonight."

"On Long Island?"

"Yeah."

"You still go out there?"

"Once in a while," I said. "I still have my people there."

"Yeah, Ah know."

"Meet me about six o'clock," I said. "It's about two now."

"Tha's nice," Brew said. "It'll give me a couple hours with Alayce."

"Yeah, how is she?" I asked. "That's a nice woman."

"A-huh. She's awright. Gets me warm sometimes, but they don't come no motherfuckin' better, in or outta bed."

"Give 'er my regards."

"Sure will."

"Well, cool it, faggot," I smiled.

Brew grinned and said, "Dozens? Evah notice how your pappy walks?"

"Nope, I've been too busy diggin' how your mammy walks."

We laughed and slapped skin going away. I watched Brew make it and then walked off toward Penn Station. Some thoughts were still working in my mind. *Jesus, if I'm a Negro, I gotta feel it all over. I don't have the "for sure" feelin's yet.* I waved to one of the cats in front of El Viejo's candy store and kept on walking.

SUBURBIA

"You and James are like houses—painted white outside and blacker'n a mother inside. And I'm close to being like Poppa—trying to be white on both sides."

14. LEARNING SOME NEW ABC'S

The next morning I was awakened by a shrill clacking. I reached out with eyes closed, found the alarm clock with the sight of outstretched fingers and, click, I killed it by turning a little knob. "Hey, Brew, get up," I called sleepily. I let my eyes open slowly, like it was a luxury they had always deserved. The soft half-light made its way into my room like a bashful intruder.

I felt my face and wished I could spit out my tongue, which tasted like shit. I scratched my belly and smothered an itch that was becoming familiar with my balls, then I jumped outta the bed and took a look at the dead clock. Its sad face said 7:45. "Come on, Brew," I said, "shake a leg." I pulled the covers off my *amigo* and gave the lifelike corpse a mighty goose and it came to outraged life.

"Hey, man, cool that shit," Brew said. "Ah might get to like it, and it'll be your fault if I'm ruint for evah an' evah." Brew very daintily got outta bed and, wrist-limp, swished his way over to where his pants were and pulled them on like a broad getting into a girdle. We both cracked up and fell all over the room on a laughin' kick.

"Hey, will you stop yelling so I can get some sleep?" a voice called angrily. "A man sleeps when he's not working. I work nights. So dammit—"

"Sorry, Poppa," I said. "It was pretty funny. You should have seen it." But Poppa had fallen out again, sound asleep. I jumped into my clothes, made it to the toilet, and went into the same old routine: 1. Take a leak. 2. Brush my teeth. 3. Wash myself—sometimes a shower. 4. Shave—sometimes. 5. A dab of Dixie Peach and a lotta brushing, always. I looked at myself in the mirror. *Damn,* I thought, *I sure favor Poppa. Wonder how come we got a last name like Thomas.* Lots of people had asked me how come my name wasn't Puerto Rican, like Rodriguez or Cruz. "Who evah heard of a Porty Rican with a name like Thomas?" Brew had said when we first met. "Ah thinks maybe your daddy is a home boy trying to earn some overseas status on a Porty Rican kick." We had tangled and dealt up a storm. I had gotten my lumps from Brew's fists. But he had caught some Thomas knobs on his side jaw, too.

I winced at the memory and attacked a patch of killer hair that refused to lie stuck under the Dixie Peach. "Man," I called, "ain't that cat up yet?" I opened the bathroom door and made it to the kitchen. I smelled the bacon and eggs and Momma's fine coffee.

"*Buenos días, hijo,*" Momma said to me.

"*Buenos días,* Momma," I said. "Smells good!" I sniffed my eyes toward the table. There was Brew stuffing his big face. "Man," I said to him, "you're eating and you ain't even washed your mouth out yet—forgetting about washing your face, which wouldn't even be noticed."

Brew looked up. "Whatta yuh think Ah am," he said, "some kinda pig? I washed my mouth. Ah drank me two big glasses of watah."

"Ugh!" I said simply.

Brew put an offended look on his face, but didn't stop eating. "Ain't yuh-all gonna eat, bro?" he asked between swallows.

"Why, shore, *panita.* Soon as you're finished, we'll stop off at some restaurant and get me some breakfast," I said.

"Man, yuh sure starts playing the dozens early in the a.m."

"Only kiddin', baby," I said. "Knock yourself out."

"Thankee kindly, suh," Brew said and continued chomping away. "I just dug your brother James make it to school," he added. "He's kind of a funny cat. Nice and po-lite, but kinda cold."

"Aw, he's all right," I said. "It's José who's the funny one. I got an idea about what's shakin'—and you know what's shaking, too. What'sa matter, forget all that shit we talked about yesterday?"

"Ah remembah," Brew said. "But it's a hard thing to try an' dig."

"Pass the bread," I said.

"Knows what Ah hate mos'?" Brew asked, handing me a slice of bread.

"What, man? Lemme have the butter."

"Ah hates cornbread and sugar watah. Ah hates cardboard in mah shoes. Ah hates wakin' scared. Man, Ah nevah had much o' schoolin', Piri; the only lessons Ah evah got was from my mom. You know, Ah used to speak some terrible English. It's only now I'm talking better."

"Your moms taught you school stuff, didn't she?" I asked.

"Naw, man, schooling was for few in my country."

"Where's that?" I asked.

"Near Mobile, Alabama. Won't say where, man, 'cause I almost forgot its fuckin' name. A black man there could appreciate what a boot in the ass and in the chest at the same time can be. But a lot of black men couldn't dig that style. Some left for here, and others hadda leave. Anyway, my mom showed me some lessons she figured would keep me and my brothers alive and well. Kind of an ABC."

"Damn, man," I said, "you coulda left me some bacon."

"Ah did. Here you is," Brew said, handing me an inch-long piece of bacon. I gave Brew a grateful smile. "Mom was asking us to cop a plea to the white man," he continued. "A—accept. B—behave. C—care."

"Care?" I asked.

"Yeah. Mom wanted us to do all three, but especially the last one. She wanted us to care for the white man, not hate him. Goddammit, *care* for those motherfuckers! That's what dear, sweet Jesus does for our people:

> We is all God's chillun,
> So we gotta care.
> We is all God's chillun,
> So we gotta share.

Poor Mom," Brew added. "We shared awright—white man got the sun and we got a black night."

"Brew," I said.

"Yeah, man."

"You're sure a prejudiced Negro. You're almost as bad as me."

"A-huh. What time is it?"

"Damn, le's go, it's 8:45."

"Bye, Moms," I whispered.

"*Adiós, hijo.*"

"Bye, ma'am," whispered Brew.

"*Adiós, hijo.*"

"Thanks for the breakfuss."

"*De nada,* you welcome any time," Momma said, and added, "*Hijo?*"

"Yeah, Moms?"

"*Ven acá.*" I walked back to Momma and she whispered, "Why do you always have to go back to the *Barrio?* Ever since you leave the hospital you are in the *Barrio*. Why don't you get a job here? You seventeen years old now. Where do you get money?"

"*Caramba,* Moms, I told you I work at the dock unloading ships with Soto's old man. He's the shape-up man and he gives me plenty of work. I make out good," I lied. How could I tell her I was pushing pot and making good bread? "And besides, Moms," I added, "all my friends are there. I don't dig the *blancos* around here, and they don't dig me 'cause I'm black to them."

"You are not black," Momma said, "you're brown, a nice color, a pretty color."

"Not to them, Moms. They—aw, let's forget it, Moms. Give me a kiss and your blessing."

Momma kissed me and her *benedición* breathed itself on my back.

An hour later Brew and I were in Penn Station walking quietly toward the subway. Brew was lost in thought. I wondered if maybe he was thinking about getting down South again or about when he had said, "Bye, ma'am, and Moms had put him under her wing with her "*Adiós, hijo.*" *Jesus,* I thought, *even if she's some kinda paddy, she's got some kinda balance inside. Maybe Poppa turned her inside when he made me take hold inside her belly.* "Brew," I said aloud, "let me take care of the talking at the Union. I can run it to Dickie an' we'll make out all right."

"Yeah, tha's cool with me," Brew said, and added, "Say, yuh knows what Ah been thinking?"

"Was sorta wonderin', Brew. You been kinda quiet."

"Thinkin', man, about maybe Ah's been a little hard on yuh. Ah means, that shit Ah got mad about."

"Don't worry, *panín,*" I said. "Here comes the train. Let's make it."

The train roared to a stop and all kinds of people pushed and shoved themselves into a sameness. The doors slid shut and the train jerked itself out of the station like it was sure of where it was going. I looked around. Everyone was in his own private world despite the close packing of bodies. I was squeezed in between a Chinaman and a soft broad. The Chinaman I ignored, but the *chica* was something else. Her ass was rocking to and fro, from side to side. The friction against my stomach caused a reaction, and the reaction kept time with the motion and the roaring insanity of the train.

I tried to think of other things, like cowboy flicks, lemonade and "mind over matter." *Git down, stiff joint,* I commanded. *This broad's liable to think I'm some kind of weirdo instead of a nice normal Puerto Rican.* I pushed back, away from her. "Sorry," I mumbled.

Brew was reading the subway ads so he couldn't see what was happening to me hung up between the Chinaman and the soft-assed broad. The train lurched and that soft pile of rump crashed hard against my innocent joint. *Damn, she hadda feel that,* I thought ruefully. *Hope this bitch don't start yellin' up a storm.*

She didn't. She just turned and smiled expressively. It was a very damn-liberal smile. She didn't move away, and I could feel my joint playing it cool between her thighs. She pressed hard against me and let herself roll with the train. Man, I did the same. The train rooshed-sooshed to a stop at 42nd Street, and the doors slid open. Nobody got off; instead, more people piled in, and the pressure of the added closeness pushed me into the corner of the train. The softness before me went the same way. "Sorry," I said.

"It's all right," she said sweetly. "Let me see if I can get my balance."

I pushed back against the Chinaman and he, in self-defense, pushed back against the enemy. I held the weight back long enough for the girl to shift her weight and turn to face me. She looked flushed, and she smiled.

We said nothing else. The great weight came back and pushed us close together again. I felt her breasts hard against me and my joint bursting its wide vein between her thighs. Pressed together, we let ourselves roll in that hung-up closeness. I looked at her. Her eyes were closed. I made my hips dance a slow grind, and I let my hand think for itself and bite those liberal breasts. The whole motherfuckin' world was forgotten in the swingin' scene of stress and strain, grind and grain on a subway train.

We were roaring into the 14th Street Station. *Hurry, hurry,* our bodies urged, and *swoom-ooo-mmm*—girl and me and train got to the station at the same time.

I felt her tremble and shiver as I boiled over. The train slowed down, and we held on tight. I dug her face, her paddy-fair face. Her eyes were still closed, and her teeth were biting into the corner of her lower lip.

Thc train stopped and the opened door shitted people out, releasing the pressure. We were swept out onto the platform and separated by the going-everywhere crowd. I reached out to touch her one more time, but the broken dam of people wasted the distance between us.

I tried to see which way she was cutting out, but all I caught was a pin-look see of her looking back for someone. I thought of calling out her name. But I didn't know her name, and I couldn't just start yellin', "Here I am, paddy girl." She disappeared, and I heard a voice call, "Piri! Hey, man, here Ah am. What you-all lookin' ovah that way for?" It was Brew. He chuckled and said, "Yuh lookin' for me an' here Ah am right behin' yuh."

"Yeah, Brew," I said absently, "ain't that a kick?" I felt kinda weak, like you feel when you've seen something glittering down a subway grating. You figure it's worth something, but you ain't got nothing to get ahold of it with. So you comfort yourself by saying, "Aw, it probably was a washer or something," and you never know whether or not it was for real.

"Man," Brew sighed, "I sure am glad to be off that mother-loving train. I-mag-ine," he added mockingly, "havin' to be crushed up by them smelly white folks! They should have a special train for them. Ah's gonna write a letter to the N-A-double-C-P and have the law changed. Ah don't mind their havin' equal rights, but we black folks draw the line at havin' ta socialize." People looked at us cracking up and that made the crack-up even worse.

"Come on, let's get over to 17th Street," I said.

"Yeah, Ah hope we can cop them seamen's papers," Brew said.

"Don't work up a sweat, Brew. It's in the pocket right now," I assured him. "But say, ain't you the cat that wasn't so sure about going down South?"

"Ah still ain't too sure. It's damn hard leaving the South and harder still goin' back. But now that it's come down to it, Ah'd like to see what's shakin' home. What's your feelings?"

"Like I said, I wanta find out why I'm sharing the pain."

"You're startin' again?" Brew asked suspiciously.

"No, *señor!* I'm lookin' to end it," I said.

"There's the place," Brew said. "National Maritime Union."

We walked in, and a couple of hours later we walked out feeling like able-bodied seamen. "Whatta'd I tell you?" I said. "Wasn't it a cinch?"

"Yeah, but it sure took a lotta walkin' an' talkin', man. Ah sure is tired."

"Yeah, but we got the papers."

"Man, this sure don't look like me," Brew said, looking at his Coast Guard pass picture.

"Sure doesn't, *panín*. You're more ugly."

"Fuck you, man," Brew said with malice and friendship. "But it ain't bad," he added. "You think I oughtta shave my pussy tickler? It don't look too good in the picture."

"What mustache you talkin' about?" I sounded.

"This one, man," Brew said, carefully smoothing down the thin line of hair on his upper lip.

I looked at it critically. I even ran my fingers over it as if to convince myself there was something there. "Man, I don't know what to say. It don't show too much," I said. "Maybe it bein' black hair and, er, eh, you, er—well, er, kinda bein' the same, uh—you know—shade . . . Do ya think maybe if we painted your pussy tickler blond it, er, would stand out a little bit better?"

Brew threw a friendly punch. I ducked and threw a couple

of dummy punches, and Brew came back with a flurry. We stopped before it got serious, slapped skin, and kept walking. Brew put his arm around my shoulder, and I put my arm around his. I wondered what was the name of the girl on the train.

"You know, Brew," I said, "Dickie said we'd have to make it down to Norfolk, Virginia, for a ship. Shipping is slow right now in New York."

"When we leaving?" Brew asked.

"How about tomorrow?" I said. "I'll go home now and tell my folks."

"Your folks don't know you're goin'?"

"Not all the way. I've been running the idea to Momma about joining the army or something. That something is now gonna be the merchant marine."

"Think they'll come for the idea?" Brew asked.

"Hope they go for it," I said. "But if they don't, I'm making it anyway. We're gonna need some bread," I added. "You got any bread, Brew?"

"Ah got about $63 put aside. Think that's enough?"

"Should be," I said, "with the 118 *pesos* I got from hustling the pot I had. Bus fare is about $17 one way."

"One way?"

"A-huh. What we gonna need a round trip for? We gonna get us a ship, ain't we?"

"I almos' forgot that," Brew said.

We got to the corner of 14th Street. "Well, cool it, man," Brew said. "Ah'm splittin' here. Think Ah better make it up to Alayce's."

"Why don't you come over to my house and cop some good-o Porty Rican cookin'?"

"Nay, man, Ah better see her while Ah can, cause after we leaves, there ain't no mo'; besides she got some good grit waiting for me."

"Yeah? like—"

"Like greens, an' black-eye peas, an'—"

"*Papipas,*" I broke in.

"Wha's tha'?"

"Ham hocks, Daddy-o."

"Later, turkey. Be good."

"Yeah, baby, take it slow," I said. "I'll pick you up at Alayce's tomorrow morning." I cut down the subway steps and walked up to the turnstile. I took a quick look at the cat in the change booth and, like a million times before, when I was a kid, I jumped the turnstile so fast and smooth that it looked like I'd paid. The subway platform was almost empty. The herds of working slaves were still working. I looked down the tunnel and saw the little green lights of the train going from side to side, getting bigger and bigger. I was thinking about that paddy girl.

The train jerked to a stop and I got in. I looked around, expecting to see the broad again, and sat down across from a wino who was spread out all over the seat. He looked a mess and I dug how peacefully dirty he was.

An hour and some thirty minutes later I was turning up the walk to the house in my other world. I whistled like always and heard Momma's voice.

"Is that you, *hijo?*"

"*Sí,* Moms." I kissed Momma a noisy kiss on the back of her neck. "Hey, Moms, is Poppa home?" I asked.

"Not yet," Momma said.

I decided to wait till he got home and break the news all at once.

"Wan' to eat before you wash?" Momma asked.

"Later, Moms. I want to take a shower first," I said. I undressed and got into the shower and let the water dig into me like shotgun BB's.

My shorts were stiff and starchy from the great strain on my vein, so I soaped and rinsed them and tossed them into the washbowl. The memory of that train ride stirred my joint again. I wondered if the broad was rememberin' how great it was, or if she was tellin' her friends how she made a horny

Porty Rican climb the side of the wall on a subway train just by wiggling her white snatch against his black cock. I frowned. I'd thought "black cock," and that meant the broad was prob'ly sayin' "nigger" instead of "Porty Rican." I had a mental picture of all her friends hanging on her every word . . . "*You know, of course, that niggers got pricks two and three times as big as a white man . . . I tell you, girls, even through my dress I felt like I had about half of it inside me . . .*"

I shut my eyes to keep the soap out and saw her face clearly, her eyes closed and her teeth bitin' her lower lip . . . "*And when he grabbed my breast, I almost screamed, but I didn't want him to stop . . .*"

"*Oh! I'd die if it were me,*" said one of the listening broads.

"*I almost did,*" said my broad. "*I felt myself tremble all over and that black boy pushing all the weight of his thing into me and I felt my knees get weak and I'm pretty sure he had an orgasm, too, because he sort of sagged against me.*"

"*And what happened after that?*"

"*The train stopped and I got swept out along with him. We were separated. I'm glad 'cause I couldn't bear to have him say anything to me after my practically going to bed with him.*"

"*Don't be foolish, that's not the same as when you're with your husband.*"

"*I know, but regardless, it was with a* colored *boy. I just got away from there. I looked back once to see if he was following me and saw him looking over the heads of people as though he was looking for someone. In that one second, I was never so ashamed of myself.*"

"*Oh, you needn't feel that way. It was just one of those nasty-delightful things one does in rare moments.*"

"*You don't understand. I was ashamed because I wanted to fight my way back to him.*"

I bent down and turned off the water tap, satisfied on the ending of my mental production of "Beauty and Black's Best." But inside me, I felt hot and real stink about this funny world and all the funny people in it.

15. BROTHERS UNDER THE SKIN

My daydreaming was splintered by my brother José kicking at the door in sheer panic. "Hey, who's in there?" he yelled.

"Me, man, me," I yelled back. "Whatta ya want?"

"Let me in. I gotta take a piss so bad I can taste it."

"Taste good?" I asked softly.

"Dammit, open up!"

I laughed, and reached out a dripping hand and flipped the latch. José rushed in like his behind was on fire. His face had a pained look on it. "Chri-sus sake," he said, "you made me piss all over my pants."

"It'll dry, man, it'll dry."

"Aggh," he said as he relieved himself. "That feels good." I looked at my brother. *Even his peter's white,* I thought, *just like James's. Only ones got black peters is Poppa and me, and Poppa acts like his is white, too.*

"Poppa's home."

"Yeah. Hand me the towel, simple."

"Damn, Piri, you made me piss all over my pants," José said

again. He pulled back the towel he was offering me and began to wipe his pants with it.

"Man, turkey, what you doin'?" I said. "You drying that piss and I gotta wipe my face with that towel."

"It'll dry, man, it'll dry."

I yanked the towel outta his hand and carefully wiped with what seemed to be the part he hadn't used. "You know somethin', José?" I said.

"What? Jesus, I hope this piss don't stink when it dries."

"I'm goin' down South."

"Where?"

"Down South."

"What for?"

"Don't know all the way," I said, "except I'm tryin' to find somethin' out."

"*Down South!*" He said it like I was nuts.

"*Sí.* I want to see what a *moyeto*'s worth and the paddy's weight on him," I said.

"Whatta ya talking about? You sound like a *moto* who's high on that *yerba* shit. And anyway, what's the spade gotta do with you?"

"I'm a Negro."

"You ain't no nigger," José said.

"I ain't?"

"No. You're a Puerto Rican."

"I am, huh?" I looked at José and said, "Course, you gotta say that. 'Cause if I'm a Negro, then you and James is one too. And that ain't leavin' out Sis and Poppa. Only Momma's an exception. She don't care what she is."

José didn't look at me. He decided that looking at the toilet bowl was better. "So whatta you got to find out, eh?" he said. "You're crazy, stone loco. We're Puerto Ricans, and that's different from being *moyetos*." His voice came back very softly and his hand absent-mindedly kept brushing the drying wet patch on his pants.

"That's what I've been wanting to believe all along, José," I said. "I've been hanging on to that idea even when I knew it wasn't so. But only pure white Puerto Ricans are white, and you wouldn't even believe that if you ever dug what the paddy said."

"I don't give a good shit what you say, Piri. We're Puerto Ricans, and that makes us different from black people."

I kept drying myself even though there was nothin' to dry. I was trying not to get mad. I said, "José, that's what the white man's been telling the Negro all along, that 'cause he's white he's different from the Negro; that he's better'n the Negro or anyone that's not white. That's what I've been telling myself and what I tried to tell Brew."

"Brew's that colored guy, ain't he?" José said.

"Yeah—an' like I'm saying, sure there's stone-white Puerto Ricans, like from pure Spanish way back—but it ain't us. Poppa's a Negro and, even if Momma's *blanca*, Poppa's blood carries more weight with Mr. Charlie," I said.

"Mr. Charlie, Mr. Charlie. Who the fuck is he?"

"That's the name Brew calls the paddies. Ask any true *corazón* white motherfucker what the score is," I said.

"I'm not black, no matter what you say, Piri."

I got out of the shower and sat on the edge of the tub. "Maybe not outside," José," I said. "But you're sure that way inside."

"I ain't black, damn you! Look at my hair. It's almost blond. My eyes are blue, my nose is straight. My motherfuckin' lips are not like a baboon's ass. My skin is white. White, goddamit! White! Maybe Poppa's a little dark, but that's the Indian blood in him. He's got white blood in him and—"

"So what the fuck am I? Something Poppa an' Momma picked out the garbage dump?" I was jumping stink inside and I answered him like I felt it. "Look, man, better believe it, I'm one of 'you-all.' Am I your brother or ain't I?"

"Yeah, you're my brother, and James an' Sis, and we all

come out of Momma an' Poppa—but we ain't Negroes. We're Puerto Ricans, an' we're white."

"Boy, you, Poppa and James sure are sold on that white kick. Poppa thinks that marrying a white woman made him white. He's wrong. It's just another nigger marrying a white woman and making her as black as him. That's the way the paddy looks at it. The Negro just stays black. Period. Dig it?"

José's face got whiter and his voice angrier at my attempt to take away his white status. He screamed out strong, "I ain't no nigger! You can be if you want to be. You can go down South and grow cotton, or pick it, or whatever the fuck they do. You can eat that cornbread or whatever shit they eat. You can bow and kiss ass and clean shit bowls. But—I—am—*white!* And you can go to hell!"

"And James is *blanco*, too?" I asked quietly.

"You're damn right."

"And Poppa?"

José flushed the toilet chain so hard it sounded as if somebody's neck had broken. "Poppa's the same as you," he said, avoiding my eyes, "Indian."

"What kinda Indian?" I said bitterly. "Caribe? Or maybe Borinquén? Say, José, didn't you know the Negro made the scene in Puerto Rico way back? And when the Spanish spics ran outta Indian coolies, they brought them big blacks from you know where. Poppa's got *moyeto* blood. I got it. Sis got it. James got it. And, mah deah brudder, you-all got it! Dig it! It's with us till game time. Like I said, man, that shit-ass poison I've been living with is on its way out. It's a played-out lie about me—us—being white. There ain't nobody in this fucking house can lay any claim to bein' paddy exceptin' Momma, and she's never made it a mountain of fever like we have. You and James are like houses—painted white outside, and blacker'n a mother inside. An' I'm close to being like Poppa—trying to be white on both sides."

José eased by me and put his hand on the doorknob.

"Where you going?" I said. "I ain't finished talking yet."

José looked at me like there was no way out. "Like I said, man, you can be a nigger if you want to," he said, as though he were talking with a ten-ton rock on his chest. "I don't know how you come to be my brother, but I love you like one. I've busted my ass, both me and James, trying to explain to people how come you so dark and how come your hair is so curly an'—"

I couldn't help thinking, *Oh, Crutch, you were so right. We shouldn't have moved to Long Island.* I said, "You and James hadda make excuses for *me?* Like for me being *un Negrito?*" I looked at the paddy in front of me. "Who to?" I said. "Paddies?"

Lights began to jump into my head and tears blurred out that this was my brother before me. The burning came up out of me and I felt the shock run up my arm as my fists went up the side of his head. I felt one fist hit his mouth. I wondered if I had broken any of his nice white teeth.

José fell away and bounced back with his white hands curled into fists. I felt the hate in them as his fists became a red light of exploding pain on my tender, flat nose. *Oh, God!* I tried to make the lights go away. I made myself creep up a long sinking shit-hole agony and threw myself at José. The bathroom door flew open and me, naked and wet with angry sweat, and José, his mouth bleedin', crashed out of the bathroom and rolled into the living room. I heard all kinds of screaming and chairs turning over and falling lamps. I found myself on top of José. In the blurred confusion I saw his white, blood-smeared face and I heard myself screaming, "You bastard! Dig it, you bastard. You're bleeding, and the blood is like anybody else's —red!" I saw an unknown face spitting blood at me. I hated it. I wanted to stay on top of this unknown what-was-it and beat him and beat him and beat him and beat him and *beat beat beat beat beat*—and feel skin smash under me and—and—and—

I felt an arm grab me. It wasn't fair; it wasn't a *chevere* thing to do. In a fair rumble, nobody is supposed to jump in. "Goddammit, are you crazy?" a voice screamed. "Goddamn you for beating your brother like that. My God!—"

I twisted my head and saw Poppa. And somewhere, far off, I heard a voice that sounded like Momma crying, "What's it all about? What's it all about? Why do brothers do this to each other?"

I wanted to scream it out, but that man's arm was cutting my air from sound. I twisted and forced out, "Lemme go, Poppa. *Coño*, let me go!" And the arm was gone. I stayed on bended knees. My fists were tired and my knuckles hurt at this Cain and Abel scene. As the hurting began to leave me, I slowly became a part of my naked body. I felt weak with inside pain. I wondered why.

"José, José," Momma screamed, and I wondered why she didn't scream for me, too. Didn't she know I had gotten hurt the worst?

"Why in God's name?" Poppa was saying.

Fuck God! I thought.

"Why in God's name?"

I looked at Poppa. " 'Cause, Poppa," I said, "him, you and James think you're white, and I'm the only one that's found out I'm not. I tried hard not to find out. But I did, and I'm almost out from under that kick you all are still copping out to." I got up from my knees. "Poppa," I added, "what's wrong with not being white? What's so wrong with being *tregeño?* Momma must think it's great, she got married to you, eh? We gotta have pride and dignity, Poppa; we gotta walk big and bad. I'm me and I dig myself in the mirror and it's me. I shower and dig my peter and it's me. I'm black, and it don't make no difference whether I say good-bye or *adiós*—it means the same."

Nobody said anything; everyone just stood there. I said, "I'm proud to be a Puerto Rican, but being Puerto Rican don't make the color." Still there was silence. "I'm going," I said.

"Where?" Poppa asked.

"I don't know . . ."

"He's going down South," said José, sitting on the floor with his head in his hands and the almost-blond hair, the good, straight hair that could fall down over his forehead.

"*Where?*" Poppa asked.

I looked at José and felt sorry for me. I looked at the wall and said, "Down South. I joined the merchant marine and me and Brew's going, and—"

"Who? Brew? That's that colored boy, ain't it?" Poppa said.

"—and I wanna find out what's happening, and . . ." I wondered why everything I was saying didn't sound like it was so important to anybody, including me. I wondered why James wasn't there. I wondered why Sis wasn't there . . .

I walked away. Momma put her hand on me and she asked, "Why does it hurt you so to be *un Negrito?*"

I shook my head and kept walking. I wished she could see inside me. I wished she could see it didn't hurt—so much.

16. FUNERAL FOR A PRODIGAL SON

Breakfast the next morning was kinda quiet. The whole scene looked strange. Poppa, who worked nights and never sat at the kitchen table unless it was Saturday or Sunday, had joined us. It was like a Puerto Rican funeral for a baby, when everybody plays games like pinning twisted paper tails on people and setting fire to them, then making a roar of soundless laughter and drinking coffee and eating *tocino* sandwiches.

Momma put everything on the table as though she had never done it before. James tried hard not to look at anyone. José tried, through a swollen eye, not to look like he'd made a choice between a brother and a color. *I love you all,* I thought, but nobody heard my thoughts, so I said aloud, "I love you all. I just can't dig your—"

"Please, Piri," Momma said, "don't start this thing again."

"Sure, Momma," I said, "I'm just trying to say I don't wanna leave no bad-tasting feeling in any of you after I ain't here anymore." I tried to look everybody in the face at the same time. I made words: "You understand, Momma—I gotta find me. Maybe if I had come outta you with the same kinda color as them"—my eyes swept across my paddy-fair brothers—"maybe I wouldn't feel like I do. Who knows? Maybe I'm jealous. Maybe I hate 'em for what I'm not—"

"*Dios mío*," Momma said, "you speak of hatred against your own *familia*—"

"Not against my family, Moms," I said, "just against their color kick. Like Poppa, for trying to show what's not inside. Goddammit, can't he see that the whole white world don't care what he feels like inside? Poppa, they don't care how you feel inside. They don't care if you look white. No mix, no mingling—for Christ's sake, even your shit gotta be practically white!"

I looked at all the faces. Nobody said anything. "Ain't nobody gonna say *nada*?" I asked. The silence was a bitch, unbearable. Intolerable, like prejudice. I pulled my chair back.

"You haven't eaten anything," Momma said.

"Sorry, Moms, I—" What the fuck could a guy say under all that strain? A strain that had been a long time coming. And now it had happened and it couldn't ever be forgotten. "Er, I gotta be going," I mumbled.

I looked at each of their faces—Poppa's, Momma's, José's, James's, and Sis's. Momma came toward me and took my face in her warm arms and just looked at me. She was quiet for a long while, then she said, "Be *un hombre*, wherever you go."

"*Sí*, Moms, I'll be a man."

"God bless you and guard you."

"*Gracias*, Momma."

"Son," Poppa said, "there's a lot of things I'm right in and there's a lot of things you don't understand just yet. Maybe you see something in me I haven't seen yet, or maybe won't admit yet. I don't like feeling to be a black man. Can you understand it's a pride to me being a Puerto Rican?"

"What kind, Poppa, black or white?" I didn't want to get mad, but I couldn't help myself. I was trying to blame somebody for something that was hurting me, and I couldn't say it in words without getting mad. "What kind, Poppa?" I repeated. "Don't you say you're mixed with Caribe or Borinquén

Indian blood. Poppa, don't you know where you at? Or are you seeing it, Poppa, and making like it's not there? If you're really so sure you're white, come on down South with Brew and me and see where you're really at. You don't even have to go down South. You can see where you're at right here. Only thing you don't hafta worry about is sitting in back of trolleys or buses. But then, you only go to places where you're sure you ain't gonna have no trouble. You protect your lying dream with a heavy strain for a white status that's worthless to a black man. You protect your dream, Poppa, protect it, but that's all it is—just a dream. You gonna have to wake up to the fact that you ain't white, but that's all right, Poppa, that's all right. There's pride galore in being a Negro, Poppa."

I looked at Poppa's face and saw it get kinda tight, and I waited for his big hand to smash into my mouth. But Poppa just got up from the table real slow and mumbled, "I'm not very hungry, Momma . . ." He walked away, hurt for having had this truth pushed out at him by a son who looked like him but didn't want to be like him. Suddenly he stopped in mid-step and turned around. "Uh, do you need any money?" he asked me. His voice was flat, neither calm nor angry.

"No, Poppa," I said.

"I have a few *pesos*," he said.

"I got some money, Poppa."

Poppa turned away and his voice trailed behind his back ". . . think I'll get some sleep . . . working nights is tough . . . hard to sleep daytime . . ."

Poppa, I thought. *I'm sorry, but I can't help it. I want you all to share my hurt.* "Poppa," I said, and took a step toward him. He kept on walking and mumbling ". . . be good to work days . . ."

I felt a hand on my shoulder. It was José. "Piri," he said, "I can't help what I am, or what I look like, or how I feel, any more than you can. You wanna be black. You wanna find out if you can fit better. That's you. You're still my brother, if you can overlook my color. That's me. I'd like to hug you, but it don't seem right. At least not right now. One of us might think we don't mean it."

"Thanks, José," I said. "I don't have no bad feelings. At least I won't like me to have any. One thing I do know I got. I got some bad confusions going on inside of me."

José's fingers started to tighten on my shoulder, then relaxed. I thought, *José got my fist in his eye and I've put a doubt on him, like something he might forgive but won't forget.*

I made it to my old bedroom and threw a few things into a suitcase. I looked at my wallet and counted $118. With Brew's $63 that was plenty. We'd get us a ship going coastwise through all those southern ports. *You gotta have faith, brother. You gotta have faith, saith the good book. Why?* I thought. I picked up my suitcase and made it into the kitchen. James was looking at the wall. José had his swollen eye. And Momma and Sis were crying softly. Nobody except Poppa had moved. Courtesy is a must at a funeral. *Poppa's got a way-out dream,* I thought, *and Momma's got his pain—an' us kids share both.*

I let the suitcase feel the floor and walked over to Poppa an' Momma's room. "Poppa," I called. He was on the bed. My Poppa, a man who had put some kinda seed in Momma; a seed named Piri. I called louder, "Poppa!"

"Uhhhh?"

"You ain't asleep, huh, Poppa?"

"No, honey," he said.

Honey. Poppa only called us kids "honey" when he was feeling something big, like hitting the numbers or getting a raise. Or real sad. "Poppa, forgive me," I said. "You try to understand me. I can't fool me any more. I can't dig another color and make it mine just 'cause it's some kind of worth. It's not my worth. My own is what I want, nothing more. If there's anything in between, and it makes me belong, then that's what I want. I don't wanna choose Momma's side and I don't wanna pick your fooling dream. Poppa, I don't mean to be disrespectful, but I gotta say it like it is. I got something that's been growing inside of me for a long time. It started growing in the

Barrio and it got going out here in Long Island. I got two big kinds of hate getting bigger inside me, Poppa, understand?"

Poppa was quiet. He turned over slowly.

"Poppa," I said. "You favor the other kids over me, don't you?"

"I love you like I love the rest," he said.

"Sometimes, Poppa, didn't you favor them a little more?"

"I—I got pride in you, *hijo*," he said slowly. "Maybe I—I mean, maybe it looked like I did, or maybe deep down I have. I don't know. Maybe." Poppa's eyes were on his hands, and one fingernail was trying to peel the broken fingernail from another finger. "I ain't got one colored friend," he added, "at least not one American Negro friend. Only dark ones I got are Puerto Ricans or Cubans. I'm not a stupid man. I saw the look of white people on me when I was a young man, when I walked into a place where a dark skin wasn't supposed to be. I noticed how a cold rejection turned into an indifferent acceptance when they heard my exaggerated accent. I can remember the time when I made my accent heavier, to make me more of a Puerto Rican than the most Puerto Rican there ever was. I wanted a value on me, son. But I never changed my name. It was always James Thomas. Sometimes I was asked how come, if I was Puerto Rican, I had James Thomas for a name."

"What'd you say, Poppa?"

Poppa's one fingernail finally peeled the broken fingernail off the other finger. In a voice like crying, he said, "I'd say, 'My father was so proud to be an American that he named all his children with fine American names.' God, I felt like a *puta* every time. A damn nothing." Poppa started looking for another broken fingernail.

I believed everything Poppa said 'cause I'd never heard his voice cry before. I didn't know what to say. I felt ashamed, but I didn't know who for. I had a going-away pain of wanting to be some place else.

"—even said I had Indian blood in me," Poppa mumbled.

That's what José had said. I backed away from Poppa's bed.

"Bye, Poppa," I said. It didn't sound gentle enough. "Bye, Poppa," I said again, more gently.

Poppa didn't answer. He was way back when he was a young man and running into his own kinds of walls. I walked back into the kitchen. "I'm going," I said. I hugged Momma and Sis. I half put up my hand for a good-bye to my brothers and thought I saw James do the same. José winked and maybe even smiled. I made it out the door.

I hate funerals, I thought. *Too fuckin' sad.*

DOWN SOUTH

I felt like maybe I bought a ticket to the wrong Technicolor movie.

17. GONNA FIND OUT WHAT'S SHAKIN'

I walked up to the brown-faced building on 118th Street and Lenox Avenue where Alayce lived. Her windows on the second floor were covered with newspapers instead of shades. I whistled, and Brew's face appeared between the newspapers and he motioned me to come up. I took the worn marble steps three at a time, and when I reached the second floor, Brew was leaning on the banister.

"Real modern joint you got here, Brew," I said with a straight face.

"Don't knock it, rich boy," he laughed. Then he saw the lump on my face where my brother had scored. "Man," he said, "who jumped you, a Red Wing? Them paddies got to go."

"It was a paddy all right, but no Red Wing."

"Jus' one paddy?" We went inside. "Ah hopes yuh busted his dick string. Who wuz it? Anybody Ah knows?"

"My brother José," I said. "And he didn't jump me. I cooled him first."

"Wha' cause the shit?"

"Same old shit—the black an' white story; but let's forget that. I got my suitcase from El Viejo's candy store. Ready to make it? We can cop a Greyhound bus for Norfolk, Virginia, and be there in seventeen hours if—"

The toilet door opened and Alayce came out. "Hi, Piri," she said and came over and hugged me. "What Ah heah about you two goin' to Norfolk?"

"Damn Alayce, you always sure do look fine. If you ever want to leave that Negro and make it with me, we can swing. Us Puerto Ricans can make some bad lovin'—"

Brew cut me off with a pillow looped into my face from across the room. "Down boy," he grinned, "les' Ah lay a heavy hand on yuh."

"Now, Brew," Alayce said, smiling, "yuh all knows Ah'm yours and an' yours alone. What time yuh gonna pick me up, Piri?"

Brew's face went into a comic look of betrayal. Throwing one hand across his eyes, he began beating his chest with the other, moaning, "Mah best frien' and mah only gal. But Ah won't stand in your way. Be happy, mah chillun, fo' as long as you both shall live. An tha' ain't gonna be fo' long. Whar's mah shotgun?"

We all cracked up laughing and couldn't look at each other without splitting our sides.

We sat there quiet for a while, and then Alayce asked again: "What's this stuff about goin' to Norfolk, Virginia?"

Brew looked at me sideways. "Din't Ah tell yuh, baby?" he said to Alayce.

"No, you din't tell me, baby."

"Ummm. Wal, it's like this, honey, Piri wants to go on down South to find out what's shaking."

"To find out what's shaking? What's he wanta find out, an' why you gotta go, too?"

"About Mistuh Charlie, an' peoples. An' Ah sorta promised Ah'd go along."

"What people?"

"Our people."

"He makin' some kinda research or something?"

"No, baby—Ah mean, yeah—Ah mean, our people is his people and he wants to be sure about whar he's at, 'cause his momma's a paddy and his poppa ain't, an' he's got trouble with his brudders 'cause they feels to be paddies and they's overlookin' the fact they got some tar-brushing on 'em, and his poppa doan' wanna believe that, an'—"

"What the hell you-all talkin' about, Brew?" Alayce burst out. "He's a Porto Rican and that's whar he is. We's Negroes and that's whar we're at."

Shit, I thought, *this broad sounds just like José.*

"Hold on, baby," Brew said. "Sure he's a Porty Rican, but his skin makes him a member of the black man's race an' hit don't make no difference he can talk that Porty Rican talk. His skin is dark an' that makes him jus' anudder rock right along wif the res' of us, an' tha' goes for all the rest of them foreign-talkin' black men all ovah tha' world. When you're born a shoe, yuh stays a shoe."

I lit a cigarette and sat back on the beat-up sofa. A lotta lovin' had broken its back.

"But honey," Alayce insisted, "Porto Ricans act different from us. They got different ways of dancin' an' cookin', like a different culture or something."

"What's culture gotta do with the color of your skin?" Brew asked sarcastically.

"I dunno, but Ah've met a whole lot of dark Porto Ricans, an' I ain't met one yet who wants to be a Negro. An' I don't blame 'em. I mean, like anything's better'n being a li'l ole darkie."

"What you say?" Brew said. He got a funny wasting look in his eyes. "Bitch, did Ah heah you right?"

"I said what I felt, honey. It's hard to be just plain black."

"Yuh think Ah doan' know that? Ah'm a black man, gur-ell."

"It's harder bein' a black woman," Alayce replied. Her voice was soft, like she knew her man was getting mad but she couldn't stop, or she didn't want to. "Ah ever tell you what happened—"

"Goddammit!" Brew said, "it don't make no fuckin' difference what happened, yuh supposed to be proud of being a Negro. Don' yuh know that's what red-neck Mr. Charlie wants us to feel? Yee-ah, be so fuckin' ashamed of being black you lose all your damn worth and git to feel lesser'n shit so's when they han' y'all that shit yuh jus' take it, 'cause shit is shit an' his own can stant his own."

I took a long drag and stared at a picture on the wall. It was a picture of Christ kneeling with his hands clasped together and looking up at the sky with a hangdog look. The picture was covered with dust and a pair of Alayce's stockings were draped over one side, making it hang lopsided. The Christ in the picture was paddy. I blew smoke toward the picture and watched the blue smoke form clouds around the kneeling figure. I half expected the Christ to cough. He didn't.

"Honey," Alayce said, still softly, "you once told me about yuh momma an' how she raised so many kids and taught you all something you call ABC's, remember?"

"Yeah. So what?"

"How proud you feel, honey, smiling at Mr. Charlie from clear down yuh asshole?"

Smack! I looked down from Christ's picture in time to see Alayce go sliding across the room on her ass, blown there by Brew's big-handed slap. Brew stood there, his face twisted, and I couldn't tell if he was fighting to keep the tears in or to let them out.

"You bitch!" he said.

I looked at the picture and thought, *Pray for her, Christ, she's gonna get wasted.*

"You bitch!" He blew it out with real tears. "You think Ah didn't feel all that shit? Ah ate and lived with that ABC bullshit Momma put down, an' one day I couldn't no more. Ah was about sixteen yeahs old. Ah was comin' down the back road headin' home and two motherfuckin' crackers were comin' toward me. One yelled out, 'Hey, niggah, whar yo'-all goin'?' An' Ah smiled and smiled clear down to my ass, jus' like

Momma said Ah should. Man, Ah almost tore my ass off, Ah wagged it so hard."

Alayce was still sitting on the floor; Brew was trying not to blow his cool; I was looking at the picture on the wall; and Christ was still praying.

"One of the white boys," Brew continued, "put his hand on my haid and rubbed it jus' like he musta done a thousand time to one of his dogs, an' then he winked at the other white boy and said, 'You know, John, I bet heah's one of them good nigras. Ain't you, boy?'

"Ah said through a smile, 'Yassuh.'

" 'An' bein' a good nigra, you-all won't mind doin' a favor for us . . .'

" 'Guess not, suh.'

" 'Fine, fine. Jus' take your pants down an' we jus' do a li'l corn-holin' with you-all.' "

I looked at Brew. He was like one of those statues in Central Park. Only the tears running down his cheeks made him real. He went on talking. " 'No, suh, Ah couldn't do that.'

" 'Why not, nigger?'

" ' 'Cose Ah'm a man.'

" 'Wal, nobody'll know, boy.'

" 'Ah'll know.'

" 'Ketch holt of him, John—'

Brew's big fist was pressed against his palm. I looked at Alayce. She was still sitting where Brew put her. There wasn't any expression on her face. She just kept her eyes on Brew.

"You-all know what Ah did, Alayce?" he said. "Ah kicked John daid in his balls and got aholt of the other cracker's neck and squeezed and squeezed until his goddamm red face got redder and he went limper'n a motherfucker."

"You kill him, Brew?" I asked the wall.

"No, Ah din't. He jus' laid thar like he was snorin'. Ah got me a big rock an' walked over to the white boy named John. He was holdin' on to his balls an' twitchin' all over. When he saw me standin' over him with that big rock, he began to whine like one of his dawgs. 'Damn, boy,' he said, 'we's only funnin' with you-all. We warn't goin' do you no harm at all. Please, boy, don't drop that damn rock.'

" 'Say *suh*,' I told him.

" 'Suh.'

" 'Say, *Youh better'n Ah am—suh*.'

" 'You're better'n Ah am—dammit, boy, I tole you we was funnin—'

" 'Say, *A black man's better'n a white man*.' He sat there lookin' at me funny-like. Ah raised the rock an' said, 'Say it!'

" 'A-black-man-is-is-bet . . .' *You goddamn black bastard! I won't say it, you goddamn nigger!*"

Brew stood there and his hands slowly let go of an imaginary rock. "Ah dropped that fuckin' rock dead on his mouth and watched him spit out blood an' teeth, an' then Ah went home an' tole Momma what I done, an' next thing Ah was in a car with mah Uncle Stevens drivin' like hell ovah the state line an' on a train to New Yawk. That was three years ago . . ."

"Goodness," I said in a fake voice, "that was a close shave, *amigo*. You almost lost your cherry."

Brew laughed, and with that his body relaxed. I looked at him *serio* and said, "Lucky you didn't kill him."

"Same thing, Piri. Hittin' a white man down thar is same as killin' him."

"How about your folks? Nobody tried getting even?"

"Naw. They din't know who Ah was, an' as for discriptions, 'One nigger looks like anudder.' "

"Going down South now ain't going to put you in no binder?"

"Naw. Ah was big then, but Ah'm bigger now. 'Sides, that was three thousand years ago."

Alayce said from where she was still sitting, "Ah'm sorry, honey."

"What for, girl? Paddies gotta be sorry, not us."

"Ah mean Ah'm sorry for not being proud of what we are.

Ah guess Ah can't forget the so many times them white boys tried to pull me into the bushes like Ah was one big free-for-all pussy. Ah can't forget the one time they finally did. Ah fought them as hard as Ah could. There were four of them, an' Ah was fifteen, an' they hurt me an' hurt me an'—"

Brew walked over to Alayce and bent down and picked her up gently. He looked at her face and his big hands made her look at him. They didn't say anything, not a word. Brew put his arms around her. I'd never seen my boy so gentle.

"Alayce, honey," he said, "there ain't nothin' so bad can happen that'll make one ashamed of what they is, if they's proud enough."

I almost couldn't hear Brew saying it. Alayce held on to him real tight and they walked over to the newspaper-covered window. Brew's fingers gently tore the paper away and they both stood there, looking out. I dug Christ's picture. He hadn't moved. I got up and walked over to the door. "Brew," I called.

"Yeah?"

"You don't hafta go down South with me."

"Ah'd like to see Momma again."

"She'll surely be happy to see you again," said Alayce.

Brew looked at Alayce. "Ah wants to find you waitin' right heah when Ah gets back," he said.

"Be right here waiting for you, Brew."

"Pack mah stuff, girl. Want a drink, Piri?"

"*Chevere!*"

Brew got a bottle.

"I wonder if I gotta right to be as mad as you, Brew?" I said, thinking aloud.

"Man's got a right to what he feels. Your mad is jus' as important as mine or anybody's."

I pointed toward Christ's picture. "You think he was prejudiced against something?"

"Ah dunno, man." Brew kept his eyes on the picture for a long while and finally added, "He was white, wasn't he?"

I waited downstairs while Brew said his good-byes to Alayce. After a long time, he finally came down. "Man," I said, "how long do your farewellings take?"

"Ah made out with her one more time. Have yuh seen your broad yet?"

"No," I said, "and Trina ain't no broad. She's damn fine and she's good. She don't go in for shackin' up with everybody."

"Jus' close frien's, huh, buddy?"

"I'm serious, Brew. She even goes to mass and stuff like that."

"Man, Piri, she must of got off at the wrong station. She shoulda kept right on goin'. Like heaven-bound."

I laughed. "I mean it, Brew. I really dig her. She ain't hip and that's what I like."

"So, daddy-o, you-all gonna be the first one to break cherry."

"Hey, man! Nothing like that. I ain't gonna *chinga* her till we're married."

"You-all that close already?"

"Not yet, man, not yet. But we will be. Hey, let's cop a cab an' pick up my suitcase at El Viejo's and make it to the bus terminal." We got a taxi, and ten minutes later we turned into 104th Street. "Right there, cabbie," I pointed, "on your right."

"A-huh," he muttered, "will you be gone long?"

I laughed. "Don't worry, cabbie. This ain't gonna be no *bomba*. I'll even leave my good *amigo* here for security."

"Oh, hell, I didn't mean it that way," the driver said quickly, "I just meant—"

Brew laughed and said, "Tha's all right, mistuh, we knows what you meant. There's all kinds of turrable people in this heah neighborhood."

I walked into El Viejo's, got my suitcase, and said *adiós* to my boys. The driver had the trunk of the taxi open and I put my bags in and started to climb into the cab when I saw Trina.

"Hold it, Brew," I said, "I'll be right back," and I called Trina and ran up to her. She looked oh-so-fine.

"*Cómo está*, Piri?" she said.

"Fine, Trina," I said. "Look, I'm leaving town and I wanted to say so long, an'—"

"Wait!" she said. "No talk so fast the Engleesh."

I apologized and repeated in Spanish what I had said.

"Is for lon' time?" she asked.

I told her maybe, maybe not, but that I would write to her, if that was okay.

"*Sí*, if you like," she said.

"Will you answer my letters?"

"*No comprendo*—ans-sur?"

I said it in Spanish.

"*Sí*," she replied, "surely."

"Hey, Pi-ri!" Brew called, "shake your ass, man. This heah meter is countin' his mother off."

"Hold it, man," I shouted back, and then to Trina I said, "*Mira*, I wanna tell you something. I ain't got time to tell you what I should've when I had time, but I dig you a whole lot."

"*Deeg* you?" she asked, puzzled.

I explained to her what it meant and told her that I would write it to her in Spanish and say it like it was. "*Adiós*, Trina," I said, and I touched her hand and held it for a hundred years.

On the way downtown to the Greyhound terminal, Brew asked me, "Piri, your girl, Trina, she's white, ain't she?"

"Yeah. So?"

"Ah mean, ain't you-all so down on paddies?"

"Trina's Puerto Rican, Brew."

"But still white, man. Jus' like a Porty Rican spade is still a spade."

"Shit, Brew," I said, "you getting things all fucked up. Trina ain't like the other kind of *blancos*. She's different."

"How many kinds is thar, Piri?"

"Good-o an' bad-o. *Trina's* good-o."

"White is white," Brew insisted.

I didn't answer him. I just dug pretty girls until the cab rolled into the terminal.

We got our tickets and boarded our bus, which was bound for Washington, D. C., and points south. I started to sit in a front seat but Brew caught my arm and motioned me to follow him. He walked all the way to the back of the bus and sat down. "What's the idea?" I said. "Don't you know back seats on buses are the bumpiest?"

"Yeah, baby, I know," he said. "But let me tell yuh like it is. Once we all cross the Mason-Dixon line, all spades will commence to sit their asses in the ass of the bus. I thought it right good fo' yuh to git used to the idea from the jumps."

I laughed and said, "Dig it." But in my mind I hadn't thought it was gonna apply to me.

We changed buses in Washington, and when we started to roll again, the colored people, who had sat wherever they wanted to on the bus from New York, were not sitting where they wanted to any more. It was black from back to front and white from front to back. I looked at Brew and he said, "Getting used to the idea, Piri?"

"Who the fuck can get used to any shit like this, man?"

"Wal, baby," he said, "forget 'Glory, Glory, Hallelujah' an' quick memorize 'Dixie.' "

I looked through the darkness of the bus and took another slug of the whisky which we had brought with us. I wondered about Poppa and Momma and the kids, about Harlem, about Trina. "Hey, Brew," I said.

"Yeah."

"That stuff you was saying about Trina being a paddy—"

"What 'bout it?"

"She ain't prejudiced. She don't dig that kinda shit."

"Yuh sure?"

"Sure, Brew. There's a lot of light Puerto Ricans married to dark Puerto Ricans."

"You-all think she'd marry a dark cat who wasn't no Porty Rican, like me, fo' instance?"

"I believe it, Brew, if she loved you."

"Thar's a lotta white Porty Ricans that's prejudiced, Piri."

"Yeah, I know. But they caught that played-out sickness over here."

"Sure?"

"I'd like to believe it, Brew."

"Likin' to believe it don't make it so, man. Ah'd like to believe Ah ain't prejudiced, but Ah am. Ah'd like to believe a lotta things, but they jus' ain't that way. You're prejudiced, too, Piri."

I didn't answer that; I went back to Trina. "There's plenty like Trina," I said. "It's like Alayce said, 'Puerto Ricans got a different culture.' "

"Don't git too hung on that idea, man," Brew replied. "They may have a different culture, but they's probably got some different way of discrimination. Maybe them that got bread are down on them that got none. Dig it?"

I let it rest.

An hour later we checked into a Negro hotel in Norfolk. We grabbed some breakfast—it was still early morning—and made it down to union headquarters on the other—the white—side of town. On the front of a small, wooden building hung a "National Maritime Union" sign. We walked up to a window and waited for the cat behind it to give us some attention.

"Yee-ah," said a paddy with a colored voice.

"We'd like to ship out," I said.

"Le's see your union books."

"Ain't got any yet. We're trip cards."

"Wha' kinda ratin' y'all got?"

"Messman, wiper, an' ordinary seaman."

"No good. Ah got calls fo' three AB's, one cook, and an oiler. An' besides, union memba's come first. Maybe tomorrow."

Brew got close to the window and said, "Think we can git us a ship tomorrow? We got us about twenny dollas left—er, twenny apiece—an' if we could get us a ship real soon, we shore wouldn't need no money on the ship. Say," Brew added, "maybe you could take the money and donate it or somethin' to the Seamen's Fund."

"Whar y'all lookin' ta ship out to?" the paddy asked.

"Coastwise—anywhere around southern ports," I said.

"Some ship due in a couple days an' thar's a pretty good chanct fer you two . . . Tell you-all what. Come back day afta tomorrow. Purty good chanct you-all make out all right."

"Wal, thanks a lot, mistuh," Brew said.

" 'S'all right. Ah likes ta help fellers jus' gittin' started." I started to turn away. "Uh, wait a sec," the paddy said, "didn't y'all say somethin' 'bout how you'd like to contribute about forty dollas to the Seamen's Fund?"

"Now?" I asked. Mr. Paddy smiled a big "now." Brew and I looked at each other, wondering if this could be a hyep, like him takin' the bread an' not coming through. But it was a risk we had to take. I nodded my head and Brew pulled out forty *bolos* and smiled at the cat. "We almos' forgot," he said. "We sure got some bad mem'ries. Hope we all don' forget we gotta be heah day afta tomorrow so's we can ship out. Tell you what, Piri," Brew added, looking innocent, "you remind me an' Ah'll remin's you so we don' forget."

I grinned at the paddy and said, "Thanks a lot, mister. We really appreciate your giving us a hand. Lotta people wouldn't give a damn."

"Tha's all right, boy. Glad ta help out."

I started to give him a funny look at that "boy" shit, and Brew put his arm around me and moved me toward the door, saying, "Ain't it great, man! We're gonna ship out." Outside he said, "Piri, what'd Ah tell you about that jumping stink? These paddies call us 'boy' jus' as nat'ral as they calls us niggers. It's jus' part of they vocabulary. Jus' don' blow your cool, okay?"

I promised I wouldn't.

18. BARROOM SOCIOLOGY

That night, after a nap, we walked around the colored part of Norfolk. The night air was cool and everything was living and going someplace. It reminded me of Harlem. We were on our way to the Blue Bell, a place Brew remembered from another life. It had a dance floor, a hot combo, and some rooms nearby for sitting out dances.

It wasn't a big place, but it swung. Inside it was dark except for red and blue light bulbs that gave the walls the shadows of the patrons. Brew and I got to a table and almost right away a waiter came up to us. "May I help you, gentlemen?" he asked.

We gave him our order, and a few minutes later he returned with our drinks. He spoke so well I asked him if he was from New York.

"No," he said, "I'm from Pennsylvania. But I can tell you're from New York, and," he added, looking at Brew, "you're not."

"Yuh right," Brew said, "Ah's a home boy."

"Been here long?" asked the Pennsylvanian.

"Couple of days," I lied. "We're on business. How about you?"

"Well, I've been here—excuse me, somebody's waving for

service. Look," he said as he moved away, "I have my relief in a few minutes and if you don't mind, I'll join you for a chat."

We nodded "okay," and the Pennsylvanian saluted his thanks and drifted off through a mass of bodies. I eye-drilled a hole in the dress of a pretty baby leaning on a jukebox across the dance floor. "I'd like to get workin' with her like real fast," I said. "Dig, she got my eye."

"Well, play it cool," Brew said, " 'cause tha's what she's heah fo', to ketch yo' eye an' yo' bread."

As I rolled my eyes around the broad's curves, the Pennsylvanian returned with fresh drinks. He sat down and told us he had been in Norfolk about three months. He looked about twenty-five or twenty-six. "I'm writing a book on the Negro situation," he said, "and I came down for the sense of personal involvement. I wanted the feel of what it means for a Negro to live here in the South. Background and such, you know what I mean?"

"Damn, man," Brew said, "yuh sho' coulda picked a tougher place than Norfolk fo' your book. Ah means a place whar you li'ble to get a kick in yuh background."

The Pennsylvanian smiled. "Oh, I'm not looking for that kind of personal involvement," he said. "I'm not seeking violence but rather the warmth and harmony of the southern Negro, their wonderful capacity for laughter and strength, their spiritual closeness to God and their way of expressing faith through their gospel singing. I want to capture on paper the richness of their poverty and their belief in living. I want the words I write to blend with the emotions of their really fantastic ability to endure and absorb the anguish of past memories of the slavery that was the lot of their grandparents. I want to write that despite their burdens they are working with the white man toward a productive relationship."

I glanced at Brew. He was studying the shadows on the walls. I took a good look at the Pennsylvanian. He was tan-colored and not really very negroid-looking. I got a funny, almost proud feeling that I looked more negroid than he did.

The Penn State man continued, "You see, I really feel the large part of the publicity being given the southern situation is adverse and serves only to cause more misunderstanding. I realize that there have been incidents, and white men have been cruel and violent toward the Negro, but only an ignorant and small minority—"

Brew broke in quietly with a wave of his hand, "You not a southe'ner, are yuh?"

"No, I'm not."

"Evah bin down South before?"

"No, I haven't."

"Evah notice any of these problems you was talkin' 'bout up No'th?"

"Well, I suppose there is some bigotry up there, but it's not the same, or at least I find it doesn't have the same meaning as here in the South."

"Ah sees," said Brew, barely hiding a growing disgust. "You-all been any other places inna South?"

"No, but I've been making plans to go to Atlanta, and—"

"You oughta go to some of them small towns whar a rock better fuckin' well know his place."

"Well, I don't think that's totally necessary. The problem of the southern Negro is the same whether he's in the large cities or in back-wat— I mean, backwood counties. I believe that the southern Negro of today is marshaling his dignity and preparing himself for a great social revolution."

"Yuh-all gonna be a part of it?" Brew asked.

"I certainly feel that my book will contribute in some effective way to the Negro's cause."

"Ah means," said Brew, "if it comes down to fightin' an' havin' black an' white mixing their blood on big city guttahs or goddamn dirt roads?"

"If in looking for a solution to this problem," the Pennsylvanian replied, looking at me, "it comes to the point of violence, I know that many will die, especially Negroes. Those that fight, of course. And that will be their contribution to their cause. Some whites may die, and that will be their contribution to their cause. But it falls to others, black or white, to contribute in some other way. Perhaps one of these ways is by writing. By writing I will be fighting."

"About what? an' foah who?" said Brew. "Yuh gonna write 'bout Negroes' warmth an' harmony, an' their won'erful ability to laugh an' rejoice, an' that shit 'bout the richness of their poverty? Yuh gonna write 'bout their fantastick 'bility to endure fuck-up mem'ries of slavin' an' smilin'? Prissy, wha's your name? Mine's Brewster, Brewster Johnson."

"My name, Mr. Johnson, is Gerald Andrew West," the Pennsylvanian said in such a way to let Brew know that he didn't like being called "Prissy." It was like the way you let someone know your name when you think he's inferior to you.

There was a fifth of whisky on our table. It hadn't been there before, or had it? It was almost empty, and I felt high, and Brew seemed high too. "You-all don' mind if ah calls yuh by your first name, eh, Ger-rul?" he said.

"If you like—er, Mr. Johnson—I hope I haven't caused any misunderstanding between us. I didn't mean to cause any resentment. I hope . . ."

Brew didn't answer.

"Don't worry, man," I said, "say it like you feel it," and I nudged Brew to keep his cool. He smiled gently, like a hungry tiger, and I knew he'd stay cool. "*Suave, panita,*" I added to Brew.

"Oh, you speak Spanish," Gerald Andrew West said to me, "Mr.—"

"Piri—Piri Thomas. Yeah, I do."

"How wonderful! Are you of Spanish descent?"

"No, just Puerto Rican father and moms."

"I speak a little Spanish, also," said Gerald Andrew West. "*Yo estoy estudiano español.*"

"Ah di'n't order any more drinks," Brew said as another fifth of whisky found its way to the table.

"This is on me, Mr. Johnson. Uh—do you speak Spanish fluently, Mr.—Piri? May I call you by your first name?"

"You 'ready did," said Brew. "Damn p'lite prissy."

I nudged Brew again; he made pop eyes and mumbled, " 'Scuse me." Gerald Andrew West looked like he hadn't heard him or like Brew wasn't there.

"Yeah, you can call me Piri—uh, Gerald," I said.

"You know, Piri, I've been taken for Spanish many times, and Indian, too. I know that many dark people say that, but it's really happened with me." Gerald smiled almost too pat and added, "So you're Puerto Rican?"

I looked at the shadows over Brew's head and then at the jukebox. Pretty baby was still leaning on it.

"A-huh," I answered, "Puerto Rican *moyeto*."

"*Moyeto?* What does than mean?"

"Negro," I said.

"Oh—er—do Puerto Ricans—er—consider themselves—uh —Negro?"

"I can only talk 'bout me," I replied, "but *como es, es como se llama*."

Gerald thought for a second and translated, "Like it is, is how it's called. Am I right?"

"Word for word, *amigo*," I said. "I'm a Puerto Rican Negro."

"Wha' kind is you-all, Gerald?" Brew said, smiling.

"What kind of what?" Gerald asked. "I'm afraid I don't understand you, Mr. Johnson."

"Ah means, what kinda Negro is yuh?"

"Oh! I understand now. Well, uh—according to—er—my —according to a genealogical tracer—you know, those people who trace one's family tree back as far as possible—well, according to the one my parents contracted to do the tracing, I'm really only one-eighth colored."

Brew was shaking his head slowly up and down. He made a move with his head at the bottle and Gerald said, "That's what it's there for, Mr. Johnson. By all means, please be my guest and help yourself."

"How's that work?" I asked Gerald. "I mean, tracing and all."

"Well, you see, they check back to your grandparents and get information so they can trace back to your great-grandparents and so on. For example, my great-great-grandfather was an Englishman named Robert West. He was on my father's side. His wife, my great-great-grandmother, was from Malaya. You can see my eyes have an Oriental cast about them. Well—"

"A-huh, Ah sees," Brew said absently.

"—he—my great-great-grandfather—was a ship's captain and married his wife on one of his trips to Malaya. Then his oldest son, my great-grandfather—his name was Charles Andrew West—married a woman whose father was white and mother was half Negro. They had children and their second son, my father, married my mother, who had Indian blood, from, uh, India, and, uh—some Spanish blood and uh—some Negro, colored blood. I—really—I'm so blended racially that I find it hard to give myself to any, ah—well, to any one of the blends. Of course, I feel that the racial instincts that are the strongest in a person enjoying this rich mixture are the ones that—uh—should be followed."

"What is your instinks, ah, Gerald?" asked Brew, staring at our blended friend.

Gerald laughed nice-like and answered, "I—rather—feel—sort of Spanish-ish, if I may use that term. I have always had great admiration for Spanish culture and traditions. I—er—yes—feel rather impulsed toward things Spanish. I guess that's why I have this inclination to learn Castilian. Of course, I don't disregard the other blends that went into the making of me, which—"

"Yuh evah been mistook fo' a Caucasian?" Brew interrupted.

Gerald smiled politely and answered, "Well, like I said, I'm always being mistaken for one of Spanish, uh, origin, or Puerto Rican. It's the same thing, I guess, and—"

Unpolite Brew broke in again, "Ah said *Caucasian.*"

"Er, I rather think that Spaniards, even though some are swarthy like Italians from Sicily, uh—are considered Caucasians. Yes, I probably have been taken for white."

"How 'bout gittin' mistook fo' a Negro?" Brew asked. He was tight and his voice sounded like it did that day on the stoop in Harlem when he was sounding me on the same subject.

"Well," Gerald said hesitantly, "I've seen looks of doubt, and I've had some rare unpleasant experiences. But I find that I am mostly taken for a Negro by Negroes. I guess there are many like myself who, because of their racial blends, find themselves in the same unique position."

"An' what's your answer when yuh ast?"

"By the Caucasians?"

"Naw! Ah can figger what yuh tells 'em. Ah wanna know what you says to the rock people."

"Why, I say 'yes.' I—er—couldn't possibly say anything else under the circumstances. It would at best create resentment if I attempted to explain that I don't feel one hundred per cent Negro, since I am only one-eighth Negro."

"Don' yuh-all feel a leetle bit more Negro than that?"

Gerald looked at me for assurance that this wasn't going to be one of those "under the circumstances" situations that would lead to resentment and make his "personal involvement" physically painful. I smiled at him that I'd do what I could to keep everything cool.

"Don' yuh-all feel a leetle bit more Negro than that?" Brew repeated. "Tell me, is the book you're writin' gonna be frum the Negro's point o' view? It's gonna be a great book. Yuh-all fo' sure show the true picture of the workin's toward a productive relationship 'tween the Mistuh Charlies and the rock people. Ah am sure that your book will tru'fully show who all is enjoyin' the producin' part from that there relationship."

Gerald stayed quiet for a long time, then he said, "Mr. Johnson, I'd like to tell you something." For the first time he sounded like he was going to say what he had to and fuck Brew and whatever he thought or whatever he was going to do. Brew looked at him *carapalo*. "I'm not ashamed for the so-called 'Negro' blood in me and neither am I ashamed for what I feel myself to be. Nor how I think. I believe in the right of the individual to feel and think—and choose—as he pleases. If I do not choose to be a Negro, as you have gathered, this is my right, and I don't think you can ask or fight for your rights while denying someone else's. I believe that my book will contribute. I believe that the so-called 'Negro writers' are so damned wrapped up in their skins that they can't see the white forest for the black trees. It's true I don't look like a true Caucasian, but neither do I look like a true Negro. So I ask you, if a white man can be a Negro if he has some Negro blood in him, why can't a Negro be a white man if he has white blood in him?"

Gerald tenderly squeezed the flesh of his left shoulder with the fingers of his right hand. I dug the jukebox and its ornament. Brew watched Gerald.

"I believe the Negro has the burden of his black skin," Gerald continued. He was in focus now. "And I believe the white man has the burden of his white skin. But people like me have the burden of both. It's pretty funny, Mr. Johnson. The white man is perfectly willing for people like me to be Negroes. In fact, he insists upon it. Yet, the Negro won't let us be white. In fact he forbids it. Perhaps I was a bit maudlin in describing what I was looking for in the southern Negro, and this may have set you against me. But I would like you to know that if, because of genetic interbreeding, I cannot truly identify with white or black, I have the right to identify with whatever race or nationality approximates my emotional feeling and physical characteristics. If I feel comfortable being of

Spanish extraction, then that's what I'll be. You might very well feel the same way, were you in my place."

People were still dancing and Gerald was still tenderly squeezing his shoulder. I was thinking that Gerald had problems something like mine. Except that he was a Negro trying to make Puerto Rican and I was a Puerto Rican trying to make Negro.

Gerald got up. "Do you know, Mr. Johnson," he said, "it's easier to pass for white down here than up North. Down here, a white man thinks twice before accusing another white openly of being a Negro for fear of getting slapped with a lawsuit or worse. And the Negro only has to think once for fear of just the 'worse.' But up North it's not an insult according to law, and I've never seen or heard of the 'worse' happening. Anyway, I've come down here to find what I couldn't find up North, and I think I've gotten what I came looking for. I've wanted to taste, feel, and identify with what was fitted for me. Even Negro. But I cannot. Not only do I not feel like a Negro, but I cannot understand his culture or feelings or his special kind of anger. Perhaps it's because I was born and raised in the North and went to white schools and white boys were my friends from childhood. I've mingled with colored boys up North, but I never felt like I was one of them, or they of me. Tonight, Mr. Johnson, I started out of place. The same feeling I've lived with a long time. And I found out tonight that I *am* out of place. Not as a human being, but as a member of your race. I will say that you hit it on the head when you insinuated that I was trying to be a Puerto Rican so I could make the next step to white. You're right! I feel white, Mr. Johnson; I look white; I think white; therefore I *am* white. And I'm going back to Pennsylvania and *be* white. I'll write the book from both points of view, white and Negro. And don't think it will be one-sided. That one eighth in me will come through; it's that potent, isn't it?"

Gerald stood there waiting for Brew or maybe me to say something. Brew was looking at a fat broad sitting at the bar.

I looked at the jukebox. Gerald smiled at the shadows on the wall and said, "Good night, Mr. Johnson . . . Piri. And good-bye and good luck."

"*Adiós*, Gerald, take it smooth." I waved a hand and wasn't sure I meant it. But I found it hard to hate a guy that was hung up on the two sticks that were so much like mine. Brew just nodded his head and watched a self-chosen white man make it from a dark scene. "Ah guess he's goin' home," he said and downed his drink. "Le's go see what pussy's sellin' fo' by the pound."

I heard Lady Day singing from the jukebox. The broad was still there, still coming on. I thought, *pussy's the same in every color*, and made it over to the music.

19. LAS AGUAS DEL SUR

Two days later I woke up all burned out. Brew was staggering around too. This was the shipping-out day that our forty *bolos* had bought us.

At breakfast our heads cleared a little and our memories began to focus through the haze of a thirty-six-hour hangover. And it wasn't the *chicas* we remembered, but Mr. Gerald Andrew West, the blended wonder.

"Ah still hates his mudderfuckin' guts," Brew said, "but at least he got the heart to make a choice."

"Yeah," I said, without enthusiasm. My head still hummed, and besides, the memory of Gerald stirred funny thoughts. What he had said about choice had shattered my own ideas on the matter. I felt like maybe I had bought a ticket to the wrong technicolor movie. Brew must have sensed my hang-up 'cause he asked me:

"How 'bout you, Piri?"

I forced myself to think about it for a while, a long while. "Brew," I finally said, "I've been wanting it to be like there ain't no doubts at all, but . . ." Brew looked at me, his eyes trying to break up what I was saying. I went on. "I'm . . . still trying to find what's my kick. I'm still trying to find my own stick of living. Man, Brew, you gotta understand. I want to be wanted—not by them motherfuckers but by me! But I ain't got rid of that fuckin' status that I got brought up on. I don't mean at home alone. I mean like I envied it on the streets, I dug it wherever it meant anything to be better than just a wrong color. I feel like shit. It ain't just that I don't wanna be what I'm supposed to be, it's just that I'm fightin' me and the whole goddamn world at the same time. Jesus, Brew, I don't know if I'm makin' any sense at all, but everybody knows paddies are prejudiced against Negroes—and Negroes want to be prejudiced right back."

"Yeah, but them paddies are nuttin' but fuckin' ignorant."

"Like you and me, eh?" I was trying to keep from getting excited. I didn't want to turn my ace-coon boon against me, but all my life I had wanted to be for real. I had wanted to be proud of feeling just the way I'm supposed to feel. "Am I going down wrong with you?" I asked Brew. "You wouldn't want me to bullshit you?"

"What yuh mean 'like you an' me'?" he said.

"You and me," I said. "You hate Gerald's guts because he don't wanna be a spook and you hate whites for the reason known to a whole certain race that you happen to be part of. And I feel the same because I'm hung up. I still can't help feeling both paddy and Negro. The weight feels even on both sides even if both sides wanna feel uneven. Goddammit, I wish I could be like one of those lizards that change colors. When I'd be with Negroes, I'd be a stone Negro, and with paddies, I'd be stone paddy. It ain't like with Gerald. He got used to his choice even before he had made it, so it's all over for him inside. It ain't like that with me. Mine is startin' for real an' I'm scared of this hate with one name that's chewing me up. So dig it, Brew, if I'm talking one way one time and another way another time, it's only 'cause I wanna know, 'cause I ain't been born but this one time. Understand?"

Brew picked up his napkin and, looking at it intently, said,

"Ah unnerstands, Piri. Yuh-all still sounds like yuh tryin' to walk a fence. Yuh can't do that, man. Yuh knows damn well yuh can't make it like a Caucasian due to your nappy hair—better'n mine, but still nappy. Your nose ain't the right shape; it ain't as flat as mine, but it's still flat, an' your color can't pass as a suntan even if yuh-all had a letter of recommendation from Sun Tan Oil Incorporated."

Brew put down his napkin and we made it out into the street. The sun was nice and warm. A trolley came along and I thought, *There's the trolley and it got some empty seats in the back.* We got in it and sat in our state-appointed seats. Fifteen minutes later we were standing in front of the forty-dollar window.

"Ain't any jobs opened yet; come back tomorrow," said our friend behind the window, without even looking up to see who was there.

"Remember us?" I said. "We're supposed to see you about a boat. We were here a couple of days ago an'—"

"Ah rememba, ah rememba," whispered the treasurer for the Seamen's Fund. "Go on an' set fo' ten or so minutes, then go on 'round the back an' Ah'll see you there."

Ten minutes later we were waiting at the back door. After a while Mr. Forty Bucks stuck his head out, took our trip cards, and handed them back with a piece of paper clipped to each one, "Heah you are, boys," he said, "the address is there on them slips. Ship's on Pier 4. It's a tanker an' yuh both signed on as mess boys. Have a nice trip."

The name of our ship was the *James Clifford.* We walked up the gangplank and at the top some cat asked us what we wanted.

"We're signed on this boat," I answered.

He looked at us and said patiently, "You must be new mickies 'cause you don't call a ship a boat. Le's see your papers. Messmen. Go on back aft and see the steward. He'll take care of you."

"Er, where's aft?" I asked. Brew said, "Tha's inna back,

Piri," and the sailor pointed patiently toward the back of the ship and let out a sigh.

"Thanks a lot, mate," I said, just to let him know I knew something about the sea jazz.

The steward was a paddy with a lotta white hair and just as much beard. We showed him our papers, and after staring at them for a while he said, "Okay, boys, follow me and I'll show you to your fo'c'sle. You fellers got any rain gear or work clothes?"

"We got some clothes," Brew said, "but none of that rain gear yuh-all talkin' 'bout."

"That's all right. You can get what you both need out of the slop chest later."

"Slop chest?" said Brew. "Sounds like a hawg pen."

The steward smiled and said, "It's like a store aboard ship. You can buy shoes, shirts, smokes, and so on; you know, toothpaste, brushes, blades, and so on. And incidentally, if you have no money, you can buy against your wages. Here we are. You're on the port side, midship."

We looked blank, and the steward, showing his nice smile, said, "I know you're first trips, but don't worry, you'll get used to sea gab." We stepped into the fo'c'sle. It had two double-decker bunks, a little table, and four lockers and three little round windows. "You're bunking with the utility and the pantry man," the steward explained.

"Nice room," I said.

"Fo'c'sle," gently reminded the steward.

"Fo'c'sle," I gently repeated.

"I'll give you two a tip," said the steward. "Keep your portholes closed in rough weather or you'll have the whole damn ocean in here."

I cool-walked it over to one of the little round windows and opened it, just to let the steward know that I knew all the time them little round windows were portholes. I got no kind of victory outta that. All he said was:

"When you've finished stowing your gear, come over to the galley and I'll show you both your duties."

Half an hour later we were in the galley. "Brewster," the steward said, "you'll work in the crew's mess hall, and Thomas" —the steward already had given up on "Piri"—"you'll work in the officers' mess." He showed us where everything was and how to set a table. "When the ship sails," he concluded, "you get up at 6:30 a.m., set up your tables, get everything shipshape, and then stand by. Breakfast is at 7 o'clock. You clean up after breakfast and then knock off till about 10 o'clock. Then get started for lunch. After you clean up again, knock off till 3:30, set up again, stand by for supper, clean up again, and then you're off till next morning at 6:30. Got that? Oh, one more thing," he added to me. "Always serve them *hot* coffee. 'Specially the Old Man—the captain. You give these officers good service and when the trip is over they'll tip you pretty good."

I nodded up and down that I would serve my "massahs" well.

"Well, boys," the steward said, "just do your jobs right and you'll find that I'm not the kind of man to be breathing down your necks. Take care, and good sailing." He left and I turned to Brew and said:

"Ain't a bad old cat, huh?"

Brew didn't answer, but I was glad I could still feel good about a white man.

The next morning I was at my appointed station, dressed in a white jacket and serving my "massahs."

"Messman," called the captain.

I turned away from the toaster and walked over to his table. "Yes, sir," I said.

"Son, please bring me a cup of coffee and make it—"

"Yes, sir," I cut in, "black, hot and no sugar."

The captain man smiled and said, "Looks like the steward's been working on you."

I smiled back and nodded. I looked at the chief mate and asked, "Will you also have coffee, sir?"

"Yes, I will, er—thank you."

I let my eyes go over the rest of the officers to see if anyone else wanted my cool service. Nobody said nothing. I went out and brought back coffee. With a good feeling, I watched everybody finish dessert. Everything had gone well. I hadn't forgotten to serve from the right and take from the left. Then the chief mate fucked up my whole meal. He put up one finger and said, "Hey, boy, let me have another cup of coffee."

"Yes, sir." I didn't look at him. I just went to get it.

"Here you are, sir."

"Er, thank you . . . Say, this coffee is cold."

"Is it, sir? I'll get you another cup."

I came back. There was no "thank you" this time.

"Say, fella, this coffee's still cold."

"Can't understand it, sir! Don't worry, I'll get you another cup."

"Never mind."

"It's no bother, sir, I'll be glad to." *It'll still be cold*, I thought.

"Never mind." His lips looked kinda clenched.

"Yes, sir," I said meekly. *Any of you cats that call me "boy" is gonna get the same treatment.*

After everybody had left the dining room and I had cleaned up, I went out on deck. I saw Brew and started to head for him when I heard somebody call me.

"Messman."

It was the chief mate.

"Yes, sir?"

"Look, fella, I got a feeling you brought me cold coffee both times on purpose. Why?"

"Ya really want to know, sir?"

"Yes, I want to know—really," he added sarcastically.

"Well, it's this way. When I was a little kid, my momma told me that someday I'd grow up to be a man, and if I was a good boy and ate a lot, I'd grow into a real *chevere* man. Well, I've done what Momma asked me and I've grown into a man.

If Momma is right, and I believe she is, I ain't no longer a boy. You understand, *sir?*"

I got no answer; he just clenched his lips tight like before and showed me his back.

"Sir," I called, "I don't think your coffee will be cold from now on, unless you want it like that."

He didn't like that, but I guess he liked cold coffee less, because he stopped calling me "boy." Actually, he didn't call me at all unless he couldn't avoid it, and then he just ordered what he wanted without any preliminaries.

We hit Mobile, New Orleans, and Galveston on the trip. Mobile was Brew's home town. "You know this place pretty good, eh, Brew?" I said.

"Like a book, man, like a book," he said. He spoke low and wouldn't say much. I kept tryin' to force some kind of conversation out of him; I figured a guy oughtta be happy to talk about the place he was born in, no matter how bad it was. But Brew wouldn't string more than four or five words together about Mobile. Maybe he was scrapin' up old, long-ago memories. You can share good memories with an ace-boon coon, but not the bad ones.

We went ashore at Mobile and got stoned. On the way back to the ship I got hungry and walked into the first restaurant I saw. It was a white place. There wasn't a black head in there, just a neat row of *blancos* sitting on stools in front of a long counter. I perched on an empty stool at the end of the counter. Brew had warned me about going in, and I could see him through the plate-glass window, standing outside, waiting, with no expression on his black face, the only black face around. I was the alonest.

I heard the walking of shoes and I looked in the direction of the noise. It was the counterman. He passed me right by. I waited until he came my way again and I said, "Two hamburgers an' a Coke." I timed it, I thought, just right.

Nobody said a word.

I repeated my order. Still silence. I raised my fist and

smashed it on the counter with all my Puerto Rican black man's strength. I felt a sense of somebody coming up behind me. Thinking it was Brew, I started to say, "Whatta ya want *to eat, panín*—" when a voice full of Alabama candy cut me off.

"Boy—er—ah—we don' serve nigras heah . . ."

A hand touched a little part of my shoulder. I looked around and a skinny white face said, "Y'all don' want no trouble, do you, boy?" Nobody else said a word.

I jumped off the stool and spilled a lot of bad words, mostly in Spanish. All the eating, smiling, and talking stopped and a mean-sounding murmur rose from all those *blancos* sitting on stools. Brew, who had been watching from outside, came in and gently led me out with looks to the *blancos* that said, "He's a stranger here . . ."

"Brew," I said, but I didn't have to finish. He dug what I was thinking.

"Ah tol' yuh, man. Ah tol' yuh. Why don' yuh unnerstan' that you ain't nuttin' but one mudderfuckin' part of all this hurtin' shit?"

I couldn't answer. I just stood outside that greasy grittin' place that served two kinda menus and tried to keep nutty things that were running all over me from fuckin' my mind up. I wanted to go back into that place and jump on that counter and run down its holy length and kick white plates and cups of coffee into all those paddy laps. The bombs blowing up inside of me made some room for Brew.

"That ain't the way, man, it ain't the way," he said. "If y'all goes back inta that place, it's like stickin' your ass in the hosse's mouth." Brew sounded like he didn't really expect me to believe him. I listened to the noises coming from out of me. They sounded like death, like hollowed-out words which one can only hear in a room with no goddamn way out.

New Orleans was our next stop. I was getting pretty fed up with this two-tone South. Brew, too, seemed to have lost something, maybe in Mobile. We downed a bottle and picked up a couple of octoroon snatch that reminded us of Gerald Andrew West. That was our only laugh in New Orleans. The snatch had separate pads, so we split, and agreed to meet on the ship. Brew never made it. I don't know what happened. Maybe he was gonna pick peas on a prison farm or maybe he went back to Mobile for something he forgot the first time. I waited by the gangplank until they pulled it up and the ship began to slide away from its pier; I searched the darkness for my black brother, my ace-boon coon. But he didn't show. I never saw him again. When I got back to New York, Alayce had disappeared, too. Maybe they went back home together.

A couple of days later the *James Clifford* pulled into Galveston and I went ashore by myself. All that I knew about Texas was what I had seen in cowboy movies. I just walked through town and when I stopped walking I was in the middle of a carnival. I drifted over to a tent where some cats were pitching pennies into a circle for prizes. I threw a few pennies and one of them went into the circle without hitting a line. "*Bueno, hombre, bueno!*" said a cat next to me. He was a Mexican, and we traded names and wandered together through the carnival. We went to a *cantina* and had some drinks—he, tequila, and me, to be true to all *puertorriqueños*, rum. We got on a high and I asked my newfound *amigo* if he knew a cathouse, a white cathouse. I wanted to break out against this two-tone South; I wanted to fuck a white woman in Texas.

"*Sí,* I know one," he said. There was a slight hesitation in his voice and I knew why immediately. He was olive-skinned and his hair was like silk and his nose was straight and fine; then there was me. I looked at him and he said, "Do you know how it is down here? *Qué es tu nacionalidad?*"

"*Puertorriqueño,*" I said. "I know that my hair ain't good and my nose is too flat and my skin is too dark." And very quietly I told him what I wanted to do.

He looked at me and said, "Okay, if that's what you want. If you do not speak a word of English, you may pass for Puerto Rican."

I smiled at that crack. Maybe inside he dug me for a home boy.

We walked down the street and into a nice white hotel. The man at the desk said to my friend, "What do you want?"

"We would like a room and a couple of girls," he replied in a soft Texas drawl.

The clerk said, "What does this boy here want?" He just looked at me. "What's your name?" he asked.

I looked blank. Then, playing my role to perfection, I looked at my Mexican friend and said in Spanish, "What did he say?"

"You don't understand English?" the clerk said. "Where you from? *Dónde tu eres?*"

I lit up my face like I had just come off a banana boat.

"Puerto Rico," I said, smiling.

The clerk sidled over to my Mexican friend and whispered to him, "He ain't a nigger, is he?"

My friend assured him that I wasn't. I looked blank. The clerk told my friend, "Well, you know, we got all kinds of people coming in, all kinds of foreigners, and Spanish people who come from Argentina and Colombia and Peru and Cuba, and that's all right, but we got to keep these damn niggers down."

So we each got a room, and with it a broad, and I fucked my white woman. It cost me $10 (and $5 for my Mexican friend) and the broad thought she was taking me because probably nobody had paid her $10 in the last six months. But the money didn't mean anything to me; I wanted to prove something.

After I had blown my insides into her, I got dressed and told my friend in the next room in Spanish to make it. He asked me why. "Don't ask," I said in Spanish, "just go if you don't want to get killed," and I went back to my room.

A few seconds later my friend popped in. He didn't know what I was going to do, but whatever it was, he knew it was insane. "*Cuidado,*" he said. "Take care."

"All right," I said, and heard his feet running down the

stairs. Then I stepped in front of the mirror and put my jacket on. The broad was still on the bed, wondering if I was going to make her again. When I walked to the door, she smiled and said in broken Texas Spanish, did I like it and did I want more? I opened the door and said, "Baby, I just want you to know"—and I watched her smile fall off and a look of horror fill the empty space it left—"I just want you to know," I repeated, "that you got fucked by a nigger, *by a black man!*" And I didn't wait to hear her gasp or to watch her jump up out of that bed. I ran, I disappeared, because I learned a long time ago to hit and run right back to your turf, and my turf was that god-damned ship.

I made the trip back to Norfolk and caught a ship to the West Indies, signing on this time as a coal fireman on a black gang. Damm-sam, I never knew what a slave was until I began to shovel that black crap. I worked four hours and was off eight, around the clock. But during those four hours I was in hell, and after a few shifts I figured I better do something quick to get outta this coolie labor. I reported sick to the purser, who doubled as the ship's doctor. I told him that I was physically fit but that I couldn't stand heat and could probably die from it. I thought I had signed on as an *oil* fireman. The purser talked it over with the captain and the chief engineer. "Don't worry about nothing, kiddo," the chief told me. "How would you like to work as a coal *supplier?*"

"What's that?" I asked.

"You just supply the coal to the chute that the firemen get their coal from," he said.

I said okay, and someone gave me a shovel that looked like a hoe and led me to an open hatch. I peered in and saw nothing but blackness. The chief gave me a pat on the back and a lamp that burned a wicked smell and a bright light, and down I climbed into a mountain of coal. For the rest of the trip I breathed coal dust, ate coal dust, and sweated coal dust.

About halfway out I got into an argument with one of the firemen, a big Swede. He complained that I wasn't supplying him coal fast enough down his chute. "And you break up the fucking coal"—some chunks weighed fifty pounds—"before you send it down," he added. "You hear?"

A West Indian messman—Isaac was his name—had told me never to take shit from anybody on board or I'd become a flunky. So I shouted down to the Swede that the only thing I would break up and send down the chute in little pieces would be his faggot ass. That did it. He cursed me out good, ending with, "I'll see you on deck, you lousy basturr. By jiminy, I break you just once in half."

"Shove it out," I yelled back, and I felt like I was back on my block.

"Watch out for him, boy," Isaac later warned me. "He may want to out the light for you."

I sized up the Swede. He was a tall man, pretty good build, not young, maybe fifty or fifty-five. But I didn't count too much on his age; these old cats fool you sometimes. I thought it might come when we were off duty, smoking or lounging on deck. But it happened as I was carrying my mess tray from the galley to the mess hall. The Swede had left his food in the mess hall. When I came into view, he met me and knocked my tray out of my hands and all my grit mixed with the fish oil on deck. He hit me upside of my head. I dug the message and copped a handful of throat and punched with my right and wrestled. I dug I was stronger than he was and I decided to strangle him a little. I wrestled him to the deck and wrapped my legs around his waist and got a choke hold around his neck and squeezed. Some spittle began to gurgle out of his mouth. I got shook. *Suppose I kill this* pendejo, I thought. I looked around. If I continued to squeeze, I'd kill him; if I let him go, he'd probably kill me. I saw Isaac, one of the onlookers.

"*Caramba,* Isaac," I said. "I don't want to kill this cat." Isaac nodded to a couple of seamen and they broke it up.

The old Swede had had it and I was feeling flush, like after a rumble when you win. Isaac took me aside. "Piri, I think you are yellow," he said softly.

I felt cold all over. "What do you mean, yellow, you little bastard? Didn't I waste that chump?"

Isaac said just as softly as before, "I think you're yellow not because you didn't kill him but because you didn't *want* to kill him. You'll learn, boy, this is a hard life for a black or brown man. I'm black, you're brown. Unless you're willing to kill at the exact moment you have to, you'll be a pussy bumper for the rest of your life. You got to have the heart not only to spare life but to take it. You can only spare it now, but maybe you'll learn. I don't mean you're yellow in heart, just in instinct."

I said, "If the time comes an' I gotta cool somebody for good, I'll do it, but it gotta be a good reason. I've learned everything I know and if I gotta be a killer to dig myself, I can learn that, too."

I learned more and more on my trips. Wherever I went—France, Italy, South America, England—it was the same. It was like Brew said: any language you talk, if you're black, you're black. My hate grew within me. *Dear God, dear God,* I thought, *I'm going to kill, I'm going to kill somebody. If I don't kill, I'm going to hurt one of these paddies.* I was scared of the whole fucking world. *Brew, baby, you were right!* I cried. *Where the fuck are you, baby? Damn, man, you're my ace, you're my one brother; Jesus, man, I hope you ain't dead. You ain't, are you, Brew?*

HARLEM

Jesus, I thought, *I finally shot some Mr. Charlies. I shot 'em in my mind often enough.*

20. HOME, SWEET HARLEM

I came back to New York with a big hate for anything white.

The first place I went to was *El Barrio*. I had been away for seven months and I wanted to dig the inside of my long block. But I was so fucked-up inside of myself I changed my mind about making it to the block and went instead to see my aunt on 110th Street. She told me that my momma was very sick and in the hospital.

I went to the hospital and found a momma wasted by some killing germs. "Ay, Piri," she said to me, "I prayed to God for He to send you before I die." She was very weak and the doctors wouldn't let me stay long. So I sat at her bedside on a white chair and she held my hand and I read her Bible to her, and she made me promise to go home to Babylon with Poppa and the kids. When I left the hospital, I did a lotta walking around. I got back to my aunt's after midnight and lay across the bed in the extra room thinking about my momma, the little fat Moms I used to know.

A knock at the door about 3 a.m. brought back the realness of that hospital scene. "*Quién es?*" I heard my aunt ask. "Telegram," a voice answered. A few minutes later my aunt walked quietly into my room holding a piece of yellow paper. I sat up and put on the light.

"*Hijo*," she said, and I actually heard her tears fall, "*tu madre se ha muerto*."

"Yeah, I know, Momma died," I said flatly. Hurt can make a cat scream out or cool him into a *cara-palo* stick.

At the burial I hung back after everybody had made it to their cars. I wanted to say something so last and special to Momma, but all I could say was "*Bendito*, Momma, I'm sorry."

I stood there staring down into that uncovered hole in the ground. In my mind the past words of the preacher turning out some fast words of "ashes to ashes and dust to dust. I looked deep into the hole in the ground and hurt-like stared at the individual flowers dropped on Momma's coffin-box by all who loved her. I couldn't remember Poppa's having dropped one too.

"Piri, are you coming?" It was *Tía*'s voice.

I raised my hand in a "wait a minute" sign.

I heard Mom's voice . . . almost.

It said, "Your father has another woman."

"Naw, Moms, it ain't so. Man! Pops is only for you."

"Piri, *vente*." It was *Tía*'s voice.

I said good-bye with my eyes to the hole in the ground.

I stayed at home for a couple of months. I tried to make everything like the same as it was before. Except I had a burning, yearning desire to see what Poppa's other woman looked like.

I broke into Poppa's things. I remember the woman's name. I found her picture. I heard a warning from a brother or sister that I shouldn't go into Poppa's things. I didn't hear them. I just stared at the picture and her name was written there. I wondered if she knew Momma was dead. Her eyes seemed to say, "I am very sorry to hear of your mother's death." *You fucking pig*, I thought, but I just nodded and stared at her picture. She had light-brown hair and green eyes, a thin nose, and a very white skin.

I walked out the house, the picture of Poppa's other woman held almost gently in my shirt pocket.

"Where are you going, Piri?" Sis's voice was somewhere behind me.

I walked down the road without answering. The night was swinging; a three-quarter moon lit up everything. I stopped and took out her picture and stared at it for a while. "She's pretty, all right, but she's shit compared to Momma," I said aloud. I tore up the picture in little shitty bits and flung them up and watched the shitty bits of her make it every which way.

I got home and climbed into bed, feeling glad that I had met her. Now, knowing what she looked like, I could hate her more clearly. I fell asleep on the good-o thought of little shitty bits of her falling to the sidewalk.

Suddenly, in my sleep-blurred mind, I heard cursing and I felt someone hitting me. I was being dragged out of bed. "Okay, where is it?" Poppa's voice came in clear.

"Where is what?" I asked. My hands were partly up. The light bulb on the ceiling went on.

"The picture! You know what I mean. Where's your wallet?" Poppa's face was mean-looking. He picked up my pants and pulled out my wallet. I made a grab for it.

"Hey, Pops, gimme my wallet," I said. "You ain't got no right to be going into my wallet."

I got a slap in the mouth, and wondered who had squealed on me.

"*Qué está pasando?*" said a girl's voice. It was my sister, Miriam. José and James were mumbling something from the next room. I jumped out of bed. "Pops, I ain't kidding, gimme my wallet." Blap, I got another shot in the mouth. I wondered how it'd feel to punch Poppa in the mouth.

He didn't find nothing in my wallet. He picked up my pants and looked through them and still found nothing. "Where's that picture?" he said.

"I ain't got no picture." I smiled. "Besides, I don't know whose picture you're—"

"You little bastard, you know whose picture."

"What the fuck would I want that old bag's picture for?"

Splat, I got another shot in the mouth. I really hated that bitch now and, Pops or no Pops, I was gonna hit him. I lifted closed fists.

Sis saw it and jumped in, crying, "Please, stop, Poppy! Piri! Please . . ."

I saw right there in Sis's good-o-moms, and I relaxed my fists. "Sure, Sis," I said, I ain't gonna—"

"Where's that picture?" Poppa said again. He sure was lost on that kick.

"Goddamnit," I exploded, "I ain't got no picture! If you don't believe me, kill me. Dammit, I wouldn't touch that fuckin' paddy bitch with a ten-foot dick."

Poppa looked at me and just stood there, his fists clenching. I felt higher and higher. "Please, *por Dios*," my sister pleaded.

"If he lays a hand on me again, I'm gonna off him," I said to my fists, and all of a sudden he was gone, just like that. I was shaking all over and Sis was crying. I couldn't. Tears are only for when you feel something. I felt dead. "Go to bed, Sis," I told her, "nuttin's gonna happen. I'm leavin' this fuckin' house and he can shove her up his ass. Come on honey, go to bed."

I didn't sleep that night, and in the morning a hard silence hung over the house. I wanted to get back at Poppa somehow. I found my chance. James was talking about walking me to the railroad station and I answered him in a southern drawl, "Why, sho' man, if'n yuh sho' 'nuff willin', you can sho' 'nuff go wif me all."

"Stop that goddamn way of talking," Poppa shouted.

"Why sho', Pops," I said, "if y'all doan' like the way Ah's speakin', I reckon Ah could cut it out."

That did it. The next second Pops was on me. He grabbed me with both his arms and lifted me off my feet. "Damn you,

I'll teach you," he yelled. "I'm throwing you out of this house and you come back no more. Talking like you came from some goddamned cotton field."

"Is that where you came from, Pops?" I teased him. "Ain't that what bugs you? Ain't that what bugs the hell out of you, Mistuh Blanco in natural black-face? Let me go, Pops, or I'll put my knee in your phony white balls."

Pops dropped me and swung out. I felt his hard fist on my face and the cutting edge of his ring. My head rocked. I felt my face and the blood on it, and everything got red with hate. I ran to the kitchen 'cause I didn't want to hit Pops; I wanted to kill him. "Where's a knife? Dammit. Where's a knife?" I screamed.

Sis was hysterical, José was stone-quiet and James was standing there white with fright. I grabbed a kitchen knife and met Pops running into the kitchen with a baseball bat, and measured.

"Stop it! Stop it!" Sis screamed, and jumped in between us. Her voice was way out. "Stop it, do you hear? I'm going crazy and you're the cause of it. Oh God! Mommie, what's going to happen to us?"

I watched the tears roll down my sister's face and Pops looked at his shaken princess. It took the fight out of us; only the "never forgetting" remained. I just packed my stuff and said good-bye to Sis and James and José. I didn't even look at Pops because he wasn't there for me. I just said a low, " 'Bye, Poppa." It was the most I could do.

21. HUNG DOWN

I made it back to Harlem after that, back to hallways, rooftops, and *amigos'* pads—and real back to drugs.

Heroin does a lot for one—and it's all bad. It becomes your whole life once you allow it to sink its white teeth in your blood stream. I never figured on getting hooked all the way. I was only gonna play it for a Pepsi-Cola kick. Only was gonna use it like every seven days, that is until the day I woke up and dug that I was using it seven times a day instead. I had jumped from being a careful snorter, content to take my kicks of sniffing through my nose, to a not-so-careful skin-popper, and now was full-grown careless mainliner.

At first it was like all right, because I had some bread going for me, but them few hundred bucks melted real fast and all I had was a growing habit. I still had some clothes and a wrist watch but they went the same way the money went. I got a job for a while, but forty bucks or so weren't enough and the more I used, the more I needed.

Yet there is something about dogie—heroin—it's a super-duper tranquilizer. All your troubles become a bunch of bleary blurred memories when you're in a nod of your own special dimension. And it was only when my messed-up system became a screaming want for the next fix did I really know just how short an escape from reality it really brought. The shivering, nose-running, crawling damp, ice-cold skin it produced were just the next worst step of—like my guts were gonna blow up and muscles in my body becoming so tight I could almost hear them snapping.

I could make a choice of stealing or pushing to support my new love. I picked pushing. I walked up and down the streets looking for a guy named Turkey. He'd earned his name from having kicked the habit cold-turkey a few times running in the Tombs City Prison. I finally ran into him in the poolroom on 106th Street. I made a sign for him to come outside. He eased out onto the sidewalk and with his eyes asked me, "How much stuff ya want?"

"I wanna push stuff," I whispered.

"Ya mean ya wanna buy a piece and push it for yourself?"

I shook my head no. "I can't, Turkey, I ain't got the bread. Let me push for you and give me my cut in stuff."

Turkey rubbed his nose like giving me a lot of thought. "Wait for me in front of the school on 105th Street," he finally said. I walked away from him feeling saved or something.

About a half hour later, Turkey walked up to me and in the darkness of the schoolyard pushed a packet gently into my hand. "There's twenty-five bags of good stuff here. For every five bags you push at three bucks apiece, you cop one bag for yourself. You can get rid of twenty bags by *mañana*. Bring me sixty bucks back and you can pick up some more. If you get a hold of some cat that is strung out and you can hook him for more on a bag, the difference is yours." I shook my head up in yes-time.

"If you don't blow your profit, you can put enough bread away to get a piece for yourself and then make enough for money and your veins."

I started to walk and he put a hand on my elbow and said in a real friendly voice, "I'm trusting you, baby; if you blow this stuff on yourself, you're in trouble. Play it cool and I'll trust you much more."

I was back to the next *mañana* with Turkey's sixty bucks and he trusted me much more.

In the months that followed, I was selling nice. I was supporting a habit that ran to about fifteen bucks a day. I shot up every day and I was pleased in a funny way that my arm wasn't tracked up like a trolley-car run. I had cultivated a crater and always shot through the same hole. It sure looked awful, though. The word that I had good stuff went around and I had cats looking for me. A lot of my sales weren't for cash. I took clothes, jewelry, radios, or you name it. I'd buy their things for about a tenth of what it was worth and sell it to a fence up Jackson Avenue in the Bronx for a nice profit. He always paid off in cash and always said the same greedy words, "I'll take all you can bring." You had to be a lot harder to be a pusher; you couldn't have a soft heart, like "no dough, no glow."

Everything was going as good as could be expected. I had a little furnished apartment, and some of us would shoot up and dig red-cloud sounds of whatever our favorite music happened to be. Or we'd make it to a flick, and have a ball looking at whatever was showing or just nodding through the whole scene.

Everything was going as good as could be expected, till the panic hit. There was a short go of heroin on account of some big wheeler-dealer with millions of dollars' worth of the stuff had gotten himself busted and this caused a bad shortage. All the little pushers like myself were either saving the stuff we had for ourselves or were selling it for four times the selling price in the hope that the panic would soon be over and we'd be far ahead with a big profit. What happened was that the panic hung around for weeks and them that had sold for a big profit and users were now paying double the profit they had made. That is, if they could get. Everybody was buying and nobody was selling except the gyps, and they were mixing milk sugar with quinine and selling this ca-ca for the real thing. But not too many got away with this shit kick. They got fixed up one way or the other. And it wasn't a nice way. Some got free

O.D.'s, others just got away with a broken arm or leg. Like it ain't nice to take advantage of people's suffering.

By the time the panic was over, I was in as bad shape as before pushing. I think I was in a worse-off mess. I was broke, had no stuff, and the oodles I had used up didn't belong to me. Turkey wasn't gonna trust me no longer. I let him know where I was at. He didn't say much; he just smiled and said, "Like bring me my money in so many days or *adiós amigo*." I felt sick and walked away thinking maybe I could find somebody to give me a *cura*.

I walked down the streets and looked in through the window of the automatic laundry on Madison Avenue between 103th and 104th streets. Trina was washing some clothes in the machines. I walked in and sat there waiting for her, and my God, I was sick, sick—so goddamned sick. My back was twisted up with pain and I couldn't keep the water out of my eyes and nose.

"What's wrong, Piri?"

"I don't feel so good. I think I got *la monga*."

"*Bueno*, we'll get some medicine from the *botica*."

Jesus, I thought, what I need is a fix, and Trina doesn't know this, or does she? How many times can you hustle money from your girl and she doesn't get an idea of what's happening? Maybe she doesn't want to know.

"Look, Trina, I'll see you later."

"But aren't you going to wait for me?"

"I can't. I'd better go see a doctor." *I'd better go see my connection.*

"I'll see you."

And I walked out of that laundry like if death was there. I walked down toward 104th Street and Lexington Avenue and I saw Waneko.

"Hey Waneko, hey man, wait up."

Waneko waited and I crossed the street. He saw me like I was and said, "What's happening?"

"I'm sick, man."

"Yeah, you've been looking like real shit warmed over for a couple of days."

"Yeah, that *tecata*'s got to me. Jesus Christ, man, I'm hooked and I've been trying to get off but I can't, like if I'm in love with this bitch."

I sniffed and thought how I wasn't gonna get hooked. How I was gonna control it. Why the hell did I have to start playing with stuff? Who wants to be a man at that rate? Hell! All for the feeling of belonging, for the price of being called "one of us." Isn't there a better way to make the scene and be accepted on the street without having to go through hell?

I wiped my nose. The water kept oozing out and my eyes were blurred. My guts were getting wilder all the damn time.

"Man, Waneko, I gotta quit. I just gotta quit."

"Look, man, don't be a jerk and try to kick the habit all at once."

My mind went back and his voice blended into the background of my thoughts. I thought of all the hustling I had gone through for the sake of getting drugs, selling pot, pushing stuff, beating my girl for money. Man, I was sick all over, inside and outside.

"Like all you gotta do is get off the habit a little at the time. Get a piece of stuff and break it up. Each time take less and less and bang, you've kicked, cause trying to kick it cold-turkey is a bitch. Do it this way and—"

"You sure?"

"Yeah, I'm sure."

"I'm gonna try it, but I gotta get some bread so I can cop some stuff. You got anything?"

"Yeah."

"How about it?" I was trying to act cool. I wanted the stuff bad, but no matter how hard I fought it, everything in me was crying out for that shit's personal attention.

Waneko's hand went into his pocket and I dug the stuff in his hand. I felt my throat blend in and out with the yen.

The taste that takes place even before you get the junk into your system. All of a sudden, I felt like nothing mattered, like if all the promises in the world didn't mean a damn, like all that mattered was that the stuff is there, the needle is there, the yen is there, and your veins have always been there.

I went up to the roof of number 109, running up those stairs like God was on that roof, like everything would be lost if I didn't get up there on time. I felt the night air and my eyes made out the shadows of others like me. Cats I knew and yet never really seen before. Their forms made word noises.

"Got any shit, Piri?"

"Yeah, but I need it all, man. I've been fighting a fever. I'd really like to split with you all, but I'm really strung out like I'm swingin' between hell and the street."

"Yeah, baby, we understand, it's okay."

But I knew they didn't really understand. But it's got to be okay; if it was them, it would be the same.

A little later I felt well, like normal. I was looking at the Triborough Bridge and all its lights and thinking about when I was a little kid and how I used to stand up there on the roof and make believe and there I was, almost twenty years old, and I was still going to that roof and still making believe.

I looked toward Madison Avenue and thought of how close it was to Christmas. I thought about shipping out as soon as I could.

"Funny," I said half aloud, "it's like I've been kinda hanging around waiting for Brew to show up. Hope that Negro's okay."

I felt good about something else—me and Trina was making a steady scene; we really dug each other. My eyes crossed Park Avenue and got nearer Trina's house. I thought about being hung up on *tecata* and Trina kind of noticing that I was acting way out. *Coño,* like the time at the flick. I was goofing so bad, I couldn't hold my head up and just kept going into my nod.

"*Qué te pasa,* Piri?" she asked.

"Nothing, girl, just sleepy—tha's all."

I saw Trina come out and stand on the stoop. I felt mad at me for not being satisfied to just snort or a "just once in a while skin-pop." Naw, I hadda be hitting the main vein.

Man, a thought jumped into my mind, *mainline is the best time.* I pushed that thought outta my mind, except for the part of the way out feeling when that good-o smack was making it with you, that nothing in the whole *mundo* world made no difference, nothing—neither paddies nor Poppa and strange other people.

My mind fell back on my pushing stuff to keep my veins happy, and how I was on a certain cat's shit list for taking some stuff from him to sell, and instead, I shot up for as long as it lasted. I mean, like down people know a cat can't help it when *embalao,* like strung out every which way when you need it—that's it, you just need it. But that's a bad bit, cause them people that give you the stuff to push gotta have some kind of trust in you. Even a junky gotta have some kind of dependable, he gotta have some kinda word.

I sat down on the edge of the roof ledge. My mind refused to get off its kick of reminiscing. Man, like how many times some cat's come up to me with his old man's watch or sister's coat and swap for a three-cent bag. Heh, a three-cent bag—like a grain of rice crushed to powder, that's how much it is for a cost of three dollars, and you couldn't beat down that hell-like look as the begging took place in exchange for that super-tranquilizing ca-ca powder. I sniffed back a tear that came out of my nose. And how about the time I plowed through that falling snow with no pride at all in my Buster Brown shoes—like brown on top and bustered on the bottoms—knowing without a doubt in the world that the only thing that would get me warm again so I could care about being cold was the connecting—the blending of my vein's blood and dogie drug.

Shit, man, how far can pride go down? I knew that all the help in the world could get that stuff out of my system, but only some kind of god would be able to get it out of my swinging soul and mind. What a sick mudder scene! If you didn't get gypped outta your stuff, you'd get beat on some weak, cut-down shit. If you didn't get dead on an overdose, you'd get deader on a long strung-out kick. Everything in the world depended on heroin. You'd go to bed thinking about stuff and wake up in the morning thinking about it. Love and life took second place to it and nothing mattered except where, and how soon. It was like my whole puking system had copped a mind bigger than the one in my head.

I walked toward the roof landing. I was thinking. I was gonna kick for good. "I can do it. I swear ta God and the Virgin. Gonna get me li'l shit and cut down good. *I ain't no fuckin' junkie.*"

I went looking for Waneko. I found him in *El Viejo*'s candy store. I put my want to him in fast words.

"Help me kick, man?" It was a question. Waneko knew how it was. Even though he was pushing now, he wasn't using, but he'd been through that kicking road *mucho* times. Waneko nodded, "Sure, *panín*—sure I will." We walked into Waneko's place. He explained to his moms what was shaking. She smiled nice-like and said everything was gonna be all right. Waneko followed that assurance up with, "Moms helps most of the cats that want to kick and even some of the chicks. She should be some kind of church worker or something." He laughed. I tried a weak smile.

They put me in a room that just had a bed and chair and a window that had a metal gate across it to keep the crooks out and kicking junkies in. I laid down, and after a while Waneko brought in a small radio so I could dig some music, to take my mind off what was coming. Both he and I knew that the li'l taste of stuff I had shot up on the roof a while ago was gonna wear off and then World War III was gonna break out inside of me. Billie was wailing some sad song. I wailed along with her in a soft hum. Then some kinda time started to go by and my system was better than a clock. And then Judgment Day set in . . .

Man, talk about wantin' to die—everything started off as it should. First like always, the uncomfortable feeling as you knew your system wanted its baby bottle. And nose running ever so gently at first and the slow kind of pain building up not so gently. I tried hard to listen to some wailin' on the radio, but all I could hear was my own. I got up and went to the door. It was locked from the outside. "Hey, Waneko, open the door," I yelled.

"*Qué es?*"

"I feel real bad, like in bad, man."

"Man, lay down, you ain't been in there long enough to work up any kind of sweat. I'll tell you when, and only then I'll give you a li'l taste to ease you off. So cool it, *panin.*"

I don't know how many hours ran crawling by. I just knew I couldn't make it. *But I hadda. I just hadda.*

"Lemme out, Waneko—lemme out, you motherfucker." I swam to the door and hit at it.

"Waneko is not home right now." It was Waneko's mom.

"Let me out, *señora.* I kicked already."

"He said not to let you come out until he comes back, *hijo.*"

"Did he leave something for me?" My voice sounded like tears. I went back to the bed and just rolled and moaned all alone.

I don't know how many hours ran crawling by. It was a lot of them. At one time I heard the lock being taken off the door and heard it fall from some one's hand. I felt Waneko's mom's voice—I felt her cool hand on my face and felt her wipe my cold sweating face. I heard sounds of comfort coming from her.

"*No te apures, hijo,* you weel soon be fine."

I tried to get up and make it, but she was faster. I felt the iron gates on the window. I shook them. I turned and flopped back on the bed. I was shaking. I was in bad pain. I was cold and I couldn't stop my snots from flowing. I was all in cramps and my guts wouldn't obey me. My eyes were overflowing real fast.

"Lemme out, Waneko—lemme out, you motherfucker." Shit, I was like screaming out of veins.

Nobody answered and I just lay there and moaned and groaned all alone and turned that mattress into one big soaking mopful of my sweat.

I don't know how many hours went crawling by. Millions maybe. And then a real scared thought hit me. Waneko wasn't coming back. He was gonna let me make it—cold-turkey—*a la canona.* I kept trembling and my whole swinging soul full of pain would make my body lurch up and tie itself up into one big knot and then ease itself almost straight and then retie itself. I felt like a puke coming afar. I thought, didn't I puke before? I felt it come out of my mouth like a green river of yellow-blue bile. I couldn't control nothing, and all the strength I had was enough just to turn my head away. I think I made some soft ca-ca on myself. I think I made some hard ones too.

Sometimes I think I heard Waneko telling me, "It's almost over, baby, it's almost over—we got it beat." But I couldn't answer. I'd just hold myself together with my arms holding me tight and rockaby baby myself to some kind of vague comfort. In a dream, I'd eat mountains and mountains of sweet, sweet candy. I opened my eyes and Waneko had me sitting in a chair and I saw Moms cleaning the toilet I had made out of the room—and then I was back in the bed. I still had all the pain, all the cramps. I still had the whole bad bit, but I knew I was gonna make it. I rocked myself to and fro.

I don't know how many hours ran crawling by. Jillions maybe. At last the pain cut itself down. I felt all dried out. Waneko came into the room and rubbed my body down, like trying to work all the knots to straighten out. Waneko and his moms kept me with them for a week or so putting me into shape with hot pigeon soup, liquids, and later heavier stuff like

I mean, rice and beans. They were great, Waneko and Moms. My body was kicked free from H—gone was dogie. They said it takes seventy or so hours to kick a habit. I think it seemed like seventy years. Now all I had to do was kick it outta my mind.

I left Waneko's house after really thanking them from way down. I hit the street thinking, "Wow, dying is easier than this has been. Never—never—*nunca más*."

22. REAL JESSE JAMESES

I was standing in front of the *cuchifrito* restaurant on 103rd Street, a couple of months later. I had gotten a job there peeling grease off dirty dishes, pots, and pans. Pay was small, but I was paying my rent and eating up a storm. I was really feeling good, feeling clean. I was clean. There was nothing left of the habit, except the temptation, and I was fighting the hell outta that. I dug Li'l Louie coming in through the side door of the *cuchifrito* joint and I waved to him. He walked toward me like he was afraid I was gonna hit on him for some coin for a fix. I nodded and laughed:

"Naw, babee, I'm clean, like nothing for the last two months."

"Damn, Piri, like I'm glad, baby, like you don't need that shit to move one. *Chevere.*" Louie's face got hung up on a big grin.

"Buying some *cuchifritos?*"

"Naw, just some straights." He walked over to the cigarette machine and got some smokes. He offered me one and while we smoked he said:

"Come on over to my pad when you get off from work."

"How'd you know I worked here? I ain't seen you for a while, least not since I got this job."

"That's right, man, like I've been swinging up in the Bronx, but you got *cuchifrito* grease coming out your pores. Besides, some of the cats told me they'd seen you working here. I didn't know you had kicked, though."

"I'll come up about six o'clock, okay? Or you want me to come up later?"

"Naw, six o'clock is fine." Louie slapped skin with me and walked away. I watched him cross the street and stop to make some kind of time with some kind of broad.

I went up to Louie's pad after work. He got some cold Manischewitz wine and put some sounds on and we just started to bullshit. We got around to talking about the old days of cops and robbers. We got around to talking about the lack of coins in our pockets.

Louie got up and went to the mirror and combed his hair.

"Man, there must be a way to make some good bread," I said.

"So let's get together," Louie said as he knotted his tie, "and make some fast *pesos*."

Little Louie, the smooth coolie. I sat on the edge of the bed and watched his fingers go through the twists of a Windsor knot. We had become skin-tight *amigos* since the days of our grocery-store *guiso*. Louie was about a year older than me and taller by about three inches, which made him close to six feet. He had the good looks that made broads bounce.

"Jesus, Piri," he said, straightening his tie, "all the times we've talked about being big-time . . ."

"Yeah, yeah, I know," I said. "I go for the idea of making fast *pesos*, but like how?"

I thought to myself of how I was getting tired of *cuchifrito* grease.

"Stick-ups."

"Wheow, man! There's easier ways of making bread."

"Like junk?"

"That's one way, but run it to me anyway."

"Well," Louie began, "I've been thinking about the things that some good coins could bring. Whatta ya say, Piri?"

"Hell, man, you down, I'm down. Now all we gotta do is get us—"

"Wait a minute, Piri, it ain't us alone."

"Uh-uh," I grunted warily. "I gotta be tight with anybody for this kinda *guiso*, I sure gotta know him before I trust him."

"It ain't exactly one guy, it's two guys. And these cats are experienced at pulling stick-ups."

"Real Jessie Jameses?"

"Yeah, they're from Newark, and they done time in the state pen."

"Say, *panín*, how come you know criminals like that?" I asked.

"Same place you know yours," he slipped back.

"Hell," I said, shrugging my shoulders, "I've been thinking about going into a lot of things lately, like pushing junk. I was using more and more up to last month, but like you know, I cut it down to *nada*." I made a face, not wanting to remember the pain that went into that cutting down. "But I can't trust myself to even get near that shit in no way."

"Yeah, Piri, I know," Louie said. You should have just stuck to pot once in a while instead of *tecata*."

I changed the subject. "What about your friends? And how soon do we get together? Who knows, maybe this is the beginning of something, eh?"

"Oh, just one thing, Piri," Louie said.

"Yeah?" I looked at him doubtfully.

"These guys ain't spics like us."

White or *moyeto*, a spic was a spic to Louie. "*Moyetos?*" I asked.

"No, *blancos*."

"Paddy boys? Man, Louie, I don't know." I shook my head from side to side.

"Look, Piri, I know Danny."

"Danny?"

"Yeah. My friend's name is Danny and his friend's name is Billy. I can vouch for Danny and Danny vouches for Billy."

"Louie," I said, "what we spics got in common with paddy boys? How far can we trust them?"

"Jesus, Piri, at least talk with 'em, will ya? Here's a chance to make some real *plata.* Ya don't hafta be prejudiced all your fuckin' life. Who knows, maybe these cats got a colored mammy way back." Louie laughed, and I almost laughed. And three days later we met Danny at a bar on 110th Street.

He was a couple of years older than us, a small guy with a polite smile and a feeling of coldness, like he was fronting for himself. I looked *cara palo* at him. Being a down stud, I wasn't gonna break words first.

"So you're Piri," he said. "Louie's been telling me a lot about you."

I looked cool at him and said, "So you're Danny. Louie talked a little about you."

"How'd you like to work with us?" Danny said.

I lit a cigarette and inhaled for enough time to think about it. "I don't know; who's boss?" I said finally.

"Nobody's boss. We're democratic. Everybody puts in their ideas, everybody plans jobs."

"How about this friend of yours in Newark?"

"You wanna know who he is?"

"Yeah, I would."

"I like you, Piri," said Danny.

"I like me, too," I said, and I let a little grin slip out.

"Yeah, you look like a Porto Rican with heart. You are Porto Rican, ain't you?"

"Whatever I am, we all got heart; very little of us are without heart," I answered, still smiling.

Danny laughed and said, "*Aya en el Rancho Grande.* See, I talk a little Spanish."

"That's cool," I said. "I talk a lotta English."

Danny looked a little hard at me, but it was just a quick shadow and he broke into a wide smile.

"I like you, Piri, I like you. Let's drive out to Newark and talk with Billy."

We walked out of the bar and Danny led us to an old green Oldsmobile. We got in. That Olds was smooth; it had a boss engine. We rode and talked, or rather Louie and Danny talked. I played my cool role. I didn't feel the picture much. It was like mixing rice and beans with corned beef and cabbage.

We picked up Billy and started driving back to Harlem. I almost liked the big gringo. He had a warm, easy way with him. I didn't trust him all the way, but I almost liked him. We talked and made plans, and when it was over, Danny looked at Louie and me and said, "You know, we're like a League of Nations. Billy's a Polack, I'm Irish, Louie is a white Porto Rican, and you"—Danny looked at me—"who the hell knows? But we're sure gonna—"

"I'm me, Mr. Charlie," I said, feeling hot in my chest.

"Whooo, smooth down, friend," Danny said. "I didn't mean no insult. I mean, like you're mixed with two or three races and—"

"Yeah, Piri," said Louie, "he didn't mean nothing. Practically all Puerto Ricans are mixed."

But in my mind, Danny's words, "and you, who the hell knows?"—were burning. *He's right,* I thought, *this bastard's right—who the hell knows?* That kept going through my mind. Then I heard voices breaking through my *pensamientos* and I dug Louie saying, "Well, if we gotta be proved . . ." And I said, "Proved in what?"

"Ain't you listening, Piri?" Louie said. "Danny and Billy feel on account they got *mucho* experience they know what they can do, but they haven't seen us work."

I said, "I ain't seen them work, either."

"Yeah, Piri, but they've been in jail."

"So, shit, what's that prove except maybe they ain't so good? But it's okay with me. What's the big *prueba?*"

"Well, you guys pull a job," Danny said, "and we'll watch from across the street and see how it goes, 'cause we don't want to take a chance with guys that may not have what it takes when the pressure is on."

I looked out of the car window and saw a cigar store on Third Avenue. I said, "You wanna see heart, eh, Mr. Charlies? Okay, park the car. Me and Louie is gonna pull a score right now."

"Man, Piri, we ain't ready yet," said Louie.

"You got that baby piece, Louie, that twenty-five cal?"

"Yeah, but it ain't loaded."

"Fuck it, we goin' shit for broke." I looked at the two paddies and winked at them. "This one's on us," I said. "Come on, Louie!"

Louie walked alongside me and he was talking a mile a minute. "*Caramba*, man, this is stupid, we ain't ready yet."

"When does one get ready for this kinda shit, man? You just jump into it with both feet. What do you expect, Louie, to go to school? You just start, *vente!*"

Danny and Billy were right across the street where they could watch the action. *Man,* I thought, *even if it was a bank, I'd pull it, just to shove it down them paddies' throats.*

Louie and me walked into the cigar store. There was only the owner there. "Walk to the back," I whispered to Louie. I stood near the candy counter, picking out candy bars.

"Can I help you?" said the owner.

"Yeah, *amigo*, you can give us your bread, money!"

He turned white. "Are you guys kidding?"

I said, "Listen, *maricón*, if you wanna die, then we're kidding; otherwise we're not. Just put the money in a paper bag. Your wallet, too. Louie, if the motherfucker makes a move, fuck him up good."

Louie just stood there, like he wished he was some place else, but for that matter, so did I.

"Show him the piece, Louie."

Louie pulled out the *pistolita* and it looked even smaller. "Look, mister, no more shit," he said.

"Don't shoot, please, don't shoot."

It was hard to say who was more scared, him or us.

He put the money in a bag and handed it to us. We locked him in a back room and made it. Just like that we had over $100 for a couple minutes' work. Woooie! We walked down toward the car and I felt Louie straining to start running.

"Cool it, man," I said. "If we run, them paddy boys are gonna think we ain't got heart."

Danny and Billy were sitting in the car with the motor running. Louie and me strolled over, smooth-like, opened the door, cool-like, and sat down. "Candy, anybody?" I softly asked, while that heart of mine was beating like crazy.

We were in. I could see it in the paddies' eyes. I counted the money as we drove. Danny was watching me through the rear-view mirror. I said, "Pull over to the curb, man."

"What for?"

"Gotta see my *muchacha*," I said. Danny smiled and started to say something smart. "Don't say nothing," I added, "if it ain't nice, Mr. Charlie."

His smile washed off. "What's this 'Mr. Charlie' stuff you've been throwing around?" he asked.

"It's just a name, man, like one kinda people got for another kind of people. Ain't you down?"

He didn't answer. I got out of the car and handed Louie $75. "We split four ways, even."

As I walked down Madison Avenue, I thought, *Shit—splitting with paddies: Brew should see me now.*

A year went by. With time, we got badder and cooler. I stopped counting the scores. We hit small bars, East Side, West Side, all around the paddy town. I took a room on my old block with an old lady for a few bucks a week. She was all right.

I gave her a lot of hell, but she loved me like a son—she said. I believed her, so I acted like most sons do in Harlem—I paid her no mind.

Our stick of working was simple. Each of us had a job. Danny and Billy took the back of the place, Louie stood in the middle and I covered the door. Anyone could come in, nobody could go out. We emptied the johns and pushed everyone but the bartender into the back and cleaned them like Rinso of anything that was worth money. Meanwhile Louie would have the bartender opening the safe if there was one, or showing him where the cigar box of hidden cash was. Just before leaving, we pushed them all into the ladies' room and stashed a cigarette machine or jukebox against the door to give us time to make it without sweat.

But sometimes it was a sweat thing. Once I was sitting on a bar stool near the front door of a place, drinking a beer and playing chickie the cop while the guys took care of business in the back. I held a *pistola* in my lap, out of sight. As we were ready to leave, I looked out the window and a *hara* passed by. He looked up and saw me. I kept drinking my beer calmly with my left hand, my right hand resting on my gun. He moved on and I breathed easy—then he stopped and turned around. He was gonna come in for a beer, I guess, or to use the john. I thought, *Oh, shit, oh,* hara, *don't come in.* As he stood there, undecided, my mind clicked off what to do if he came in. *I'll tell him to put them up and I'll take his piece. But what if he still goes for his piece? I'll hit him for the big one, in the head. Don't come in,* hara, *go away, go away, cop . . .* I drank more beer. Finally, the cop turned and walked on.

When we left, he was standing at the corner, near our car. I remembered a movie I had seen. "Let me play drunk," I said, "and you guys play high, and we'll make it. The cop may feel something's wrong, but he won't be able to place it." We rolled out, not too noisy, 'cause the cop would stop us, but politely high and good-natured. I even smiled at the cop and mumbled something like, "Man, that's enough beer for me, gotta work tomorrow." And away we split, with $800 or so in cash and jewelry.

That was one of our better scores. Most of our jobs copped us more like $250 to $400. The right score, the big-money one, just ducked. I began to get tight nerves. We all were on edge. Then one day we were punching the clock out on a job on the West Side and as we were taking the bartender to the back to lock him up, he dashed up a stairway leading to an upstairs apartment. Without thinking, we blasted at him. We missed and we ran like hell. As I cut the corner, I looked back. The bartender was screaming and blasting away at us with a piece. I got to the car as Danny was pulling away. "For a lousy $75," I said. "It ain't worth all this heart failure. Man, we almost killed us someone for a lousy $75." Then I asked myself, *Suppose you had killed him for $75,000—would that have been worth it? Ain't no bartender got 75 gees,* I answered.

My nerves got tighter. I began skin-popping, promising myself that I wouldn't go mainlining again. Trina suspicioned I was back on stuff, but wasn't sure. She kept asking what was wrong and I kept telling her, "*Nada, nada.*" In between we talked of marriage. I hadn't copped her. I wanted her, but I wanted her right—church, white dress, the whole bit. She was one thing the streets weren't gonna make the mean way.

The shooting shook us up, so we laid off for a while. But when the dust settled and the money ran out, our shooting scene seemed *chevere* to us instead of stupid, and we went back into business. Danny had wrecked his Olds, so we needed a new car. We thought of copping one from a private garage, but we decided it wasn't worth the risk. I got a bright thought. We could buy a car, then one of us could stay outside and, after the sale was made, come in and beat the seller for the bread and whatever else he had on him. We drew for some kinda honor, and I picked the short stick.

"Okay, you're it," said Louie.

"*Chevere,*" I answered with a *cara-palo* look.

Danny, Billy, and Louie left me about a block from the

used-car dealer. They had 450 bucks to spend. I waited for them to spend it.

It was a warm day and I was wearing a light windbreaker, but I still felt a chill. *Man,* I thought, *why don't them cats hurry up?* A little later they came out of the office and got into a car and drove off. They passed me and Louie signaled that they would wait for me in the next block. As I walked toward the auto dealer's office, a motorcycle cop pulled up to a diner right across the street. But it was too late to back down. I walked into the office.

"Yes, sir, what can I do for you?" the manager asked. He was still putting the $450 away.

"I'd like to know the price on that '56 Buick," I said.

"Which Buick is that, sir?" He was an old man, gray-haired, but I couldn't back down, dammit; my rep was on the line.

"It's that one next to the Chevrolet," I said, pointing outside.

The old man turned to put his order book on the desk. I pulled my piece out and shoved it in his back. "Play it smooth, mister; make it with the bread and there won't be no trouble."

The old man turned around and he didn't look scared, just angry-like. He reached out for me and hung on. We struggled. *Coño,* man, it was a hassle. The old man was strong. We both fell to the floor. I hit him with the gun again and again and then it was over. He just lay there and moaned, "Uh, uh, uh, uhm, uhmmmmmm."

I felt ca-ca green. I felt sticky, like my hands were sweating glue. It was blood. My windbreaker was lousy with blood. *I gotta get outta here,* I thought. I opened the door and walked out. Across the street the motorcycle cop was still eating. I started to walk toward the corner and stopped cold. The money —I had forgotten the money. *Run, you jerk! No,* I thought, *this ain't for nuttin', you done it for the bread. This ain't for nuttin', something gotta come outta this.* I walked back into the little office. The manager was still on the floor, moaning softly. He was full of blood. I bent down and took the gold from his pockets. I avoided looking at him because I didn't want to split with his sufferings. As I walked away from him, I kicked something; it was his false teeth. They looked like a nightmare smiling at this wild scene. I felt sorry for the old cat and I wanted to help him, but hatings of things I couldn't name wouldn't let me.

I stepped out into the street and stopped stone-cold. To the right of me, about twenty feet away, was a garage, and there was a police car there with its hood open and a mechanic and two cops huddled around the motor. "Yeah, Mike," I heard one cop say, "this damned car won't run right. I think it's the spark plugs."

"Naw, Pat, I think it's in the transmission," the other one said. "Whatta ya think, Mike?"

The mechanic rubbed his head and looked up and I thought, *How can he miss seeing me standing here all smeared with blood?*

"I think it's the valves, Joe," he said, "but I'll hafta check it. And what about . . ."

I walked away from their voices. People passed by me. *Jesus, how come they don't see I'm smeared with this* sangre? I pushed my sticky hands into my pockets and crossed the street. The motorcycle cop was coming out of the diner. He looked all around. *Don't see me,* hara. *Don't look at me.* I reached the other sidewalk and saw our car halfway down the block. Louie was smoking a cigarette and leaning against the fender. Outside I was *cara palo,* but inside I heard Momma's voice saying, "*Mi negrito, mi negrito,* what have you done?"

Louie saw me and got into the car and held the door open for me. I threw myself in and lay on the floor in the back. Louie looked at me and his voice turned weak. "*Ave María,* what's wrong? All that blood—are you shot?"

"I'm okay, *coño.* Le's go, man, le's go."

All the way back to the block I lay there thinking of the old man. The car pulled up in front of my building. I waited till the street and stoop were clear and I ran into the hallway. I opened the door to the apartment and we all went in. Luckily the old lady was out. Billy and Danny sat down at the kitchen table and didn't say a word. They hadn't said a word all the way home.

I went into the bathroom and looked at myself in the mirror. I couldn't stand what I saw and I puked. The taste was bad. I wanted to say, "I couldn't help it," but I couldn't; I wanted to lie, but I wouldn't. I washed and washed, but it was not enough. I made a hard face, a *cara-palo* face, and walked back into the kitchen.

I looked at everybody, Danny, Billy, and Louie. Louie looked down, Billy looked at the window. Danny looked at me and I saw he was thinking, "Better you than me." I threw the wad of bills on the table. They stuck together with the old man's glue.

"Split four ways," I said.

23. WISH IT WERE YOU, TRINA

We decided to cool it. Louie made it to the Army. Billy and Danny made it back to Newark. I went to sea for a few months. When I came back, I started to hustle pot—light stuff, here and there a few bucks. But no mo' junk. I was gonna stay clean.

Trina took off for Puerto Rico on account of her momma was sick. I went with her to the airport, and after her plane left, I felt like shit. Like a little bit more lost.

A few months later I was at the pad of one of my boys, Chino; there was a set, a jump, going on—a few cats and broads, low lights, and a smooth fish playing. I had had some sneaky pete and some pot, and I felt pretty good. Someone introduced me to Chino's cousin, Dulcien, a pretty little girl who had just come out of some kind of home. We fished real close and felt each other up. She had a couple of kids from some other cat, so she was hip on what a man dug.

I got her some wine, and we talked quietly, and danced quietly. We couldn't get any closer grinding, and we both began to breathe hard. I hadn't had a lay for some long time and it was beginning to show. Suddenly she tore out of my arms and ran into a back room. I followed her and found her lying across the bed on her back, one arm across her face. When I touched her arm, she moaned.

"Li'l baby, what's wrong?" I asked. I knew what was wrong, but we both had to play the game.

She sobbed. "It's not my fault," she said. "It's been a long time since a man's touched me, I can't help it." I ran my hands over her body and she grabbed at me and moaned over and over, "It's all right, you can do it to me, it's all right."

We both made it, man. Like all she knew was me and all I saw was her and anything else was a dead scene. *Nada*. I heard her say from far away next to my ear, "The bed—the bed—don't make so much noise." And then she stiffened. I looked over my shoulder and saw somebody's outline standing there in the dark.

"What ya want?" I asked.

The voice came to me kind of mixed up mad and embarrassed, "It's me—Chino, and that's my cousin you're screwin'."

"So what. Am I screwin' you?—wait your turn or get the hell outta here!"

Two weeks later she went to Puerto Rico where, after a while, she began growing a belly. Naturally her mother wanted to know how come, so she wrote Chino's aunt, who made a FBI investigation and sent back a report to which Dulcien confessed.

Meanwhile, I had gone to Washington, D.C. Somebody I knew had bought a restaurant right near Howard University. I had been working there seven or eight months when I got a phone call from one of my boys, Waneko. He told me what had happened, that everyone said it was my kid. Trina, back from Puerto Rico, knew too. Dulcien, he added, had been thrown out of her home in Puerto Rico, belly and all, and she was sleeping in hallways and underneath the stars. My name, in fact, was something like shit around the block, and Dulcien's family was looking for me to cut me up with Puerto Rican machetes.

"Make it back or make it away," Waneko said.

I had been thinking about going to school. In a special exam at Howard University I had passed everything but my math, and Howard was gonna send me to Dunbar High School for a special course in trig. I had a job; here was a chance to break away from Harlem, from a way-out kind of life. Only, like it's said, Harlem don't let you get out so easy. I made up my mind. "I'm coming back, Waneko," I said.

I made it into New York about 6 p.m. and went straight to the block and stood across the street from number 109. Trina lived there, I had lived there on and off, and Chino's mom lived there—in fact, on the floor above Trina. I must have stood there a couple of hours before I saw her, my Marine Tiger. She had her coat thrown over her shoulders and was carrying a couple of empty milk bottles to the grocery around the corner. I let her turn the corner on Park Avenue and 104th Street, then I came up behind her and helped her arrange her coat, which had been slipping off her shoulders.

She turned fast, saw me, and threw herself into my arms, and just as quickly out of them. She turned that loving look into one of anger and hurt.

"I'm back, baby," I said; "ain't that what counts?"

"No, it's not that way," she replied.

"You love me yet, eh, yes?"

She nodded and said, "And you?"

"I will always."

"But what about that girl and her baby she's going to have?"

"Look, maybe the kid's mine." I figured the odds against it being mine were roughly a thousand to one. Still . . .

But Trina wasn't taking the bet. She gave me a mean look.

"Look," I added quickly, "I'll do all I can for the kid when it comes. But I don't dig her; if I marry anybody, it's going to be you."

She didn't seem impressed. "Have you seen Chino's mother? You did it in her bed, you know?"

"*Sí*, I know. Just tell me we're forever."

She hesitated, then said, "*Sí, para siempre.*"

I turned and went up to Chino's pad. His mother gave me a swinging reception. As I stepped into the apartment, she cursed me out in more ways than I had thought even a Puerto Rican knew. I let the old lady blow off steam. She was yelling something about how I had disgraced her home, and if that wasn't enough, I had copped her niece in *her* bed. "You son of a beetch," she concluded.

"*Mira, vieja,*" I replied. "I did what I did. I am a man. Dulcien gave it up 'cause she wanted to. I didn't snatch it; she got as much kicks as I did. Okay, I'm willing to go with anything that's right without marrying her. It ain't like I popped her cherry. I wasn't the first at the wall. Whatta you want me to do?"

The old lady's tears dried up fast. She probably hadn't expected me to be straight with her. "You have to send her plane tickets for her to come to New York," she said. "She gave birth already and she has no place to stay."

"Okay, *bueno,*" I said, and a week later the old lady and I met the airport bus at the ticket agency on 103rd Street and Madison Avenue. The bus pulled in about 11:30 a.m. Poor Dulcien looked beat. *It's sure tough to be a broad,* I thought, *but that's life.*

She smiled and whispered, "*Cómo estás?*"

I nodded and put my arms out and copped the kid. It was a boy, Pedro Luis. I looked at him and felt kind of proud. *If only he was Trina's and mine,* I thought. I wish I could have loved him more, yet how could I? I didn't know what that meant—want, take, love, sex, belong, have—I just didn't know.

Dulcien was walking by my side: I hardly noticed her and barely heard what she said.

"Piri, Piri . . ."

"Huh?"

"Piri, I will make you a good wife. You don't have to marry with me, just live with me; I will do all right for you."

"Look, Dulcien," I said, "I don't wanna be stone in my

heart, but *caramba,* I gotta girl and I love her. I'm sorry about what happened to you. I'm not sorry we made love; we dug each other that night and I wish I could have been careful. I used the wrong head that night, but we gotta keep living. You'll find somebody, you'll see; you ain't a bad broad, and you know how to make a man feel."

We kept walking. I took the kid to the block and showed him to my boys. They made congratulations a big deal and I felt pretty proud. After a while I went to Trina's. She went wild about the baby. I talked about Dulcien giving him up and about us getting married and raising the baby and so on. But it wasn't gonna be like that.

24. IF YOU'RE GONNA PRAY—THEN PRAY BIG

I gave Dulcien what money I could, but that wasn't much. I was in a bind. I needed money, I needed distance. If I got the money, I figured, I could buy me the distance.

Louie was back from the Army. He had caught some kind of bug and been medically discharged. I began thinking about the big job, the score that would put me over, the *quiso* that would solve all my problems.

"Look, Louie," I told him one day, "you're out of the Army now and I ain't doin' a fuckin' thing; how about going back to work again?"

"Yeah," said Louie, "let's work. I've seen Danny and Billy and I told them we might work again."

And just like that we went into business again. It had been almost a year since the car *guiso*. But this was gonna be different; no more small-time shit. We were gonna hit a big place with enough bread to take care of us real good.

We looked around for a rainbow. Danny found a night club downtown that he thought would be a soft touch. "Nothing but faggots and soft asses in there," he said. We decided to hit it on the next Friday night—actually early Saturday morning.

The night came. I went up to see Trina, who was sick with a bad cold. I rubbed her down with Vick's and tucked her under a blanket. "Don't go, Piri," she begged as we embraced, "I have a bad premonition."

"What a dope," I said. "Don't worry. I'm going 'cause I got something important to do."

Trina pressed close to me and I felt her stiffen. "What's that in your inside pocket?" she asked.

Damn, the gun, she felt the piece, I thought, but I said, "It's *nada,* honey, only the pint of whisky." I got up and packed the covers around her.

She looked up at me and said, "Be good, Piri."

"Sure, baby, always for you."

Out in the street the air was cold and I pulled my coat collar up and my hat down. It was so cold it was hard to breathe, but I decided to walk back to the block. It was early yet. Louie had copped out with a flu bug, and I didn't have to meet Danny and Billy until eleven. I walked block by block and got further and further away from Trina, and way down in my mind I worried about her premonition. I decided to go upstairs to my place and waste a stick of pot.

After a short bit I felt a little cooler, although I was still a little tight deep down in my guts, almost like I was scared. I looked at myself in the bathroom mirror and made my face as *cara palo* as I could. In the reflection of the mirror I saw behind me the old lady's little altar, with all kinds of saints and candles. *Man, this old lady is sure on a Christ kick. I wonder if it does any good.* I patted the cold chalk head of the saint, knelt down, and crossed myself. *I ain't even a Catholic, but maybe it'll do some good.*

"Saint," I said, "if you can hear me, I'm gonna pull a score tonight. Make it be a good one, with *mucho* bread, so it will be my last job. Let there be thousands—millions." *Why not?* I thought. *If you're gonna pray, then pray big.*

I got up feeling kinda foolish and like I had done something wrong. I finished dressing and went to the corner to meet the guys. Danny and Billy were there waiting for me.

"Hey, *hombres,*" I said.

"Hey, kid, how ya doing?" said Billy. Danny just flicked his hand up as a greeting. "Where's Louie?" he asked.

"He's sick," I explained. "I guess it's a touch of fever or something."

"Ah, that means he ain't comin' on this score, eh?"

"Guess not," I said. "But I got the key to the car."

We decided to cop some drinks. I took the paddies to a nearby place on Madison Avenue. We stepped into the stale smoke of a dimly lit bar where a wild mambo was blasting out of the jukebox. Right away the atmosphere got tense. In Spanish Harlem all paddies look like cops and everyone at the bar began looking our way, no doubt thinkin', *Piri's got busted and them two* haras *are looking for somebody else he knows.* I laughed and said in Spanish, "Don't worry, these guys are okay. They're paddies but they're okay. Just some business partners."

It took a little while for the air to loosen up. Finally, one of the dealers in pot got next to me by the jukebox and said, "Hey, Piri, no shit, you sure these gringos ain't *haras?*"

"Yeah, man," I said. "Got some joints?" He went white, sure now that I was setting him up for a bust. "Look, stiff," I told him, "you know me, so stop your shit. I ain't never set nobody up and I ain't starting now."

"Here man," he said, and shoved a packet of six joints at me. "It's on me."

I walked over to the table where Danny and Billy were.

"What's happening, Piri?" asked Billy.

"*Nada,*" I said, "just got us some free pot." We sat and drank and I blew some pot in the shithouse. After a while the pot started to get to me. My head felt like somebody had a rubber band twisted around it. "Come on, let's get outta here," I whispered, and Billy dropped some bills on the table and we made it out to the car.

I gave my paddy friends a stick of pot and we drove around Harlem. My high was on full blast and I stretched out in the back seat and studied the passing scenes.

"Hey," I said half aloud, "it would be better for us if it rained, eh?" That would mean less people on the streets.

"Yeah, *chico*," said Billy.

"It's gonna be a clear night," Danny said. "But it's cold as hell out there, real February weather, and there ain't too many people gonna be around at two-thirty in the morning."

At about twelve-thirty we headed downtown. My high had settled down and I was in just the right frame of mind. We parked and went down a long flight of stairs and into a long, barnlike darkened room, with red and green lights and specks of yellow and a lot of people. *Jesus*, I thought, *there's almost too many people in here to pull a stick-up*. But I kept my mouth shut.

We sat at a little round table in the back and ordered expensive drinks. When my eyes grew used to the darkness, I made out where everything was—the bar, the stage, the manager's office. At about two-thirty, Billy got the little black box where we kept our pieces. The time had come. I reached down under the table and flipped open the box and handed my white buddies the cold, color-blind pieces—two .38's to a pair of hands, a .45 to another hand. I kept a P-38.

One part of me wanted to forget about this score. So many damn people . . . But another part of me—the angry, hungry part—wanted to run it through and fuck everything. Anyway, there was no copping out now.

Everybody was watching the floor show. Some broad dressed like a man was on the stage. Around her were some men dressed like broads. The flickering lights gave the scene a nightmarish quality. I blinked my eyes and moved to the front door, thinking, *Everybody comes in, nobody goes out*. Danny moved toward the stage; Billy covered the bar.

Then, Danny pushed up onto the stage, shoved the broad

away and grabbed the microphone. "Everybody keep quiet and you won't get hurt," he shouted. "This is a stick-up." His voice sounded like bombs falling.

Attaboy, Danny. The next step was to collect all the cash in the manager's office, then make all the people, the whole couple of hundred of them, drop their wallets and jewelry into a big tablecloth Billy would be passing around. But it didn't go that way at all. The customers thought Danny was part of the floor show and they began to laugh. I almost felt like laughing myself. Then Danny fired twice over everyone's head and into the mirrors and everything suddenly got quiet. "I ain't kidding," he shouted. "There's six of us pulling this job and some of us are sitting next to you, so just be quiet and you won't get hurt."

Smart, baby, real *chevere*, that's using your *cabeza*. Then a woman screamed and, as though she had touched a match to a gasoline tank, everyone began to scream. The people sitting near the back began to head for the door where I had stationed myself. I pointed the P-38 at them and roared out, "Stop, don't come any closer or you'll get lit up." They kept coming, so I lowered my piece and fired into the door. That stopped them.

The bunched-up people looked at me like watchful buzzards, afraid to move in but ready to pounce if I should cop out. A nice-looking chippy, drunk as hell, staggered toward me and tried to put her arms around me, saying, "Wha's the matta, eh, you jus' a gangster—oh, gee—I just love gangsters . . ." I tried to push her away, but she just stood there, trying to put her arms around me. *If she ties me up,* I thought, *somebody will sure jump me.* Suddenly I felt my left hand ball up in a fist and crash into her jaw. She went down and I didn't see her any more.

I strained my eyes to see if Danny and Billy had copped the dough. And then, through the pot, through the liquor, through the haze, I saw a movement to my right. I turned slightly. There was a man, on one knee, near the bar. He had something in his hand and it was pointing at me. I just barely saw it flash, then I was spun halfway around by something that crashed into my chest.

My God, what did he throw at me? The rest came fast. My body swiveled back, my hand tight-held my P-38, and my finger squeezed. The gun jumped in my hand and the man on one knee grunted and slammed back hard against the bar.

He shot me. My fingers found my chest and I felt the hot, sticky blood spreading over my white shirt. The man slid backward and lay there. *I'm shot,* I thought, *but I shot that white sonofabitch.*

My chest got full of fire and I looked at the little hole in my shirt. I put my finger in the hole, remembering the story I learned in school about a kid in Holland putting his finger in a dike and saving the town from getting flooded. All I heard were screams and guns shooting and a loud roar covering that. An arm grabbed me from behind. I fought like hell to get away. I felt blood in my mouth. The arm dragged me to the floor, and I saw it was attached to a big vulture who was now on top of me. Suddenly I felt cool and I looked at him and then over his shoulder. "Shoot him, Billy," I yelled, "shoot him in the head," and I ducked to one side as if to get away from the coming bullet. The big man went for it and scrambled off me. I pushed myself up, the gun still in my hand. No one touched me. My legs felt like melting lard. I thought to myself, *My blood is not as much in me. I'm hit, let's make it.* I screamed instead.

I heard a voice near me, echoing like in a cave, "Go ahead, we'll cover you."

"It's my turn—I must—I have to stop the blood . . ." I turned and started climbing them long steps. *Piri, stick your finger in the hole. If the blood don't come out, you can't die. Jesus, if I can only get back to Harlem, everything is gonna be* chevere *again—just get back to Harlem and there ain't a fucking thing can hurt you there.* The cold morning air hit me and I felt some more pain. The doorman was yelling his head off.

I knocked him down the stairs and ran down the street. I was running down the middle of the street and the same thing kept beating into my head: *If I can only get back to Harlem, I'll be all right. If I can get back to Trina, everything is gonna be all right*...

"My God, it's cold," I mumbled. I heard voices from far away. "Piri, Piri, you're running the wrong way. The car's back this way . . ." But I couldn't stop running. I'd die here. I just hadda make it to my block. Near the corner I saw a cab waiting for the light to change. I yanked the door open. There was a guy and his girl sitting in the back. "Don't make trouble and you won't get hurt," I told them, and I shoved them aside. "Get going fast," I told the driver. "Take me to Harlem."

The guy in the back said, "Look, don't shoot. Is it all right if I sit next to you instead of my girl?"

My God, I didn't give a fuck who sat next to me, all I wanted was to get back to Harlem.

"Please, she's very nervous."

I looked at the girl and she started to cop a fit. *Sure, I understand,* I thought. *I got a girl myself, her name is Trina and she lives in Harlem, where I live, and* . . . "Cabbie," I said, "get going to Harlem fast or I'll blow your head off."

I felt myself going soft like jelly and everything got black. I fought the darkness and when my eyes cleared I saw lights going on and off. It looked so strange . . . and then I knew. The cabbie was blinking his headlights on and off—a signal for the cops.

I didn't care any more. I just felt I wasn't gonna make it to Harlem that morning, or maybe any morning. I felt blood sticky in my mouth, in between my fingers. I wiggled my toes inside my brand-new suede shoes and they felt sticky, too. I thought about Moms, that she shouldn't have died because I needed her very much to tell me that I am her *negrito*, and that she would never change me, not even for five *blancos*.

The cab stopped and the driver started screaming. I stumbled out and he grabbed at me. I hit at him and pointed my gun at him and pulled the trigger. But nothing happened. I pulled the trigger again and nothing happened again. I looked down at my hand and there was nothing there, only my hand holding the position of a gun, like when I had been a kid playing cops and robbers. I'd point my finger and curl it and say, "Bang! bang!"—and here I was doing the same thing, only it wasn't a game.

I saw a man leaning on the fender of his car, smoking. I walked toward him. It was a cop. I pointed my hand at him, but it didn't fire. *Piri,* I thought from somewhere, *you got no gun, only the position.* I didn't know why, but the hand that wasn't holding back the blood went ahead of me. I stood there looking at the cop. The sky of the morning looked very high; it was cold, and the blood was cold on my chest and hand, and all the noises of the sirens and the glare of the lights didn't bother me at all. All I could think of was the cop in front of me, and I wondered if I should ask him for one of his cigarettes . . . then everything melted together and I fell asleep.

When I awoke I was in a car. I opened my eyes just a little bit and I saw a cop looking at me. My wrists were handcuffed. I tried to move my hands to my chest so I could plug up the hole, then I fell asleep again. When I opened my eyes again, I was back in the night club, sitting in a chair. All around me were screaming and scared people and overturned tables. The cop next to me called over a faggot and gave him a salad bowl. "If he moves, bash him," he said.

I smiled at the thought of a big coolie being guarded by a damned faggot. A rough hand grabbed at me. It was a big plainclothes man. He bent down and I could feel his spit breeze my face. "Do you think it's funny, you black bastard?" he said.

"I thought I was *Puerto Rican,*" I whispered. "If you don't mind, I'm a Puerto Rican black bastard." I didn't know whether or not the sounds were coming through, but I felt my mouth working.

"You lousy dirty black bastard, you lousy black spic, why I oughtta kill you. That's my partner lying there on the floor."

I said something like, "So what?" or "It should be you, too, you white motherfucker," and something hit me hard on the side of my eye.

"Lay off him," a voice said. Then a man in white came up. He looked at my blood and where it was coming from, and in a tired, mater-of-fact voice, said, "Let him alone. He's got a hole through him, and that makes him a patient."

I looked down at the floor where a gray-haired guy was lying. It was the cop I had shot. I felt kind of proud for him because he had a heart. He had been alone and he still had gone down; cool stud, hard stud. *Jesus,* I thought, *I finally shot some Mr. Charlies. I shot 'em in my mind often enough . . .*

I heard ambulances yelling like mad. Then the cops brought in a guy who had been shot in the arm. "I'm not one of them," he was screaming. "Honest to God, officer, I was just trying to help you cops out, that's why I had the gun. I picked it up just to help you and—"

"Do you know him?" a cop asked me.

I had never seen him before. I shook my head.

Then I felt hands push me down to the floor. I struggled. I wanted to stand on my feet. *Piri, if you lay down, you die. I can walk.* But I was pushed down on my back and onto a stretcher. Light bulbs were flashing. With one hand I nozzled my bullet hole, with the other I covered my face. If they were taking pictures I didn't want anybody to know who I was.

I was carried up the long steps out of the night club. All I seemed to be doing was going up and down these long steps. The cold air hit my face and I peeked through my hands and saw an ambulance with the name "St. Vincent's Hospital" on the side. I was placed in the ambulance, gently, like it made no difference I was a wrong cat. Inside, I asked the attendant for a smoke.

"Don't give the bastard nothing," the *hara* said.

"I can't, anyway, he's got a chest wound."

I didn't feel the pain any more, only a dullness and very tired. The ambulance stopped and I was carried into the hospital and placed on a stretcher with wheels. There were nuns and doctors all over the place. I wondered how Danny and Billy made out. One of the cops said, "These punks shot three people." I wondered who else, besides the cop, and then I saw a guy with his hand over his chest, another guy holding his arm. I looked away. Then the cops brought two guys to me and, my God, they were the sorriest, bloody messes. They almost looked like Danny and Billy. *Oh, shit,* I thought, *it is them! I never thought paddies could waste other paddies like that . . .*

"Are these the two guys with you?" asked a cop.

"No, I ain't never seen these guys."

Danny said, "Tell 'em, Piri, tell 'em we're together, they're killing us."

I didn't know how to play it, so now I said, "I don't know them."

Billy said, "Tell 'em, *chico,* we ain't kidding."

I whispered, "Okay, I know 'em," and they all melted away.

I closed my eyes and felt the smell of the hospital. Someone put a mask over my face and told me to breathe.

"I can't breathe with this shit on my face," I mumbled.

"If you don't breathe through this, you're gonna stop breathing," said a voice.

Expert hands removed my clothes. The air was cool to my nakedness. I didn't feel ashamed to lay there naked. I felt like a little baby, almost like I was waiting to get my diapers changed. I was placed on a bed in a dark room, and a priest in black with a white collar came and stood over me. A hand placed a piece of gauze over the little hole in my chest and slipped another piece under me to cover a hole in my back. The priest held my hands and made the sign of the cross. I felt faint, sort of like I was sliding down waxed paper, like all the rice and beans in the world couldn't ever again give me color, any kinda color. "I'm not Catholic, *padre,*" I said. "I'm nothing."

"It makes no difference, son, it's all the same to God."

Dios, *I don't wanna die.*

The priest left me. I heard him ask the doctor something. The doctor replied, "His chances aren't too good."

Heads were shaking and I was drowning in aloneness. I felt someone shaving me and I tried to look down.

"It's for the operation," said a voice. Then someone put a needle in my arm. It was like taking off around the block, getting high on junk; only this shot covered me with a dark blanket.

I felt my mouth forming words, "Mommie . . . I don't . . . Mommie, *no quiero morir* . . ." I talked inside; I cried inside; I wouldn't let them see me afraid . . . then everything dissolved to nothing; I fell asleep.

PRISON

I hated the evenings because a whole night in prison lay before me, and I hated the mornings because I felt like Dracula returning to his coffin.

25. THE HOUSE OF "DO-RIGHT"

When I awoke, my first thought was that I'd have to stop using junk because it was bringing me bad dreams. I started to get up—oh, man, it was too much; I hurt and burned clear through. I dropped back on the pillow and tried to catch my breath and push away the hurt and dizziness. Then someone in white pinched my arm and I went to sleep again.

The next time I awoke I knew it was no dream; it was real. Everything was real.

"That bastard is waking up," a voice said.

"That stinkin' black spic."

I opened my eyes, but all I could see was the cop I had shot and other people who had been hurt. Why were they all together? They looked at me and their noise got louder, and I closed my eyes; I wanted to go back into the darkness. Then I heard feet moving fast, and my whole bed moved, rolled. I opened my eyes again. A couple of nurses were moving my bed, the bottles and the needles in my arms, me, right out of the room, away from those voices. I didn't have to go back into the darkness.

After a few days I began to dig myself better. The pain left and I could sit up. There was a cop always on guard, watching me with a hating look. He told me that the cop I had shot was dying. If he died, I would get the chair.

The people around me didn't say anything, nor look bad-eye at me, but they knew. I could read their eyes; some felt anger, some pity, some nothing. They weren't like me inside.

The days went by. I was helped up and made to walk, a nurse on each side of me to support me. Slowly, I got stronger. Just like in the movies—maybe I had seen too many of them—I started thinking of escaping. *I won't let them know I'm getting stronger.* I lay awake and thought, *If I can slip out of bed and crawl along the floor* . . . I dreamed I was doing it. But always, always, just when I got up to the front gate after having crawled so far, I'd get shot down like a bom-bom. Then, one day, when I thought I was ready to really try it, the cops came to question me. (They had come before, but I had been too doped up to dig their style.)

The questions came real fast and I pulled a weak act. The *hara* told me if I didn't act right he'd knock me right out of the wheel chair I was sitting in. I yelled, "Nurse, I wanna throw up!"

The *hara* looked bad at me and went away. But the next day a stretcher on wheels was brought in, and I was lifted onto it, and handcuffed.

"Where am I going?" I asked the attendant.

"Bellevue prison ward."

In Bellevue I was put into a big ward with a lot of beds and a lot of guys. At one end of the ward were some solitary-confinement cells (steel doors with a square, barred opening) and a room that had been built into cells with bars—for the wild cats, I guess. My wounds were healing, but I still felt pretty lousy. It was cold in that ward. One guy died of pneumonia during the night. I thought maybe he was better off. One of the guards had told me that the cop I had shot had died. For me, it would be *la silla*, the chair.

There was a guy called Jimmy in one of the cells at the end of the ward who walked around like a nut, talked trash, and ate his own ca-ca. Later I found out why. He had stuck up a grocery store with one of my old *paníns*, Ramón. Everything had come off; they were leaving with the money, then the grocer started heaving cans at them. Without looking, one of the boys flugged a shot to scare the grocer. He scared him too good—thc shot killed him. Ramón was being held for murder; Jimmy was trying to beat the rap by pulling a flip act. He was good. He told me to go crazy and I'd beat the chair. I thought hard on that, but I couldn't make like a *loco*. Later for that!

My aunt came to see me. Everybody, she explained, was grieved over my shame. Trina was close to a nervous breakdown, my sister was in tears, my father was mad. So I was a disgrace—but I hadn't punked out, and I was alive.

Shortly afterward, I was told I was leaving Bellevue. I was given my clothes. They still had bullet holes in them, and they were stiff with my dried blood. My hurt felt even more real now. Two cops handcuffed my wrists and took me to a police station and up a long flight of stairs. Upstairs, they asked me to cooperate in clearing unsolved stick-ups and told me they would help me make parole. Parole—that meant the guard had lied to me about the cop being dead. I asked them about it and they said he was still in the hospital but that his chances for recovery were good. All I could say in answer to their questions was, "This is my first job, this is my first job." They gave up and then I was sent to the Tombs, the House of Do-Right, on 125 White Street, to await some kinda trial.

At the Tombs, I got a cell, two blankets, and an iron bedspring without a mattress. "Just put one blanket down and cover yourself with the other," said the hack who led me in. I nodded and he closed the gate on me.

"Hey! *Aya en el Rancho Grande*."

"Danny! Hey, Danny is that you?"

"Yeah, *amigo*, how've you been?"

"Bad, man, hurtin'—but pushin . . ."

"Quiet!" the hack shouted, and I stayed quiet. Later, I leaned hard against the wall as a dizzy spell hit me.

"Hey, kid, you okay?" asked the guy in the next cell.

"Just a little dizzy, man, nothing bad."

Danny heard it and asked, "Hey, Piri, what's the matter?"

"I'm just shaky, man, nothing *malo*."

Danny started to yell, "Hey, hack, man sick on third tier."

A few more voices blended in and the hack came up to my tier, huffing and puffing. "What's the matter up here?" he said.

"The kid's sick, Major," someone said.

Major came to my cell.

"I'm okay," I insisted, "there ain't no sweat."

"Oh, you're the kid who was in on that Village stick-up and got shot up. My God! Why do you guys pull crazy things like that? Aw, shit, what's the use of talkin'? Come on," he said, matter-of-factly, "we're gonna move you onto the flats, where we can keep an eye on you. I don't want to climb these steps every time you fart."

"Hey, Piri," Danny yelled, "they're putting you on Murderers' Row."

My blood went cold. The cop hadn't died, but suppose he did? . . . I said a quick prayer for his recovery.

Inside the cell, I spread a blanket for a mattress. But the bed was so hard, my bullet hole felt like it was getting crushed. I threw the other blanket on top, but it was the same. Fuck it; I decided to sleep sitting up. Major looked at me and went away. A few minutes later he returned with four or five blankets and dropped them on the bunk.

"Thanks," I said, a little surprised.

"Why not, kid," Major said, "you've got enough troubles now."

On Murderers' Row, I met Ramón, long, skinny Ramón. He had six fingers on one hand and that had helped witnesses identify him, he told me. He also said that Jimmy had fired the fatal shot. We played cards and cursed the faggots in the tier above us who often yelled down, "Don't worry, fifteen or twenty years ain't so bad," or "The chair is quick and greasy."

I was three or four months in the Tombs, waiting for trial, going to court, waiting for adjournments, trying to deal for a lower plea, and what not. I schemed and lay awake at night thinking of the thousands of years they could pile on me. I heard Louie was in the Tombs, too. They had traced our car back to him. He had turned *chota* on me.

"They told me you was dead," he tried to explain when I saw him in court. "I figured it wouldn't hurt you." I wanted to eat his heart out.

"Yeah, baby," I told him, "we'll talk some time."

Then the big day came—sentencing time. By chance Ramón and I got sentenced the same day. I was in what is called the bullpen, waiting to go into court. I called fast as they rushed him by, "What was it?"

His answer came out long and softly, "*La silla, panín, la silla.*"

Oh shit, I thought, *you poor m.f. One way or another, some bastard puts us down.*

"Hey, you," a hack called to me, "you're next!"

The gate opened and I walked with the hack to a bigger bullpen, where Danny, Billy, and Louie were waiting. "Okay, you guys, let's go," the hack said, and all of us but Louie followed him into the courtroom.

"*Aya en el Rancho Grande,*" Danny said to me.

"Not any more, *amigo,*" *I said.* "Somebody rustled the cattle Hey! How come Louie isn't coming to court with us?"

"Maybe a deal," Billy whispered.

We stood in front of the judge. In his robe of black, way up there, he looked like a giant. I felt small, but I made my face *cara palo* and my back as straight as the pain allowed. I controlled every damn thing but my knees. They went wild. I fought their shaking; I cursed them; I willed them bony-livered knees to cool it and have heart—but they just punked out. I hoped nobody dug it. I peeked behind me; the court was empty. I sure felt alone. I wondered if Danny and Billy felt like me; probably not. They had experience. The judge wanted to know if I had anything else to say before sentence was passed. The lawyers stepped forward to cop pleas for another chance, mercy and all that jazz. I thought maybe I shouldn't look too mean, too tough; that I should look just a little bit humble. I quickly clasped my hands behind my back and bowed my head. Then the judge said to me, "John Peter Thomas."

My true name sounded so strange. He had forgotten to call me "Piri"; it was almost like he was calling some other cat.

"I hereby sentence you . . . to hard labor . . . at Sing Sing . . . for not less than five, no more than fifteen years for attempted armed robbery in the first degree."

Up came my head; there was no need to be humble, the judge didn't dig my humility. I felt two hands grab me by each arm, and I was hustled away (I guess to keep me from doing anything angry or foolish). As I was being led away, the D.A. whispered something to the judge, who called me back and put five to ten years more on my back, for felonious assault, "the sentences to run . . ."

I held my breath. If he said "consecutively," I'd have to finish up one sentence before starting the other; but if he said "concurrently," the two sentences would run together.

". . . concurrently," the judge concluded.

Puta! I was still in trouble, but at least I would do two days for one.

I was led away, and from where I stood near the door, I heard Danny get a four-to-eight and four-to-ten, and Billy get a five-to-ten. I didn't hear any more or even given a damn. My time was my worry, theirs was theirs. I walked into the bullpen laughing, playing it cool to the last eight bars.

The hack looked at me strangely. "You buys," he said, "don't this time bother you?"

"Man," I said, grandstanding, "sleeping time, just sleeping time. On my head."

Louie walked in to be sentenced alone, and a few minutes

later he came out, pale and shaken. The hack said, "He fainted dead to the floor."

Coño, I thought, *they must have buried him.* "What'd he get?" I asked the hack.

"Zip-five, zip-five."

"That *maricón* got zero to five years!" I screamed. "He'll be out in a year. And *he* fainted! Oh, that punk, that *plato*-eating punk..."

When I got back to the Tombs, the first thing I heard was: "What did you get, Piri?"

"What happened, kid?"

"How'd you make out?"

Everybody wants to know your bit, big or small, maybe to measure his hope by it.

"I got fifteen *bolos*," I yelled. I said it in despair but with pride in my ability to do so.

"Tough," or "Not so bad," came some replies.

The faggots upstairs cooed, "Ah tol' you so, honee."

"*Maricones*, go screw yourselves," I shouted.

"Ah wish Ah could, honee."

I laughed. How could I not? I had to laugh or crack up. I lit up a cigarette, dragged deeply, and lay back. At least the waiting was over. I knew where I stood.

26. BREAKING IN

The next day, after breakfast, a hack rattled the door to my cell. I was lying down on my pile of blankets, thinking about Trina . . . and that five to fifteen years was a long time.

"Thomas," the hack called, "Thomas, you're on a shipment."

Damn, I thought, *a shipment—what the fuck am I; a package or something?*

"Thomas, hey, you, can't you hear? Whatta ya, deaf?"

Cool it, Piri, don't blow your cool. This white hack is just sweating to lay his blackjack on your stone head. I said, "I'm coming." *I'm coming . . . for my head is bending low . . . I spit on your faces, motherfuckers.*

"Hurry up, we ain't got all day. You're on a shipment to Sing Sing."

Now, say, amigo, *whatta ya mean, you ain't got all day? I got fifteen years, a lotta time. I got more'n all day . . .* "Yes sir, I'm coming." *Play cool, Piri, 'cause if you don't, you're gonna get wasted . . . wait for me, Trina, wait for me . . .*

"Okay, stand there . . ."

"Gonzalez."

"Rivera."

"Washington."

"O'Leary."

"Puluskie."

"Goldberg . . . Goldberg, shake a leg."

"Yessir, I'm coming."

"Okay, let's check you guys out."

"Thomas."

"Here."

"Gonzalez."

"Here."

"Rivera."

"Here, sir."

"Washington."

"Heah, suh."

"O'Leary."

"Here."

"Puluskie."

"Present."

Present, I thought, *who ain't?*

"Walters."

"Here."

"On the gate," yelled the hack, and the gate slid open. We followed the hack out in single file down the steel corridor, down in an elevator, down, down, down, and out a big-mouthed door. "Okay, two by two," the hack said, "just two at a time, come out." Holding out four sets of handcuffs, he added, "Okay, put out your hands . . . one his right . . . and the other his left."

The air smelled like no other air had ever smelled before, but it didn't last long. We were handcuffed and hustled into a green van. The van moved off and I took a last look at the New York scene. The speed of the van made my heart leave Harlem far behind, made the rep feel like it wasn't worth it . . . then I didn't look no more until we got to Sing Sing.

"Put out your hands," the hack said. He unlocked the cuffs and my hands were free, but that was all; the rest of me was in Sing Sing, for a max of fifteen years. The first business was purification.

"Strip."

"Spread your cheeks."

"Soles of your feet up."

"Take a shower."

"Where do you want your clothes sent?"

And a talk by some warden or Big Blue Uniform about doing right or else.

I walked slow and played my cool role. But in my cell, I lay on my bunk and stared the bars down; I mixed my hope and downed my pride and checked tears back. I worked hard at keeping my mind from being eaten up by pressure and from having had to go into competition with canaries. I counted my fingers, then checked how many teeth I had in my mouth and guessed at the hairs on my head; I pulled off my shoes and pared my toenails with splitting fingernails; I flushed the toilet to make a different noise; I scratched and yanked and twisted and turned; I thought and dreamed, hoped and wanted—and tried to smash away the shit-filled feeling of "this is it."

Fifteen years on a dead chest, number 109-699. *Mr. Sing Sing, cool breeze, where you at?* I curled my fingers around the cold bars. *Uncurl them, boy, you can't heat them up . . . Why is everybody so damn quiet? We're only in jail, not dead . . . Wish I had company—a bottle of soda, a cigarette, a smell of Trina, a nickel for the jukebox, a taste of smoking, curling pot . . . One good thing, the pain's eased off . . . I'm getting a little stronger now. They ain't gonna break me. These* maricones *ain't seen heart yet. I wonder, man, how long is fifteen years? Break it up into little pieces, by months, weeks, days. Oh blip, man, its too long. How the hell can I pull this bit? It's more than standing time.*

The weeks passed and "orientation" became a blip of the past. We were now purified enough of civilian complexes to become part of the prison population. I still had trouble walking straight; the wound pulled. But the body doctors and head doctors had played me in and out and had pronounced me in good, if bent, shape. I got an assignment in the jobbing shop, working on odds and ends. The jobbing shop's specialty was green-painted coffins for newly burnt electric-chair graduates.

There was lots to do, and plenty of time to do it. We got up at 6:30, swept our cells, had breakfast and went to work at 8:00. We could work in the morning and go to school in the afternoon, or vice versa. At noon we quit for lunch and a short gab period. Then we worked (or went to school) from 1:00 to 3:30. For the next hour we were free to do anything—play ball in the yard, relax in the recreation hall or masturbate in our cells. From 4:30 to 5:00 we ate dinner; then we were locked in for the night. Bugles woke us up, and bugles signaled our lock-up; in the interval we marched to our meals to the swinging music of John Philip Sousa. I felt like a POW.

One day I was sitting on top of a food locker in the recreation hall, cooling my role, the dull pain in my chest not so mean now. I was swinging my feet ever so easy when I dug three rocks watching me, funny like. I dug their look. It was the *carcel* look of wolves digging a stone lamb. I knew what was gonna shake next. I'd be sounded and if I punked out—"game time." Any cat that punks out in jail has gotta give up his food packages, his smokes and, for dessert, his ass. *Motherfuckers,* I thought, *I got one thing left, and that's my rep, and nobody's gonna take that.*

They sat at the food locker next to mine and started sounding, like I wasn't there. Every so often they smiled wisely at each other. I let my feet swing easy, like the rocks wasn't there, and waited.

"Hey, mac, can you draw?" one of them asked me.

"Yeah, mac," I answered, "I can draw."

"Can you draw good?"

"Yeah, I can draw real good. You want I should draw you?" *Smile your pussyface smiles, I dig where you're at.* I eased off the table. I could dig their minds make me feel at ease. They would make friends, do me favors, get me in debt and then ask to cop—not right away but after a time, a long time. I picked up the pencil and looked at them cool. "Which one wants his pictured drawed?"

"Draw me," drawled one that the others had been calling Rocky. Still cool, I took the pencil and paper and with no expression on my face walked over to my food locker, looked seriously at the cat, from side to side, and drew and drew. I handed him the paper and told him, "Man, this is the way I dig you."

Again he and his boys smiled their shit grins. He looked at the paper and if this cat could have turned red he would have, but he was too dark for that. His eyeballs almost exploded out of his sockets. He threw the paper down; his boys looked, dug, and busted out laughing. I had drawn him as a funny-book black cannibal, complete with a big bone through his nose.

Rocky blew up. I still dug him cool. If he hit me, one shot to my chest, I was sure to kick the habit of living. But I had to show balls. "You yellow-faced motherfucker," he screamed.

I swung my feet easy like. "Why don't you go tell it to your mother, motherjumper?" I said. Then I looked up at him, through him, all about him—and spat at his feet.

He flipped and came for me, but his boys stopped him with, "Cool it, Rocky, here comes the hack." As his boys dragged him away, he looked at me and whispered, "Motherfucker, I'll get you."

"You're right, *moreno*," I said, "you'll get a stiff dick up your ass."

I knew that he'd wait till he or his boys could snag me alone. I wasn't going to get wasted just like that, so that night in my cell, after the last bugle that stops all yak, I knocked at the cell next to mine. The guy in it had come back as a parole violator. We had been cuffed together on the trip from the Tombs. "Hey, man," I whispered.

"What's happening?" he answered back just as quietly.

"Look, man, I need a shank. You've been here before and are hep to what's down, so cop me a shank."

"Yeah, what's happening?" he asked.

I explained, and he said, "Okay, man, you're on your own, man. I'll cop one for you in the a.m. But look, young brave, don't kill the stud, 'cause you'll cop a fifteen-to-thirty-year bit behind that. Just mess him up a bit."

"Yeah," I said, "I'm gonna mess his shitty face up nice and easy, cut it up *así y así*." I moved my hand like with a knife, like the air was Rocky *moreno*. "And whenever they see his ugly *cara*, they'll know that I did it, and every con in the joint will know I got a rep for pure *hombre* and cool himself."

"Good night, *amigo*."

"Good night, *panín*," I answered.

I didn't sleep much. I thought, *Even here I'm still rumbling, still fighting.* Caramba, *God, if you're up there, I don't dig this number. That cat might not stay cut and I may have to end up cooling him for good.* I didn't want to, but if I had to, that motherfucker was gonna pick cotton in hell.

The next morning I had the shank. It was a regular plate knife, honed like a fine Gillette. It felt cool and like death against my stomach, behind my undershirt. I had breakfast and went to work.

I was scuffling with a twenty-pound mop when a hack called, "Hey, are you number 109-699?"

I nodded yes.

"Come with me," he ordered.

I dropped the mop against the wall and followed him. *The knife*, I thought, *somebody ratted.* I wondered if my boy had copped a plea. The hack took me to my cell and locked me in it. But he didn't give me a shakedown. Instead he pulled out a small narrow card with "Keep Locked" printed on it and wove it in between my bars. "Look, man," I said, "can you tell me what's happening? Why the 'Keep Locked'?"

"Yeah, I can," he replied. "You're on a boat."

"A what?" I asked.

"A boat. You're getting shipped out of here at 5 a.m. tomorrow."

Madre, I thought, *it's like God dug my plea last night.* I waited till he left and pulled the shank out of my belt and felt a hundred pounds lighter. That night I returned the shank to my boy through the bars. I was glad I didn't have to shank that motherjumper, Rocky, but I hadn't punked out either.

The next morning I had an early breakfast. On the way back to my cell block, I saw Rocky. (He must have been a trusty to be out that early.) He looked hard down at me and whispered, "You lucky . . ."

I cold smiled him. "No, you, *amigo,*" *I* said, "*you* were shit in luck." I often wondered who was the luckiest.

In the yard leading to the railroad siding about fifty of us waited for our train, shackled in pairs by leg irons. At last the train pulled in. It was a regular passenger train, except that we were given a whole coach for ourselves. A bad-taste feeling came into my eyes when I dug them law-abiding outsiders looking at us, at me. *So this is how they go down on the chain gang,* I thought. I made myself invisible.

We boarded and, after riding two hours, we were given cheese sandwiches. Another hour and we were allowed to go to the john, one at a time. Another hour and we played cards on shaky knees. Another hour and we were home—Comstock State Prison.

The world was getting tighter and tighter to wear. It was like I was outgrowing it. My God, the only thing I could do that the hacks couldn't stop was think. And I wished I could stop thinking about the free side. *The free side—dig that!* In the beginning I'd said "outside"; now I said "free side," just like a con. Well, wasn't I a con? I guessed I was.

27. MUCHO DAYS AND NIGHTS IN GRAY

One of the worst feelings I can imagine is to be something or someplace and not be able to accept the fact. So it was with me—I was a con in jail, but nothing in the world could make me accept it. Not the gray clothes, not the green bars, not the bugle's measuring of time, not the blue-uniformed hacks, not the insipid food, not the new lines in my face—nothing.

I couldn't get used to it, no matter how hard I tried. It kept pounding on me. It came to me every morning and every evening and sat heavily, like death on living tissue. I hated the evenings because a whole night in prison lay before me, and I hated the mornings because I felt like Dracula returning to his coffin.

I tried to make believe that the days were shorter instead of longer, that the moon rose within half an hour of the sun. I hated the sight of a calendar. I tried not to count the days and weeks and months and years—and I found myself counting seconds and minutes. I counted the bolts and windows, the green-splashed bars, the hacks and cons; they added up to a thousand years. The reasoning that my punishment was deserved was absent. As prison blocks off your body, so it suffocates your mind.

My life became a gray mass of hatred. I hated sunny days because of the fine times I could have been enjoying at the beach with Trina, and I hated rainy days because they were depressing and made my cell, my clothes, even my insides damp. I hated the prison noises and the smell of the guards' dark-blue uniforms. I hated the other cons for reminding me that I was one of them, and I hated myself because I *was* one of them.

Man, what a fuckin' mess I've gotten my ass into. Jail gives you plenty of time to think, and I thought and thought about the outside and the block and Trina. *I wonder what she's doing now? What time is it? She must be asleep or getting ready for bed. If I strain my eyes, I can just about make you out, baby, with your hair down and curly bouncing like and your mouth in a point, pushed out like you're always mad at somebody . . . Strain harder, eyeballs . . . I can feel your body warmth, smell you, taste you—oh, Christ, take her out of my mind . . .*

Comstock was just like Sing Sing. Every con did something; every hack was stationed just right; and above all, every bar was in the right place—over windows and doors. For school I was assigned to study brick masonry; my regular job was on the paint gang. I was paid a nickel a day, which later was raised to a dime. The money was credited to my account, and twice a month I was permitted to make a "buy" in the amount of half my monthly wages.

If you got food from home (say, canned goods) or from the buy, you ate like a king. Otherwise you ate like a con. You ate like a con, anyway, no matter what you ate, when you ate in the mess hall. It held more than a thousand people and the combined sounds of spoons brushing against tin cups full of iodine coffee, food being chewed, men talking out of hopeful throats, feet scraping, and trays banging made the meal scene like a wild dream. But it was real. If you didn't get a care package and couldn't make a buy, you made sandwiches out of bread and whatever food you got at supper. It could be anything—spaghetti, stew, cole slaw, even soup.

The food wasn't bad once you accepted it with the same readiness you accepted your prison sentence. Sunday lunch was a pretty good meal. We got roast beef or ham, gravy, bread, potatoes, dessert, and coffee. It was the same on minor holidays like Washington's Birthday. The three big holidays were Thanksgiving, Christmas, and New Year's. For Thanksgiving and Christmas we got a great big hunk of roast chicken with the works; on New Year's Day, we got a thick cut of steak, also with the works. Usually, however, the cat that sliced the meat cut it razor thin. Our favorite joke was to solemnly hold up a letter, place a slice of meat over it and begin to read the letter through the meat.

I was jail-wise in picking my friends. There is a pecking order among prisoners. At the top are the con men, the smoothies. Just beneath them are disbarred lawyers and abortionists; their brains entitle them to respect. In the middle are the heist men. Thieves and burglers rank just below them. And at the bottom are rapists, faggots, crooked cops, and junkies.

I wanted to learn all the hustles, all the arts of knowing people and their kicks. One older guy I got to know, Sam, was one of the best con men in the business. He told me how he worked. And always he ended up by saying, "But you see, kid, I made a lot of money—but here I am." My closest *amigo* was a big black Puerto Rican everyone called Young Turk, a gentle man who was doing five to fifteen for cutting a guy up in a fight.

I also was friendly with a guy who came from a good family and had gone to all the right schools. His name was Kent, and he talked English like a college professor. I listened to him and imitated him. I wanted to speak like Kent, but not all of a sudden; that would have seemed like grandstanding. So I grabbed a dictionary and slowly learned words and tried them out in our yaks. When I first did this, Kent lifted his eyebrows and smiled slightly but not superciliously. Way down he was tickled that I wanted to emulate his stick of being, and from then on he corrected me whenever I mispronounced a word, and he smiled approvingly when I spoke grammatically. One day he said to me, "Why don't you write, Piri?"

"Write what?" I replied.

"Thoughts, ideas, poetry," he said.

I laughed. "Sure, someday . . ."

I didn't write until many years later, but I did plenty of talking. Man, in prison, everyone yakked. Yak took up time, it killed time, especially on the long days like Saturday and Sunday, when we didn't work and had a lot of yard time. And we dealt for almost anything, partly out of a desire for the stuff and partly to beat the system. Goof balls, benzedrine, phenobarbitals, splits, and green money floated around regularly. At Sing Sing we had had whisky, too, but at Comstock I never saw any whisky, bonded stuff, I mean. Instead we had fermented prunes, fruit wines, and strained shellac—all homemade, of course, but they packed a kick. Some shellac killed one con with a promising career as a sax musician and blinded two others.

Splits were common. They're round white pills with a groove across the middle, some sort of tranquilizer. If you swallow one with a glass of hot water, you get a gone high that's almost like what you get with heroin. We also dealt for red capsules of phenos, two of which, with hot water, produce a forgetting high, and for cooking mace or cinnamon, a large tablespoon of which, with a glass of hot water, closes your eyelids with a way-up-and-out feeling. Sometimes the trusties or outside gang brought in wild marijuana, which we cured and dried on the electric light bulb in the cell. But splits were the kick. One guy, Clarence, a young Negro who painted beautifully, was gone on them. Clarence really loved drugs.

"That's my woman, Lady Snow," he told me once. "I sure wish I could cop some. I got some smuggled in a while back but it was just a little piece. It's hard. These hacks check everything, even take the stamps off the letters to make sure they wasn't stuck on with paste of drugs. And you get a white shirt from home and they launder it for you, just to make sure it wasn't starched with drugs."

"Forget it, Clarence," I said.

Clarence smiled at me and said, "Dig, Piri, who do you love?"

"Me," I said.

"Well, I love Lady Snow. You can't forget about you, I can't forget about Lady Snow."

A couple of days later Clarence died in his sleep. "What happened to Clarence?" I asked Young Turk.

"That damn fool, he got some splits and it's bad enough to swallow them like he does, three or four at a gulp, but he went and crushed them and copped some works, an eyedropper and a needle, and shot himself up. His heart stopped."

I had been at Comstock two years when Clarence died, and I still had three years or more to go, depending on how the parole board decided. *Jesus,* I thought, *if only the days would vary, if only one day would be fourteen hours and another three hours long, if only daylight would come at night and vice versa—anything at all to break the monotony.* But time passed as usual. Breakfast was followed by lunch and lunch by dinner, and then the cycle started again. I could feel myself growing up; the fine peach fuzz on my face becoming a heavy stubble, my chest broadening, my voice deepening, my ideas changing. Every day brought a painful awareness of the sweetness of being free and the horror of prison's years going down the toilet bowl.

Sometimes the pressure got too much to bear, as it does with all cons, who, seeking a release from the overpowering hatred against a society that makes canaries out of human beings, let out their aggressions on each other. I had been having trouble with a con named Little. He was well named, short but powerfully built. I guess he was bugged also, and when two bugged convicts meet head on, pressure gotta come out. We got into some sort of argument, not two words were needed; he looked bad at me, I looked bad at him. I said, "Man, I'm pretty fuckin' well tired of your bullshit."

"How tired, man?" he challenged me.

"Tired enough to fight your ass to the ground," I replied.

"Okay, man, let's go to the back of the paint room and we deal."

The cons nearby heard us and dug the situation, but they made no move to let on that they did. In prison you minded your business and fought your own fights or you were a punk. Besides, they didn't want to let the guards know anything was gonna pop—and furthermore, they didn't want to cheat themselves out of a fight that would give them a break from another dull, lousy day.

Little and I walked side by side, down the ramp and into the large paint room we worked in. My guts tensed and sucked air. Casey, a big, kind, friendly guard, was on duty. He was one of the few rare human beings left in my kind of world. He looked up at us and at the casually strolling cons who wanted a good look-see at this rumble, and, sensing that something was up, eased his big hard brown wooden stick into a more favorable position. But he didn't say anything. I looked at Little, who was standing close to me for a chance to reach me fast when we started throwing punches. I pushed him away and he almost tore my jaw off with a left cross. I hadn't figured him to be a southpaw. I hit the floor hard and all I knew was to get up. I scrambled and grabbed him and punched and held, and he punched and held, and damned if I didn't feel like at last here in front of me was somebody I could take out my mad steam on; and I guess he felt the same. Little actually was my friend, one of the clique—and now we were trying to mash each other. I tore into his guts with rights, lefts and elbows; he pounded away at my face. Suddenly, it was over by silent mutual consent. We just looked at each other, lips tight and bloodied. Then Casey came over quietly and said, "You guys got it out of your systems?" Our heads shook up and down in unison. "Okay, if you guys had picked up sticks or pipes, or used anything else other than your fists, I would have wrapped this billy stick around both your heads. As it is, I've seen nothing and you've done nothing. I don't want no more of this."

I looked at Little and he at me, and we both knew we didn't want no more. Sometimes a fight between two men makes them the greatest of friends, because of the respect that is born between the swinging fists. Casey walked away. Little and I slapped skin, and I asked him in a low voice, "Little, why didn't you work my guts over in the clinches?"

"I didn't want to hit you where you got shot," he said. "I figured I might cause you bad hurt." He walked away, and damned if I didn't feel wet in my eyes.

28. SEX IN THE CAN

Everyone talked about it, most of us indulged in it solo, and some guys took their kicks with each other.

The talk was almost always reminiscences. One of the best of the bullshitters was a big con we called Ching. He had a very vivid memory. "Now dig this," he would say, biting his lower lip and inhaling a long, shuddering breath of jailhouse passion, "this broad's name was Dolores, and she was real fine," and he would paint a dream picture for us. Each of us would get a different picture of Dolores. She would be a blonde, or dark, or Puerto Rican, or whatever we wanted.

But the real action was between men. If you weren't careful, if you didn't stand up for yourself and say, "Hands off, motherfucker," you became a piece of ass. And if you got by this hassle, there always was the temptation of wanting to cop some ass. I had a Negro named Claude after me to make him my steady. "Look, why won't you be my man?" he asked me. "I'll give you the moon, the stars, the world, the uni—"

"Shove it," I hissed out. "Cut the shit out. Stop making like you was a for-real broad and get your black ass from here."

"I'll give you cigarettes, anything, baby; I'll keep you real good," he insisted.

I looked past the green bars at Claude and saw a woman's pleading, tormented face. *He wants to buy a daddy-o,* I thought. *But I ain't gonna break. One time. That's all I have to do it. Just one time and it's gone time. I'll be screwing faggots as fast as I can get them. I'm not gonna get institutionalized. I don't want to lose my hatred of this damn place. Once you lose the hatred, then the can's got you. You can do all the time in the world and it doesn't bug you. You go outside and you make it; you return to prison and you make it there, too. No sweat, no pain. No. Outside is real; inside is a lie. Outside is one kind of life, inside is another. And you make them the same if you lose your hate of prison.* "Claude," I said, "if I gotta break your fuckin' jaw, I will. They've put a wall around me for fifteen years, but I've got something real outside, and it makes no difference when I get out, married or not, she's mine, and there'll be no past for the two of us, just a stone present and a cool future. Meanwhile, I'll jack off if I gotta, but I ain't gonna marry you, faggot, no matter what."

Claude got the message and peddled his ass elsewhere. About two weeks later, he found a taker, Big Jules, a stud who was doing life for cutting somebody up into little pieces. There was a formal wedding, complete with preacher, best man, and attendants. I dug the whole scene. It was held outdoors in a corner of the yard. The sun was shining and the birds were singing. A few tables were pulled together to make a long table and all the guests were seated. The bride and groom sat behind a big cake, the bride in a clean white blouse (or was it a shirt?), the bridegroom cool and attentive. Across from them sat the preacher, a con who on the outside probably played a cool racket as a phony minister.

I looked around and thought, *Do the hacks think it's a birthday party, or do they know what's shaking and are making like they don't see it?* I heard the preacher man say, "Do you, Claude, take this man to be your lawful wedded husband, to love, cherish, honor and obey . . . ?"

"I do," Claude said softly, just like any bride anywhere. *My God, what an unreal world. Look at Big Jules's face, he really is serious. This faggot is gonna be his wife, for better or for worse, until death do them part.* And it came to me, scared and hard, that this was what I had to fight against. This farce was for Claude and Big Jules their real life, the whole of existence. *Look, they see each other as Romeo and Juliet, as though the world were a part of them and not the other way around.*

The groom slipped a ring on the bride's finger and the minister said, "I now pronounce you man and wife," and the guests offered them congratulations and best of luck. It made me sick inside. *Where to now, wedded couple? Niagara Falls, Bermuda, Europe for a blissful honeymoon? Great. Where you gonna get your break? Where will you consummate your vows? Behind the cell-hall blocks, in a corner of the workshop, during idle time?* "Oh, yesss, he's mah man now," purred Claude to a well-wisher.

A few days later I got another love problem dumped in my lap. I had been playing handball in the yard and was in the middle of a break, sitting against the great gray wall, when Little came up to me, scrunched down beside me, and asked me if I had a cousin called Tico. I didn't, but I said, "Maybe, why?"

"Well, there's a kid on the new shipment from Elmira, and he sez he's your cousin. Know him? His real name is Ricardo, and he's about eighteen years old."

"Yeah, I know him." *Hell,* I thought, *can it really be Tico, Little Red's kid brother? I wonder why he's pushing himself off as my cousin?*

Later, when I saw him, I knew why. A baby-faced, small-framed, good-looking kid who looked about fourteen years old, he was perfect prey for the jailhouse wolves. He was scared, too, though he tried not to show it. He needed a friend or a "cousin" who was established in jail, who had a rep as a down guy. I watched him huddle in a corner of the yard with all the green mickies. They were laughing loud and making talk, putting on fronts and looking blasé, like being in jail was a daily kick. I walked toward the huddled bunch of citizens and Tico saw me. He moved toward me with jerky, twitchy moves, smiling the biggest, happiest smile I ever dug. He threw his arms around me and said, "Piri, I'm glad, man, I'm glad to see you."

"So am I, Tico. How did you know I was here?"

"Oh, my brother let me know from time to time how you wuz, and where. When I heard I was on a boat to Comstock, I knew you'd be here."

"Come on over here," I said, "and we'll set."

Tico turned from me and loudly called over to his huddled buddies, for them and for the whole yard to hear, "Hey, guys, this is my cousin I wuz tellin' you about." He looked surer of himself for that identification, and his huddled buddies looked envious of him for having established residence.

I sat down on my snag bag (a cloth bag with whatever junk you carried around) and he squatted next to me. I said nothing. I took out a bag of rollies (Bull Durham) and rolled one and offered it to him. He took it and in turn took out a pack of tailor-made smokes and offered me one. I took it and we lit up, inhaled and exhaled, and then he let it out. "Piri, I hope you ain't mad about me saying you were my cousin," he said, and he looked down at the barren concrete walk.

I looked at him and thought, *Baby, don't you know I know how you feel? Don't you dig I was like you a million years ago? With a brave front and a* cara-palo *defense? Shit, my little* hermano, *if we were anywhere else, I'd take you in my arms and hold you close and tell you the facts of prison life.* I broke my own thoughts and said, "Tico, we're more than cousins, kid, we're brothers. Just handle yourself right, don't make fast friends, and act cool. Don't play and joke too much, and baby, don't, just don't, accept candy or smokes from stranger cons. You might end up paying for it with your ass."

He kept on looking at the concrete walk and his face grew red and the corners of his mouth got a little too white. "Piri, I've been hit on already," he said.

I thought, *My God, he's got a jailhouse gorilla reception already*. "Yeah," I prompted, "and . . ."

"Well, I got friendly with this guy named Rube."

Rube was a muscle-bound degenerate whose sole ambition in life was to cop young kids' behinds. "Yeah," I said, "and so . . ."

"Well, this cat has come through with smokes and food and candy and, well, he's a spic like me and he talked about the street outside and about guys we know outside and he helped me out with favors, you know, real friendly."

"Yeah," I said, "and so . . ."

"So this," Tico said, pulling from his pocket a folded piece of paper and handing it to me. I knew what it was, but I opened it and read:

Dear Tico,

Since the first moment I saw you, I knew you were for me. I fell in love with your young red lips and the hair to match it. I would like to keep on doing things for you and to take care of you and not let anybody mess with you. I promise not to let no one know about you being my old lady and you don't have to worry none, because I won't hurt you none at all. I know you might think it's gonna be bad, but it's not at all. I could meet you in the back part of the tier cell hall and nobody's going to know what's happening. I've been doing a lot for you and I never felt like this about no girl. If you let me cop you, I'll do it real easy to you. I'll use some hair oil and it will go in easy. You better not let me down 'cause I got it bad for you, I'd hate to mess you all up.

Love and Kisses XXX
You know who
R.

P.S. Tear this up and flush it down the shit bowl.

My God, I thought, *what can I tell him?* Tico had to show man or he was finished. Rube would use that first time to hold him by threatening to tell everybody that he screwed him. And if anybody found out, every wolf in the joint would want to cop. The hacks would hear about it and they would put Tico on A-1 tier where all the faggots were, and he'd be a jailhouse punk. "What do you owe him, Tico?" I asked.

"About three cartons of smokes, fourteen candy bars, some canned food, and a couple of undershirts."

"You damn fool," I said, "couldn't you see what was happening? That lousy shit was courting you, making time with you, like you've done on the outside with broads. You appealed to him 'cause you're to him like a virgin would be on the outside, a first cop."

"What am I gonna do, Piri?"

"Look, I'll get the stuff he gave you and—"

"No, that won't work. I already told him I'd give him back his stuff, and no dice; that motherjumper wants to punk me and he said if I didn't punk out, him and his boys would jack me up. So what do I do?"

"Look, Tico," I said, gazing down at the concrete walk, "there's only two things you can do. One, you can punk out and become a girl." I felt him get stiff and I knew he was looking at me, or maybe into me. "Or, you can get him off your back. Does he work in your shop?"

"Yeah, he does."

"Well, the first time he says something to you or looks wrong at you, have a piece of pipe or a good heavy piece of two-by-four. Don't say a damn thing to him, just get that heavy wasting material and walk right up to him and bash his face in and keep bashing him till he's down and out, and yell loud and clear for all the other cons to hear you, 'Motherfucker, I'm a man, I came in here a motherfucking man and I'm going out a motherfucking man. Next time I'll kill you.' "

"And?" Tico said softly.

"And nuttin', baby. You'll be free, an accepted man—part of this jailhouse scene. All the weight will be off your back. The word will get around you ain't to be messed with 'cause you got heart and you ain't afraid to deal." Ba-ra-ta-ta-ta-ta, the bugle sounded, and I said, "Let's go, cousin," and our eyes met for the first time since we had sat down on the concrete walk and he said "Thanks" with his and I said, "You're welcome," with mine. As he walked away, he didn't seem so nervous, so twitchy. I figured that even if he didn't get a chance to hurt Rube, even if Rube took that wasting stick from him and messed him up, everybody would know he had heart to stand up to muscle-bound Rube; and it was better to get hurt outside where it could be seen and attended to than inside, where it would stay all his life.

Two days later I learned that Tico was locked up in isolation. The news traveled fast: Rube had approached Tico with a "gonna-punk-out-kid" smile on his face. Tico hadn't said a word, but before Rube knew what was happening, Tico had bashed him with an iron bar. If he had caught Rube flush on the head, his brains would have been all over the place; as it was, he had caught him a glancing blow on the shoulder and the hack had jumped in before Tico could swing again. Tico had screamed out hate at Rube and anybody else that had funny ideas about trying anything with him. Now he was in, but he was gonna pay with a week of bread and water and one meal a day.

I passed the isolation cell block the next day and whispered to Tico, "How you doing, kid?"

"Great," he said, "but I'm hungry."

"Cheap price, kid, to keep your ass," I answered. I looked around fast and let a pack of tailor-mades fall to the floor. I couldn't get next to the cell; a heavy wire screen kept everyone about five feet away. But there was a little space at the bottom of the screen, and I gave a fast hard kick to the pack of smokes and it slid right into his cell. Then I kept walking.

29. NO MORE MAÑANAS FOR US, TRINA

"Numba 18193," the loudspeaker blared out, "report to cell hall desk."

I jerked out of the half-asleep mood into which I had drowsed sitting against the concrete prison wall in the warm sunshine. The order was repeated. Number 18193 was me, and the call could only mean one of two things. Either I was in some kind of trouble, or I had a visitor. I hustled myself fast and walked up to the cell hall desk.

"Whatta ya want?" asked the cell hall desk officer.

"I'm number 18193. I heard my number called on the loudspeaker."

"Umm, le's see." The hack picked up a sheet and looked at it and looked at me. I wondered what in the hell kind of trouble I was in. Maybe I had got reported for cooking on my bedsprings. But I was sure that I had used *The Saturday Evening Post* for fuel, and that kinda paper doesn't throw off much smoke. "It's a visit," the hack finally said.

My God, I thought. I had been at Comstock three years, and visits had been rare—my sister twice and my two aunts a couple of times. It was a long trip, I knew, and an expensive one, and maybe a difficult one, too. I walked up to the green-barred gate that led to the prison visiting room and said to the hack who opened the gate, "I got a visit."

"What's your number?"

I told him.

"Okay, walk toward the end of the corridor."

I walked down the long corridor—where I was frisked—and into the visiting room. The whole family was there—James and José, Sis and her husband, my two aunts, and even Pops, who was sitting there looking as nervous as hell, like the prison bars were gonna keep him there too. I copped a real big smile and walked like this happened every day.

"Piri, Piri," called James and José. I tried to walk cool and unhurried, but I had to get there as fast as I could and hug everybody as hard as I could.

"*Mi hijo, cómo está?*" asked my aunts.

"Hey, Piri," said José, "how do I look in uniform?"

"Hey," I said. "Paratrooper, eh?"

And a big smile from Sis and a little hung-up tear.

I looked at Pops and he looked at me—two old men, father and son. I wanted to hug him and make like all the past days were never as they were, but somehow we both knew it was gonna take something bigger to wipe away all the rough things that had gone down between us. "Hi, Pops," I grinned, "how are you?"

"Fine, Piri, you look okay."

"Yeah, I'm studying brick masonry and I got some studies for my high-school diploma, so when I get out I can do right." I looked at this man I called Pops. *Pops, can't you dig me? I'm trying to tell you that I wanna be like before. No, not like before—what I mean is, like we* wasn't *before. I wanna be close and like other sons and fathers. I wanna be tight, real buddy-buddies.* Caramba, *Pops, can't you see?*

Pops stood there, the perfect stranger to me, like he always was, and said, "That's good, Piri." Then he vaguely looked around and said to nobody in particular, "Jesus, I didn't like for them to take my fingerprints. Did they have to?"

"It's nothing, Pops," my sister said. "They do it every time somebody comes to visit for the first time."

"Yeah," I said, "first time," and I looked at Pops and my eyes told him that I knew he wasn't coming again. *It's like you never came, Pops.*

We all sat down and talked, but after a while I noticed something strange. A pall had settled over the conversation. "What's the matter?" I asked James.

"Well, er," said James, "aw, you tell him, Sis."

"Well, er," said Sis, "it's about—you tell him, James. You found out about it."

"Dammit, somebody tell me."

"Trina got married."

I knew it! I knew it! It had to come. I grabbed the edge of the table hard. I had spent my days and nights half-expecting it, fearing that it would happen, and yet almost hoping for it to put an end to my uncertainty. I had written to her from the Tombs telling her not to wait, to make a new life for herself. She had replied that I was the only reality in her life and everything else was an illusion. The warden here hadn't allowed me to write to her because of Dulcien and the kid I gave her, but I had hoped she would understand and dig. Now all that was down the drain.

"Piri, Piri, you all right?" James asked.

I felt a small churning inside. "Yeah, sure, I'm okay," I said. "Man, there's no problem. I was expecting it, like. *Caramba,* she waited long enough. It ain't fair for any broad to wait that long, and I got a fifteen-year sentence. If you see her, give her my best and tell her that I hope she is happy. Tell her I'm happy for her." *Oh, Trina,* I thought, *why didn't you wait? Even if I didn't write, what the hell did that matter? Jesus, girl, didn't you take into consideration the nights I've spent making love to illusions of you? Of the dreams I've had that were so real I could smell you? I've built up* mañanas *of us together and how it would be. And this made it just a little easier. Now all I got is bad dreams waiting for me in that cell, bug-eyed dreams of no* mañanas *with you and sick dreams of you in another cat's arms. Dammit, Trina, I didn't touch you 'cause I wanted it to be great when we got married—and I saved you for another cat. Dammit, dammit.*

"So will you see the board of parole?" Sis asked.

"Oh, soon, in a few months."

"Gee, Piri," said José, "I hope you make it."

"Don't worry, kid, I think I will."

"Visiting is over," a hack announced.

"Jesus," said James, "it just began."

"Oh hell, no sweat, we gotta lot of *mañanas.*" *No more* mañanas *for us, Trina.*

"Take care of yourself."

"Yeah, you all do the same."

We hugged, and everybody left. I watched their backs and I felt bad 'cause somehow they kinda took Trina with them. Like if they hadn't come, she'd still be with me. I stepped out of the room and undressed for the frisk and dressed again and made the long walk to my cell, just putting one foot before the other. Then I gently opened the green-barred door and gently closed it behind me and heard the smashing and crashing of a master lock being closed behind me; and I saw, as almost for the first time, my wall, painted buff below and cream above, and the little bed and washbasin and toilet bowl in my fantastic little six-by-eight-by-nine world. I gently lay down and stretched long, and I put my hands behind the back of my neck and thought, *Trina got married.* Then, from the cell next to mine, Young Turk said, "Hey, man, you got a visit?"

"Yeah, yeah. My family."

"Everything all right?"

"Yeah, everything is all right."

"They come to see you again?"

I wished he would shut up. He was my boy and I didn't want to get angry at him, I didn't want to hate him. But Jesus, I had to have something to kill this feeling of wanting to go mad, so I said, "Baby, you got anything, anything at all to kill the pain before it drives me between this little space of green bars? Man, I haven't got enough room even to let in air so that I can breathe."

"Yeah, cool it, man," he said. "Don't blow your cool. You go some bad news on you, didn't you?"

I said, "Yeah, baby, a little bit. The most important part of my life done died. What you got, baby, for painkiller?"

"Baby," he said, "all I got is phenos, a little wild pot, some splits, and a little bit of mace."

"Give me all of them," I said, and I sat back on the edge of the bed. A few minutes later I heard the soft scraping of Young Turk's fingernails on the side of steel and I put my hand outside the bars and drew it back inside wrapped around a few feet of toilet paper. Inside the paper were the painkillers.

I opened my thermos bottle and put the mace on my tongue and gulped some hot water; I took the split with more hot water; then I lit up that wild pot and hissed it. When I got up, I had no feelings at all, so I tried to make something come. I wanted to get high, to get stoned, to get blown away. I wanted to wash away the pain. *How the fuck dare she lay in another man's arms! Oh, Christ! I think the sweetest thing that could happen to me right now would be to die. Hey . . .* And I stopped talking and stopped caring and stopped thinking . . . and then I began remembering . . .

You know, I'm remembering the night that I stayed up at your aunt's house and I slept on the couch that opened up into a double bed and I went into your room, and you were wide awake, and I sat next to you, and you said, "It is like this that you want me?" and you put yourself and made a mold of your body and molded me next to it . . .

My sand-papered eardrums picked out the reverberating sound of echoes of "Cool it, man!" from the cells around me and of a far-off murmuring of green bars and of a generalized blue, telling another one, "It's all right, he's probably talking in his sleep."

It's not your fault, baby, it's not your fault. I'm going to remember that letter, baby, that one letter and that one sentence. What was it that you said?

"Cool it, man, what do you want to do, man, bring these people down on you?"

"Yeah, okay, man; okay, baby, okay, Young Turk . . . I'm cool . . ." And I felt the blessed stink of deep sleep wash away the pain . . .

The next morning I sat down in the great mess hall, at one of the many great tables, and kept very quiet among all the murmuring of a thousand or so men beginning one more day without time. My last thought before I swallowed the lumpy cereal and drank the acid-like coffee was, *Goddammit, Trina, why did you have to get married?* And then it went out of my mind, washed away by the reality which was the beginning of one more day that had started a long time ago and would end a long time beyond.

30. SWEATIN', MAN, SWEATIN'

At the end of nearly four years in prison, I became eligible for parole. It was my most anxious period in prison. As the big day for my appearance before the parole board drew nearer, I did everything possible to avoid thinking about it. I played cards, handball, softball; I read and worked—no dice. The thought *I hope I make parole* stuck to me, and the dreams and hopes I tried to keep suppressed burst into my consciousness. The night before my appearance I lay awake thinking how things would be if I made it. I drew elaborate mental pictures of the whole bit, from the instant I was released to the moment I stepped back into Harlem. I also thought about not making it—but not in detail. Nobody who knows what hell is wants to go into detail on the subject.

As the early morning grayish light seeped into my cell, I leaned hard on the bars and, through my tiny window, watched the sun rise. This was my day. *Jesus, this is the day,* I thought. *Oh, God! This is the day for me. Turn, baby, and look into your round two-sided mirror.* I looked into the glass and saw a small brown face, bleary-eyed from an overdose of wanting to be free; then I turned the mirror over and saw my face enlarged, bloated with prison time and scarred by squeezed pimples and long lines, my lips dry and my tongue yellow-coated from the nicotine of a chain-smoking night. I inhaled half deep and exhaled twice as much and set the mirror down and looked around my six-by-eight-by-nine home, and began shining myself up for the board.

I ate breakfast calmly, like the rest of the cons, trying not to show that this was a special day. But everyone knew it was, and I heard casual expressions of good luck—"Hope you make it, champ," "*Buena suerte, panín,* Good board, buddy." Then suddenly I was sitting on a straight-backed chair in the main cell-hall block. There were five rows of cons in chairs, ten abreast, and when one con went into the board office, everyone moved up a chair and the stiffness was eased by the noise of gray coarse pants bottoms scrunching and swooshing on the wooden chairs.

The number on my slip of white paper was 42. That meant forty-one guys before me, forty-one million years of sweating it out, of setting a slipping face into a semblance of coolness. I counted the gray faces, the blank looks, and the occasional smiles of the guys who returned from the office and I hoped that the Wise Men on the board had had a good night's sleep and no family squabbles and that they would be feeling good.

At last my number was called. I hurried in casual slow motion down the long hall and through an open green-barred door and into a hall space where the four guys ahead of me were seated on chairs. A hack frisked me. *Jesus,* I thought, *I don't even have long fingernails, let alone a shank.* Caramba, *I wanna be friends with that parole board.*

I took my seat next to the other guys. The only sounds in that little space were those of beating hearts, built-up hopes, and clinking eyelashes. I watched the guys before me as, one by one, they went in and came out of the board's office. The first guy came out smiling bitterly; he whispered, "I think I got a hit, maybe a year, fuck it." The rest of us smiled at each other, thinking that the law of averages made better our chances of not getting hit. Another guy came out crying, and I swore that even if they gave me the whole bundle of time, the whole fifteen-year max, I wasn't gonna crack. *Like in I went, like out I'll come.*

"Numba 42."

"Here," I yelled softly. I got up and thought, *I hope my damn knees don't break down on me,* and all of a sudden I was calm, cooled, and quietly tensed. I walked into the room. The principal keeper was there. *Trusty blackjack and all, probably,* I thought. *Well, gents, you'll get no trouble out of me. I don't have to be jacked up. Just look at my face and see the rehabilitation written there.*

"Sit down, Thomas."

I sat, but I only borrowed a very little bit of the chair, just the thin edge. I didn't know quite what to do with my hands, whether to put them behind me, in front of me, up to my face, or under my rump. Finally, I crossed my fingers and started looking for friendly faces on the business-suit-clad men whose hands were occupied with shifting and reshifting white papers with black letters—my records. I wondered if they had there anything good I ever did. The noise of the shuffling papers grew dim, and I saw a long time back . . .

. . . *Hey, Moms, I gotta job, a real job, Moms, in a drugstore after school, and I make $2.50 a week and here's some money and I can give you a lotta money every week to help out and maybe with me working along with you and Pops, why, no limit to what we can do, uh, Moms?*

A voice broke through my thoughts. "Well, Thomas," it said, "you don't think you're going home this time, do you?"

Jesus, I thought, *I worked a long time at the drugstore and I helped Moms and Pops out and I only quit because Moms said I was too skinny to keep it up and I was goofing on my school marks, but that's one of the good things I done . . .*

". . . And we'll consider you for possible parole next time we see you. Your case is very serious."

Oh my God, they ain't gonna let me go! Just like that. Al-

most four years in here, and in four seconds they tell me "maybe next time." I felt a tap on my shoulder from the big finger of the principal keeper and, surprisingly, I stood tall and clearly said, "Thank you very much, sirs." There was no bitterness in my voice, just a matter-of-fact, polite "Thank you," like I was all full of junk or something, numb and high.

That night, after we had been locked in and the trusty hot-water boys had made their rounds and the sandwiches had been passed around, and as talk and music from guitars, saxes, trumpets, and bongos whistled through the bars, I strummed on my guitar, trying not to wonder what was keeping the hack from bringing me the slip from the parole board telling me how much I had been hit for. At last the hack came by, laid neatly on the bars a white piece of paper, folded smoothly and stapled, and mumbled something about good luck. I smiled and kept strumming the guitar, leaving the white piece of indecision laying there. When the hack left, I put the guitar down and reached for the message from García. I very slowly pulled the staple from it and carefully opened the paper. On it was typed very neatly:

HELD FOR RECONSIDERATION

SEPT. 1956

My God! I thought, *I'm here for two more stinking years. I can't make it; dammit, I won't make it. Oh shit!*

"What's happening?" Young Turk whispered from the cell next to mine.

"Nothing, man, nothing except a deuce, two years. I'll do that on my head." I wanted to break out screaming; instead I thought, *Well, look, man, you already got a two-year bit; next time you see the board, you're sure to make it. After all, man, the law of aver . . .* "Oh, shit, shit, shit," I said, "I bet if there had been one *moyeto* or one spic on that board I'd'a made it. Do only *blancos* work on parole boards?"

In the morning, the bugle signaled the beginning of my brand-new two-year bit. I groped my way out of a hide-away sleep and found myself strangely calm and cool. I went through the ritual of washing, dressing, and making up the bed and sweeping the floor, and waited at the cold barred exit for the hack to open the new day for me with his big brass key. Standing on the cell-block tier, I made brave faces and answered the questions of "How'd you make out?" with a casual "Smooth deuce, but it beats a three-year hit."

But at breakfast it suddenly came to me, like a mad, mad feeling, like brass jazz, wild-tempoed and harsh; it blew itself up through my chest from my belly and crashed past my Adam's apple and left angry little *lágrimas* stuck in the corners of my eyes. Outside I became blank and hard and silent; inside I was like a hand grenade waiting for someone to pull the pin.

I walked back through the long hall to my shop. "How are things?" I heard behind me. My head snapped angrily and my tongue formed hating words, but I bit the brakes onto my anger. It was the prison chaplain. We had had several close talks over the years. He was the only preacher I had talked to who didn't make God stick in my throat. Tall and thin, he was white-haired and slightly stooped, as though the years had gotten the edge on him. The first time I met him, I was struck by his gentleness, then by his wisdom, his knack of getting across to you without pushing himself down your throat. But more than anything else, his face bothered me; it penetrated my hate, my damning hate and suspicion. It was like a face of God—and God to me meant something too good to be among men, especially my kind. Now this quiet, humble man stopped me in the corridor. My blank face gave him the general picture. He nodded me to one side and put his hand on my shoulder. I didn't shove it off, but my skin rejected the touch of his hand. I would have done the same if he had been God Almighty. We stood there, gospel man and con man, and looked across alien feelings, and then he said, "How long?"

"Two years," I breathed.

"Angry, huh?"

"Like a mother-jumping bomb," I answered.

"Less said, the better," he replied. "Now's the time, if you got heart, it'll show through."

I smiled. He had reached me, my warm soft spot, my coat of arms, my house of rep. I looked at him gently. "You're right, chaplain," I said, "I'll cool it."

"You'll make it, fella, I know you will," he said, "here and outside."

God! I thought, *how can . . . ?* "Thanks, chaplain," I said, and I walked on to the shop determined to make it, and maybe even without the hate. "Say, man," one of the cons said to me, "have you heard? They're gonna build a school for the cons, a new one, and it's gonna be where the recreation hall is, and they're gonna use the con students that paint or are learning brick masonry and so on . . ."

Brick masonry, I thought. *That's me. I'll talk to the civilian supervisor and sign on. It will give me something new to do, and besides, maybe it will help on my record when I see the parole board again.*

The decision to cool myself made the next two years the hardest I had done because it meant being a smoothie and staying out of trouble, which in prison is difficult, for any of a thousand cons might start trouble with you for any real or fancied reason, and if you didn't face up to the trouble, you ran the risk of being branded as having no heart. And heart was all I had left.

For a year and a half I managed to keep clean. Then, in the early spring, I came to my first crossroad. The day was bright and sunny, the kind of a day that makes a con want to be on the outside. I was engaged in the daily serious business of killing time, playing handball in the yard. Ususally this was a loose time, but that day the yard seemed like it was strung up with high-tension wires, and over those wires vibrated an undercurrent of murmuring. Riot was in the air. I played handball like I'd never played before. Everyone did what he was doing like he'd never done it before. And at the same time we all wondered what our role would be when hell broke loose.

The bugle blew, indicating that it was time for us to line up and march back to our cell blocks. But as the lines started to form, the cons' usual loud yak was not as intense; eyes looked at eyes and faces reflected reflections, and the cons hung back from their assigned places. The hacks quickly got the drift of what was happening. "Hurry up, you men, get in line," they shouted. "Come on, line up." Everywhere in the yard, the same thing was happening. Not all the cons were gonna be part of the riot physically, but all of them were going to be part of it spiritually. In the west end of the yard, cons began to leave their lines and mull together, without a word to their respective hacks. More cons left their lines and walked toward the west side of the yard. The hacks looked at each other; one or two hurried to the telephone. No attempt was made to restrain the cons from leaving their lines, and almost as one, they seemed to feel freer, like they were their own men.

I stood there watching and weighing, trying to decide whether or not I was a con first and an outsider second. I had been doing time inside yet living every mental minute I could outside; now I had to choose one or the other. I stood there in the middle of the yard. Cons passed by me, some going west to join the boppers, others going east to neutral ground. The call of rep tore within me, while the feeling of being a punk washed over me like a yellow banner. I had to make a decision. *I am a con. These damn cons are my people . . . What do you mean, your people? Your people are outside the cells, home, in the streets. No! That ain't so . . . Look at them go toward the west wall. Why in hell am I taking so long in making up my mind? Man, there goes Papo and Zu-Zu, and Mick the Boxer; even Ruben is there.*

The deadly quiet unrest had now grown to a loud roar, as the west wall began to breathe, taking on the life of hundreds of cons, young and old. The mass of men was becoming a unified monster. The blue-jacketed hacks scurried back and forth, directed by white-shirted officers, into position for a defensive stand or an offensive push. They no longer talked to the cons. I still stood in the middle of the yard. Over the loudspeaker, a hack announced, "Any of you men who want to quietly line up, can do so, and you'll be escorted to your cell blocks." Nonparticipating cons lined up two by two and walked toward the cell-hall blocks. Some of my boys came up to me. "Piri," said one, "if you go down, we'll go down."

Damn, I thought, and my face expressed it, *don't make me choose for you. I can't even choose for myself.* I pondered my predicament. I had been in jail five and a half years. In less than six months I would go before the board again. I owed them nine more years, which they'd probably make me do if I joined up with the boppers. That meant I'd be more than thirty-five years old when I got out. *Caramba!*

The sound of the west wall cons got more angry as they tore down the hacks' wooden stands and splintered them into clubs. It hit me inside. *Never punk out* was the code I had lived by; fear came second, rep came first. Hell, when something went down, I had been there; and if I had to hurt, I had hurt, too. So what was keeping me back? Was I afraid? Hell, no. Did I want to see the board and go home? Hell, yes! But was I a punk to want this? I didn't know.

"Whatta ya say, Piri?"

All I had to do to save nine years was to get on a line. I stood in the middle of the yard.

"Piri, what about it?"

Stop pulling at me!

"Make a choice, Piri, make a choice."

Oh, dammit, I've got to go, I thought, and I started to walk toward the west wall.

"Hold it," a hack said. They were now all over the place. I looked at them, the guys looked at them, we looked at each other. Our decision was being made for us, and we could save face. I let myself be molded into a line, my eyes and heart at the west wall but my mind out in the wild, wide street.

The angry shouts from the cons gathered strength and volume. "We want better food!" they shouted, loud enough to hide the fear of what they knew was a hopeless fight. It was the age-old prison gripe. I couldn't dig that. The food wasn't like the Ritz, but then, I never ate at the Ritz. No, I knew, and I guess every con that had a head knew, it wasn't food they were fighting about. They, we, all of us, in one way or another, were rebelling against time, against the locked-up feeling of being a part of a building instead of a part of life. The food was just the fuse. And every con knew what the outcome of the riot would be, but the two hundred or so rioters pushed that thought away. "We want to see the governor!" they chanted. I saw a few old-timers among the rioters, but the rest were mostly gray-eyed, healthy kids looking for a rep or a blast-out from boredom.

Oh, man, I thought, *hell is sure gonna break loose.* My last view of the riot at close range was of the cons huddled at the west wall, tense and ready-looking, and of the hacks at the east wall looking the same. Between them was the big empty prison yard. We were marched inside and locked in our cells. From outside came the roar of human voices, screaming defiance, curses, and threats. One of the hacks passed by my cell and I took a chance and asked him, "Say, what's happening out there now?"

"Can't you guys imagine?" he said.

"Yeah, we can," I muttered. And by God, I could. I could imagine the warden and the governor's aide asking the huddled cons what their complaints were, saying that everything could be worked out, if there was a legitimate beef; and I could hear the cons reply: "Go fuck yourself, you motherfucker." Then the warden would deliver an ultimatum: "Get back to your cells and we'll get to the bottom of this trouble. Go now and there'll be no retaliations." And the cons would shout: "Aw, go screw yourself, screws. Yeah—ra—ra."

Chino, Dulcien's cousin, also was at Comstock. On the

barred window in front of our cell block, I saw his reflection passing by on the tier below. "Chino, Chino," I called, "tell me, baby, what's happening out there?"

"Piri, is that you, man? I thought you were out there."

"Yeah," I answered, "I thought *you* was out there. How's it going? Them screams and yells are getting bad."

"Oh, man, Piri, it's hell out there. It's cold as hell out there, and the hacks poured cold water on the guys. So they rushed the hacks and it was murder. They had state troopers and all kinds of people out there. But they have heart, Piri, the fuckin' kids got heart. They're rushing them hacks with most nutthin' but their hands, and all they're getting for their guts are split heads and blood clots."

"Move along you," a hack called.

"Piri, cool it, I gotta make it."

"Yeah, glad you're okay, Chino."

"Yeah, baby, same to you."

The battle spread to the cell block itself, as the locked-in cons shouted their angry sympathy for a lost cause. They knew the rebels didn't have a real beef, but cons are cons and time is thicker than blood. In the reflection of the mirror, I saw a young-blood guy snatch the keys away from an old hack, push him down, and run along the cell blocks opening cell doors, one after another, shouting, "Come on, come on, come on, come on!" Some came, but many, weighing the odds, decided against the sucker bit and lay down and made believe they were dead.

The roar in the cell block was deafening. Curses and cries of "I'm a punk, I should have stayed out there" were being thrown all over the place. The fever of the riot had caught on. Fortunately for the prison authorities, the majority of the cons had been restored to their cells, but they did what they could. They drenched wads of paper in lighter fluid and tossed them out of the cells; they dropped carefully aimed bottles full of water on the hacks on the main floor, screaming their hatred at their targets. The place was like a burning hell, a bedlam, a damn nuthouse. *Why don't they shut up?* I thought, and found that I myself was screaming just as loud, that I, too, was throwing out bottles, cans, anything; every con was one.

Hacks were running all over the place. Whenever they saw something thrown out of a cell, they slapped a "Keep locked" sign on the cell. No doubt the occupants of these cells would receive special considerations later on. The cons, to avoid reprisal, stuck mirrors out of the cells to see if the hacks were there or not before flinging out their hatred. If the hacks saw the flash of a mirror, they made another "care notation." Some hacks confronted the offending cons, words were exchanged and the sound of a cell door being opened by the hacks and the accompanying sounds of pain told the rest of the story.

Suddenly the whole cell block was quiet. Just like that, like if somebody had died, there was a moment of silence. Then a voice broke out from somewhere in that great echo chamber. "Hell," it said, "its all over, our fellers lost, they're bringing them in." Straining bodies pushed against the bars on all the cells; everyone felt a touch of shame at not having shared in the pain of our gray brothers. The hacks formed a double row and the wet, cold, beaten kid-cons walked between them. Some just barely could walk. Damned if it didn't remind me of the moving pictures where the Indians stood in a long row and let the white captive run through. Only the colors were reversed.

The cons walked into the main cell block, where I couldn't see them. But the word was relayed from cell to cell: "There's guys lying all over the floor, bleeding and busted up." I sneaked out my mirror for a look and became so absorbed that I didn't see a hack walk up on me.

"Don't you know any better, feller?" he asked. It was Casey, the good-o hack. I said nothing. I waited to be marked "Keep Locked" and, later, probably messed up.

"Don't goof like that again, feller," he said.

I nodded and he looked at me, and damned if there wasn't distaste for what was going on written all over his face.

At four a.m. the hacks were still going into the cells. The

taste of tear gas was all over the place, although the rioters were all locked up, and the sound of flesh being pounded into bruises pulsated through the cold morning air. "Let them alone, you lousy bunch of bastard hacks," someone shouted.

"Who said that?"

"I did, you motherfucker. They've had it; let up off them."

The sound of a gate being thrown open and three or four pairs of hack-filled shoes rushing into a cell was followed by the grunts and groans of uneven combat. I screamed, "You *maricones,* you punk faggots. It's easy, eh? No danger, no fuckin' hurt to you—makes you all feel big and tough. Who the fuck is civilized? We're supposed to be the animals, not you."

"Let 'em alone, let 'em alone," began a chant. From time to time a *corazón*-felt cry of "Mommie" came from one of the kid-cons. Then the scene got quiet and I lay down and thought about the kids getting their teeth knocked out. Suddenly my bed was lifted up and dropped by a blue-shirted arm that reached into my cell. "Hey, get up off that bed," a hack said.

I got up, feigned sleep and stood there wearily. It was a shakedown. The hacks motioned me to stand in the corridor, then they searched in the cell, the bed, and the toilet bowl for what I had hidden in my mind. One of them turned an eye on me, and I lowered my eyes because if he had seen the *odio* there, he would have had to hit me and I was afraid I would have to hit him back, and then he would have had to kill me. So I stood quietly and looked at my bare feet and thought about outside. After they had wrecked my home they ordered me back inside it and crashed the bar-door shut on me. The hack started to turn away and caught me looking at him.

"Anything the matter?" he challenged me.

I turned my back on him and looked at the shit bowl, wishing I could puke all over the damn world.

"I asked you, feller," he repeated nastily, "anything the matter, got any beefs?" His hand was tight on his stick and I knew that he would use an answer or silence as an excuse to bash me.

I shrugged my shoulders and said, "No, nothing's the matter except I'd like to go home." I forced myself to smile, but it came out a "You can go to hell" smile.

The hack read this and moved toward the door, but Casey, the good-o hack, said to him, "Come on, give me a hand," drawing him away.

I wanted to curse. I stood there for a long time, hot tears running down heat-flushed cheeks, hating all the way from my childhood to my old age. To hate—you gotta keep living.

The next day the lid was down. There was no mail out, no mail in, no visitors, no recreation, no food in the mess hall. We got one meal in our cells, served by trusted trusties who were watched by trusted hacks. After a day or so of this, we were allowed to come into the mess hall, three or four tiers at a time, with a convoy of hacks. Talking was forbidden, but stories of reprisals spread around anyway—stories of broken arms and bruised kidneys and cons carrying their mattresses being blackjacked from behind and falling on their mattresses. Hacks and cons acted as dead strangers. Some of the hacks looked real hard and mean; others looked like they wished they were some other place. In my cell, I lay back on my bed and went over all that had happened in the last three days. All I could think of was how the riot would affect the decisions of the parole board when I saw them again. *Jesus, I wish it had been a legit beef these guys jumped stink about,* I thought, and in the back of my mind I kept thinking that it was.

The prison held on to its tight air of tension for a long time after the riot. Cons and hacks remained on cold speaking terms. We did only what we had to, everything else was a blank.

31. GOD, AIN'T YOU FOR EVERYBODY?

The months rolled by. Work on the new school was in high swing. I was working putting up partitions of cement blocks, while working for a certificate in brick masonry. I had already got my high school diploma and three or four certificates on some free courses on anything that ate up time. I also had three diplomas from some Bible courses mail-order style. More and more I had been digging into philosophy and different religions.

One night I was sprawled out on my bed in my cell hearing something that I had been hearing for a long time every night. But tonight I just listened to it harder:

Allahu Akbar, Allahu Akbar,
Allahu Akbar, Allahu Akbar,
Allahu Akbar, Allahu Akbar,
Allahu Akbar, Allahu Akbar.

I heard the chanting coming from the cell somewhere below. I knew it was Chaplin, who would rather be called Muhammad. I had heard him often enough telling cons who had addressed him as Chaplin not to call him by his given Christian name, since he was a Muslim. I knew from what I had been reading that the religion Muhammad was following was the religion of Islam and was what the Arabs believed in. I knew there were a lot of colored people in Harlem who believed in this Arab religion, but I wondered if the cats in this jailhouse were really serious about this religion, or was it just a prison fad to help while away long years.

I got a chance to find out what was shaking one Sunday afternoon out in the prison yard. I saw Muhammad sitting Indian-style with four or five guys in a circle. He was reading to them out of a book. I walked over to them and sat just close enough to be noticed. Muhammad looked up and smiled a Christ-like smile and said, "Like to sit in, friend?" I couldn't help thinking that his English was as smooth as Mr. Prissy's. I nodded a "Yeah" and the circle opened enough for me to become a part of it.

"We are reading from the Holy Quran. As you may know, we are followers of the religion of Islam." I nodded understanding and he went on to introduce those in the circle. "This is Ben Jussaf, and this is Hussein," and his finger pointed out the owners of these funny-sounding names, "and this is Jamal, Nassum, Ali—and I am Muhammad." He went on, perhaps because the look on my face was saying how come you guys give up such easy-saying names like Jones and Smith for such hard-sounding ones. "These are the believers' names we have chosen for ourselves or were given to us when we embraced the religion of Islam. The names on our birth certificates, if we had one, are what the white devil has fostered upon us. Many of us simply have an X for a last name."

"Are you the pastor?" I asked. There was a little bit of smiling in his voice as he replied, "No, we don't have pastors or reverends. We have what are called imams—er—teachers, and that's what I am. What is your name?"

"Piri."

"Piri what?"

"Piri, number 18193." I smiled.

Muhammad's gentle-like face ignored my punch line and went on: "Are you interested in the religion of Islam?"

"I'm interested in anything that will get the cockroaches of confusion outta my head. I've heard you praying in another language a lot of times. It sounded like Alla-hu Actbarr or something—"

"It was the opening words of the Adhan, or the call to prayer. 'Allahu Akbar—Allahu Akbar, Allah is the Greatest.' "

I nodded to the book in his hands. "Is that your Bible?"

"What the Bible is to the Christian, the Holy Quran is to the followers of Islam, only more so," he answered.

"I've heard of Moslems before," I said, feeling uncomfortable for not having read more and for having to feel half-blank like now.

"We are not Moslems. Moslem is the way the Western world pronounces it. We are Muslims."

Again my head went up and down in understanding. Another Negro walked up to the group. I heard him say what sounded like "Asalam-aleecum." The others in the circle replied, "Waa-lee-kum-salam." "Our brother Albert X has just greeted us. 'As-salamu alaikum' means 'Peace be on you,' and 'Wa-alai-kum-salam' means 'And on you be peace.' "

I thought of the Jews in Harlem and how close this sounded to the 'Sholom' I'd heard them greet each other with once in a while. I lit a cigarette and felt a staring of eyes. I excused myself for not sharing my pack around. They all shook their heads in polite refusals—and Muhammad the imam explained, "A true Muslim does not smoke, drink intoxicating beverages, nor eat pork, among other things."

"Sounds like my momma's religion."

"Oh, is she a true believer?"

"She was a Seventh-Day Adventist. She's dead now."

"Oh, that's not quite like being a Muslim, although Christianity has many things in common with the true religion of Islam."

I thought inside my head that so far it was a clean-living

religion. I'd seen these Muslim cons around a lot and I had never heard them curse or seen them eat pork when it was given out in the mess hall. I never once saw them take off on pills or dug them high from prison home-brew. "So where's the difference?" I asked.

"Christianity is the white devil's religion. God or Jehovah is the white man's God and he's used his Christianity as a main weapon against the dark-skinned inhabitants of this world. What his blood-letting or slaughter did not destroy, his Christianity ably conquered. Even though Abraham is called the father of the faith, there's where it ends as far as we Black Muslims are concerned."

I opened my mouth to say something, but Muhammad gently cut me off. "You and I will speak further some other time. If you will bear with us, I will teach from the Quran to my brothers."

I sat there and listened as Muhammad read first in Arabic and then in English. I later found out he was also teaching the followers how to read, write, and speak Arabic. I got to know Muhammad pretty well in the next few years. He was a light-skinned Negro, slightly built with built-in deep thoughts.

A few days later, I ran into Muhammad in the recreation hall. He was sitting at a table poring over a book. I greeted him, "As-salamu alaikum." "Wa'alai-kumu-s-salam," he answered without looking up, and then looking up and seeing me, he said softly, "Only believers greet each other this way; any other way it's like blasphemy." I mumbled an "Excuse me" and added, "I'd like to know more."

"About what?" he motioned for me to sit down.

"I've been thinking if maybe the reason for this jumping of Negroes to become Muslims is on account of maybe Allah is a black man's god."

"One doesn't have to be a Negro to be a Muslim. There are many Caucasians that are Muslims."

"Where?"

"In the Far East, where our religion was born."

"I've never heard of any in Harlem," I said.

"If there are," answered Muhammad, "they are rare. The white devil in this country had his chance to be our brother. His chance is lost. His rule is at an end. His time is running out. His rule is almost buried under six feet of dirt decorated with his famous cross. We, the Black Muslims, are coming into our own."

"Lotta black humans are Christians," I pushed.

"That's the worst mistake the black man made, in allowing his brain to be Christianized." Muhammad's face was getting tight. I nodded, thinking about my hang-ups with Muhammad's white devils. Muhammad closed his book and went on. "When the black man ate the poison of Christianity, he finally was where the white man wanted him. First he took away the black man's freedom, then his dignity and pride, then his identity. In return, he gave him a secondhand sense of values—a concept of nonexisting dignity by putting him in a certain place, like low man in anything, then taught him all about Christianity and how, as a Christian, he could bravely stand the pain of his slavery, all the time softly purring into his eyes, 'No matter how much you lose here on earth, Jesus loves you and you'll get it all back in heaven.' " Muhammad somehow reminded me of Brew and me. I listened: "The white devil has kept chanting 'All men are brothers,' while all the time he meant 'if they're white.' "

Muhammad's face had totally lost all of its gentleness. He was still speaking low, but the voice was tense, angry, and curling with the hate that millions of white devils had helped so well to cultivate.

"Christianity—white man's style isn't for the black man. Christianity is only first-class salvation for the white devil, the salvation of overabundance of good living wrung out from stripped backs and millions and millions of knees bended in the prayer of black slavery." Muhammad shook his head in disgust, and mine became a companion also. "Christianity—Christianity," Muhammad spoke the name like a curse, "it's the power of good living reality for them and the reality of pain, hunger, despair, and degradation for us black men. The white devil has claimed to have given the black man all that he has. He's right. And it's all been bad. He's exploited every source the black man could provide—his strength, his labor, his dignity, his woman, his spirit—and has done all he could to exploit even his soul."

Muhammad asked me softly, "You said you've seen Muslims in Harlem?"

"A-huh," I nodded a yes. "A lot of them wear something called a fez on their heads, others wear hats made outta Persian wool, and most of them wear a mustache and a beard, but not all. Their women don't paint themselves."

"Yes, but what else did you notice about our Black Muslims?"

"Uh, they don't smoke, drink liquor, or curse, and they dress well, like neatly pressed all the time."

"Yes, but what else?" Muhammad pushed. Before I could think of something else, Muhammad himself answered, "They all walk with dignity and quiet pride. We are a united people, and only Allah, through his beloved prophet Elijah Muhammad, could have brought this about. We are educating ourselves, not as the white devil would have it, but in a superior way. We have learned that our heritage is a great one. We are of a mighty race of people. We are superior in whatever we undertake, be it science, art, music, sports—name it, and we excel. The white devil's time of keeping us living in a lie is over. He's afraid now, because he knows his time is up now. He knows it isn't a white world alone any longer. He'd like a chance for us to get along like brothers. Well! the white man is not our brother. He doesn't know how to be one. All he knows is how to be a slave master, and now that he sees the black man coming into his own, he's afraid. And with good reason, for what cruel slave master would look forward to the day that he would be slave to his former slave. His conscience itself frightens him at the thought that he may be treated as he himself once treated. Yes, he'd like for us to be brothers now.

"Our leader is right when he said, 'White man, for two thousand years you've been on top of us like this.' " Muhammad placed one open palm on top of another, and went on: "And now that he sees his day coming, he wants it like this." Muhammad turned the two palms together like in an attitude of prayer, and went on: "He wants us to be even-Stephen, he says—to walk side by side in sameness . . . like brothers. But he's not our brother. We weren't brothers from way back then and we're not gonna be brothers from here on out. He's a white devil that's afraid. He knows the hell he's put us through—and no matter what he does to try to expiate his guilt—it's no good. It's going to be like this" . . . Muhammad turned his palms still together back on their side, only this time the hand representing the black man was on top. Muhammad's voice was now almost gentle again as he went on: "White man—for two thousand years you've been on us—and now we're going to be on you. We want a piece of this world and we're going to get it, even if we have to take it all away from you."

He didn't say another word. I didn't say one either.

The bugle blew and we each made it to our lines for the trip back to our cells.

Muhammad and I became friends, and after a time we became brothers. But first he gave me books to read on the religion of Islam and one of them was the *Hadith*, or Muslim prayerbook.

"Read the prayerbook first," he said, "and learn the one called The Adhan. As I told you it is the call to prayer."

I nodded and began to peel through the pages.

"But before you say them, learn the Wudzu, or Ablution, on page eight."

I looked at the page and it was in English, but the Adhan, even though in English, the words were hard to pronounce, and I told Muhammad so.

"Don't worry," he said, "just learn the Wudzu and we will hold classes for all the rest."

That night in my cell, I tried to memorize the Wudzu. It went like this:

> Before saying prayers it is necessary to wash those parts of the body which are generally exposed. This is called *wudzu*, or ablution. The ablution is performed thus:
>
> 1. The hands are cleansed, washing them up to the wrists.
> 2. Then the mouth is cleansed by means of a toothbrush or simply with water.
> 3. Then the nose is cleansed within the nostrils with water.
> 4. Then the face is washed.
> 5. Then the right arm, and after that the left arm, is washed up to the elbow.
> 6. The head is then wiped over with wet hands, the three fingers between the little finger and the thumb of both hands being joined together.
> 7. The feet are then washed up to the ankles, first the right foot and then the left.
>
> But if there are socks on, and they have been put on after performing an ablution, it is not necessary to take them off; the wet hands may be passed over them. They should be taken off, however, and the feet washed once in every twenty-four hours. The same practice may be resorted to in case the boots are on, but it would be more decent to take off the boots when going into a mosque.
>
> A fresh ablution is necessary only when a man has answered a call of nature or has been asleep.
>
> In case of intercourse between husband and wife, *ghusl* or washing of the whole body is necessary.
>
> When a person is sick, or when access cannot be had to water, what is called *tayammum* is performed in place of *wudzu* or *ghusl*. *Tayammum* is performed by touching pure earth with both hands and then wiping over with them the face and the backs of the hands.

I got up from my bed and tried out the ablution, and then after a few trys at it, I decided to write out the Adhan. The following words are spoken as one faces toward the East (Mecca):

Allahu Akbar, Allahu Akbar,
Allahu Akbar, Allahu Akbar.
"Allah is the Greatest" (*repeated four times*).
Ashhadu an la ilaha illa-llah,
Ashhadu an la ilaha illa-llah
"I bear witness that nothing deserves to be worshiped except Allah" (*repeated twice*).
Ashhadu anna Muhammadan Rasulu-llah, Ashhadu anna Muhammadan Rasulu-llah.
"I bear witness that Muhammad is the Messenger of Allah" (*repeated twice*).
Hayya ala-s-sala,
Hayya ala-s-sala.
"Come to prayer" (*repeated twice, turning the face to the right*).
Hayya ala-l-falah,
Hayya ala-l-falah.
"Come to success" (*repeated twice, turning the face to the left*).
Allahu Akbar,
Allahu Akbar.
"Allah is the Greatest" (*repeated twice*).
La illaha illa-lah.
"Nothing deserves to be worshiped except Allah."

There was more, but for now this was enough. In the weeks that followed, sitting in the small circle with Muhammad as the imam, I learned the pronunciation and the ceremonies that went with prayers. Then one day I was invited to join the brothers as a follower of the true religion of Islam. I accepted, and after a short ceremony I took the hand of brotherhood and was given the name of Hussein Afmit Ben Hassen. I learned to pray in Arabic. I learned the respect for the Holy Quran by never holding it with my left hand, which was only to cleanse myself after making ca-ca.

I learned many things, because it involved me. I became

curious about everything human. Though I didn't remain a Muslim after my eventual release from the big jail, I never forgot one thing that Muhammad said, for I believed it too: "No matter a man's color or race, he has a need of dignity and he'll go anywhere, become anything, or do anything to get it—anything..."

32. GREAT, MAN, GREAT; I'M THINKING LIKE A STONE PHILOSOPHER

Learning made me painfully aware of life and me. I began to dig what was inside of me. What had I been? How had I become that way? What could I be? How could I make it? I got hold of some books on psychology. Man, did we scuffle. I copped a dictionary to look up the words I didn't know, and then I had to look up the words explaining the original words. But if I had to bop against the big words, I decided—well, I had heart.

The first word I looked up was "psychology." I learned it was pronounced with a silent "p," and I smiled, because I always had pronounced the "p" in pneumonia. I read the definition:

> branch of philosophy which examines and treats of the growth, function and process, conscious or subconscious, of the mind in relation to the sensations, feelings, emotions, memories, will

and conduct, whether examined introspectively [gotta look up this word, too] or from the behavior of others under specified conditions.

It's not gonna be an easy thing to dig me, I thought. *This psychology means that people's worst troubles are in their minds. That's cool. This jailhouse is just jumping with nuts and slip-times.*

For the first time I was aware that I didn't know myself, outside of the fact that I ate when hungry, slept when sleepy, and got laid when horny. I wanted something better for my stick of living. *Maybe God is psychology, or psychology is God.*

My aunt's pastor had advised me to put myself into the hands of God, that He would make a new cat out of me. *Hell,* I thought, *New York State is working on that kick right now. God, I don't want to hurt your feelings, but, Man, I can't see You. I wanna believe You're there. In fact, Man, I believe there's something to You, but what, how, where? All around? Inside me or outside me? Here on the world or up there in heaven? Do You live in a pad with clouds for sofas and beds, or do You look like me? Really, God, run it to me. Are we really all in Your image? I mean, so many different kinds of us, all colors, all shapes? Hey, Baby, that's it. You look like us, all right, but only in the—what's the word?—in the "psyche" —the breath, life, soul, spirit. Great, Man, great. I'm thinking like a stone philosopher.*

Sure, that had to be it. God looks like all of us. Some souls are worse than others, but they all look the same; they gotta, 'cause nobody's seen them, so nobody can say differently. The soul and spirit is blood with blue eyes, dark skin, and curly hair. We're all the same when it comes to our souls and spirits. *Around the world, hear this, North and South, East and West: We are all the same in our souls and spirits and there's nobody better than anybody else, only just maybe better off.*

I was thirsty for anything that had to do with understanding. And, like a kid turned loose in a candy store, I ate of every kind of candy, till I found that they all tasted the same and I had better be more choosy in what I accepted or rejected. Accepting too much without question was just as bad as not accepting anything; a con could easily flip his wig if he weren't careful. Little, the guy I had fought with, diligently studied the Psalms. The Psalms, he told me, contained the keys to great riches, "money, gold, coins, bread, loot," and he was going to break the code. He copped candles and, late at night when the cell block was quiet, tried to decode the Psalms. He ended up in Dannemora, where the split wigs are sent.

Nobody can withstand fully the pressure of a life that's forced upon him and makes his pulse seem to belong to somebody else. Three times I almost flipped, and every time I had to fight desperately to keep my sanity. My first scare came after I had been in about three years. The pressure on me was great, for I had been living out in the street mentally.

We had been let out of our cells and I was walking down the long tier toward the steps leading down to the main cell-hall block to line up for chow when it came on me, like a flushed cold wave, a sort of pulling away from myself. I felt a great desire to pop off, to start with a hell of a giggle and jump on to a mad laugh. I wanted to laugh and laugh; I wanted to jump up and down. My face uselessly jumped and twitched. My God! I grabbed my face with both hands and leaned hard against the white-painted steel of the outside cell walls. Young Turk and another con got to my side and asked, "Piri, what's the matter?"

I looked at them through the spread fingers on my face. I felt my eyes bulging and I fought off the crazy scream that was forming in my chest. *Oh, Christ,* I thought, *get this off me. If I let go now, I ain't never coming back. Pu-leeze, God, pu-leeze, I'll die if* I go loco.

"Easy, buddy, easy, man. Damn, you look funny. Something you gritted, eh?" Young Turk said.

I looked at him from far away. He looked as faint as his voice sounded. *Shit, man, can't you see? I'm flipping, I'm blowing my top. Can't you dig them tears running, like drown-*

ing me, inside? I wanted to burst out laughing, to scream, *Oh, Mommie, Moms, Momma, come back to life and get me out of here! Sweet* Cristo, *keep this thing down.* If I could have let one little bit of the scream out, if I could have afforded one little laugh, just one tiny giggle, I would have. But I knew it wouldn't happen like that; it would burst out and pour through, and that would be game time. *Moms, what's that prayer? What's that prayer?*

> Now I lay me down to sleep,
> I pray the Lord my soul to keep;
> If I should die before I wake
> I pray the Lord my soul to take.
> Amen, amen, am . . .

It's going, oh, God, it's passing over. I can feel hard lungs melting. Thank you, Mommie, gracias, *God . . .*

"Hey, you all right?" Young Turk's voice was now perfectly normal.

"Yeah, man, sure, just got a little dizzy."

"Man, you looked goofed."

I smiled and walked down the long steel staircase. I thought on how I call on Christ instead of Allah. *Guess I've been a Christian too long.* I felt the sweat running down my face, trickling down my spine and between my cheeks. From then on, I knew that not only other cons could flip their wigs, I could too.

As the day for my second appearance before the parole board approached, I tried to play it cool and keep out of trouble. But I had "shortitis"—the impatience which makes the last few weeks unbearably long, and one of the hacks supervising the construction of the new school was on my back. I don't know how it started, but about two weeks before my appearance he wasted me with hard words, and I blew up in his face. He tightened his fist on his stick and started for me. "I ought to beat your damn head in," he said.

The cons around me stood and watched. Young Turk tried

to cool me, but my blood had come up. And, knowing that any scuffle would finish me with the board, I felt like a man who faces a firing squad—he can say his last piece because nothing worse can happen to him. So I screamed at the hack. I told him to go ahead and waste me; I told him what a bastard he was, that I didn't give a fuck what he did, that I was fed up to the teeth of blue pants and shirt-filled hacks, of gray cons and high walls, of in at night and out in the morning, of bugles and water boys, of "keep locks" and parole boards, of time and time. I felt good, like a whole man, and I waited for the heavy stick to fall on me and ease me out of this hard bit. I waited and waited, thinking that what I hadn't done in the riot I was now pulling by myself. *Okay, Jesus, here goes my parole, here I go, wash me away. Moms, is it gonna hurt much? Here lies Piri Thomas, done in at Comstock Prison by a hack dressed in blue with a big brown stick. He tried to be a war counselor again, like he always was, and he cried heart and went out with a rep, and he didn't complain 'cause he had said his piece, and after all, the law of averages was against him from the jump—oh, yeah, and this stone-hearted bopper stood his ground like a champ and whistled while the shit flew . . . Now I lay me down to sleep, 'cause this hack my head will beat . . . Hey, how come he don't hit me?*

I felt the fog break on me. I felt light and I heard the hack's voice, like a second chance, coming through, "Aw, the hell with you, you ain't worth it."

Nobody could believe it. There I was—not dead, not even bleeding. "That's heart, baby," one of the cons said. "Man, you sure stood up to that faggot," said another. Me, I didn't care. I just felt that the balls that had been torn away from me had just been sewn back on.

After the run-in with the hack, I just knew I was gonna play it smooth. But it was just like bucking a tide. I couldn't keep my mouth shut, and I got "keep-locked" for talking on line. Then, when I was supposed to be working on the new school, I found myself sitting out in the yard with "idle company" men (cons who didn't work), and I was keep-locked for that. The prison chaplain heard about this latest bust and came up to my cell to see me. "Say, young fella," he said, "what's the thing with you? You look like you're starting an epidemic of 'keep-locks.' What's the matter?"

"*Caramba*, chaplain," I said, "I don't dig it myself. I'm so short now I can taste the street, and it's like I can't believe I'm here and the rules and regulations just aren't meant for me any more."

"Well, son, I'll see what I can do. But try to hold out a few more days."

I watched his long, thin back make it down the tier and I sat back on the bed thinking that I had to make it this time or I'd flip my wig. I was getting into all this chicken-shit trouble because I was scared I wouldn't make it and I knew if I didn't make it this time my mind wouldn't take it; I'd have to get institutionalized or flip.

A few days later I was in the barbershop getting a haircut and a colored guy named Big Cot started to sound me. I blew up and quietly told him to come outside, behind the barbershop. The hack dug what was happening, but he waited for it to happen.

I walked out smooth and innocent-like; Big Cot was behind me, but to the side. I kept my eye corner-cut at his to watch out for a sneak punch. Behind the barbershop we faced each other. His expression seemed to say, *Now, man, if you start any trouble, why, how will it look, a fight just before the board? Man, like if you just haven't learned how to behave, like if you just don't care whether you make parole or not . . .* He smiled and stood there posing, hand half closed, half up.

I wanted to smash his face up but I dug the hack looking through the window, and in my mind I saw myself standing before the Board, and the Wise Men saying, *Hell, Piri, it looks like you enjoy staying here in prison, like you haven't been rehabilitated. Since you like to fight, and since you have a two-year reconsideration only, we're gonna keep you for another two years' reconsideration only . . . Oh, no, man, no, no, no.* My voice opened up and I said, "You ain't worth it, Cot. I ain't gonna deal with you."

He shrugged his shoulders and, with his open hands, made a gesture of "You copped out—it's your rep," and turned to leave.

"Cot," I crunched out, "Cot, if the board hits me, I'm gonna break your fuckin' jaw." He stopped and turned. His lighted eyes were small and I knew he was ready to deal with me. *Cot, if you make me deal with you, I'm gonna kill you. And if I can't do it today, I'll do it tomorrow. I can't take more time; six years is as far as I can roll it.*

Cot looked at me. He was no fool; he had done a lot of time and he could sense that my want of being free was almost, if not quite, at the point of madness. He stood to gain nothing by fighting with me. He knew, as he looked into my eyes, that I wasn't punking out, that I was giving him his life. "Piri, man," he said, "you asked me out here, I didn't. I was funning and you jumped stink."

"Don't fun no more with me," I said. "The next time I fun, it's gonna be out in the free world, not here, not like no animal dressed in gray."

He nodded and walked away. The hack's face disappeared from the window, and I walked back to the construction work on the school. *You gotta cool it,* I told myself. *You're pushing too hard. If you break into a fight with someone and all that pressure inside you comes out, you're gonna end up with fifteen to thirty years tacked onto your sentence for killing a guy in prison, just like Pops Hills, who came to jail in 1927 to serve out a five-year hit and killed two or three guys with a sharpened spoon and is still here twenty-nine years later. What's a rep? If you're in jail, who wants a jailhouse rep? What's it worth? It's better to be free, outside, home, with people, rice and beans, mambo music, kids laughing. It's better to wear what you want, to be able to sit on a toilet bowl in privacy, not like a monkey in the zoo who has to crap with everybody looking at him; to really smell woman smell or take long walks in Central Park and sling peanuts at squirrels and pigeons and sit on park benches and dig the parkman sticking a shiv at the end of a long stick into helpless pieces of paper . . .* Yeah, I could take a little more shit for that, but only a little more.

In a few days I was sitting for the second time before the Wise Men. Again, I heard the rustle of papers and saw the faint white faces above the dark business suits. I heard murmuring, low voices . . . *Jesus what's it gonna be? Stop wasting time and get to the point. I mean, like I got things to do and places to make it to and you all got me sitting here wasting time. Slam, bam, people—let's get to the point. Is it so hard to say, "Okay, Piri, we're gonna let you go," or somethin' like that? God, I'm sweating inside. Don't move, Piri, don't squirm and shuffle in that chair. Don't scratch your nose or pull your ear. Don't look up at the ceiling. Don't clear your throat and don't yawn. Don't pick at your fingernails. Don't look from face to face and don't try to read your wants on their lips. You're a down stud, man. Don't breathe, if possible, just make yourself like part of the scene. Think of any old thing:*

I got time, you got time
All God's children got *mucho* time . .
Time, time. lots of time.
All God's children sho' got time.

Dammit, hurry up, blancos, *I ain't got all day. Hey, God, you listening? All your children got time. I'd like to spend mine out in my* Barrio, *you know, like home sweet home. Take this like a prayer, Man, I wanna be a free Puerto Rican . . .*

"Well, Thomas, how would you like to go home?"

What, man? Who said that? Face, oh my face, stay cara palo *till you hear it again. Let your eyes make it to the face that pushed out them words. I think it's the face with the gray hairs on top . . .*

"Well, how'd you like to go home?"

My face cracked and smiled and something dry like words came out low and quiet. "I'd like that," I said. "It's real nice, sir." But inside I was exploding: *Wooiee, people, I'm made. I'm coming home after six long years in the penitentiary . . .*

"Yes, outside of a few infractions of the rules . . ."

Yeah, a few, not counting the couple of million I never got caught on . . .

". . . you've really strived toward rehabilitation. Ah, of course, Thomas, we're going to release you to some, er, I believe it's two warrants for armed robbery in the first degree in the Bronx County and . . ."

God, I forgot about them things. Man, why'd my boy have to rat on me? But at least I'm getting out of here . . .

"So, Thomas, what do you say?"

"Thanks a lot, sir." *Man, I forgot about them warrants . . .*

"Well, good luck to you, Thomas. This board feels you'll make it in society, and . . ."

At the entrance to the big yard I met Young Turk. He searched my face, looking for anger and, finding none, he said, "How'd you make out, Piri?"

"Great," I replied. "I made the board. But I gotta go face some warrants."

"Ow, but don't let them fuckin' things bug you. Why, man, it's been six years since you pulled them deals, and there ain't no court judge gonna screw you after so long. You gotta get a break. Dig, man, you've been re-ha-bi-li-tated, like, uh, you're a changed cat, a credit to the human race."

I smiled at him and thought, *Jesus, buddy, you don't know how right you are. I ain't ever gonna be the same. I'm changed all right.*

NEW YORK TOWN

They had been mutilating my turf while I was gone, but the heart was still there. New faces and old hearts.

33. FREE SIDE IS THE BEST SIDE

On the big day, I awoke early and sat by the bars and looked out, like for the last time. I had been through processing, had been fitted in a shirt, suit and shoes (and had been photographed in them, for future reference, if necessary), and had been promised a letter from Reverend Winch to the judge in Bronx County who would decide my fate. I was happy, almost trembling, but only inside.

Breakfast was smooth, and when I left my cell for the last time and walked down the long corridor toward the tailor shop, I felt like I was leaving home. Home! Brrr, I shuddered at the thought.

A short time later I was dressed. I fumbled with my tie. I almost had forgotten how to tie a Windsor knot. I looked in the mirror. I was me, except I shaved every day now and I had lost some teeth and I was filled out like a twenty-eight-year-old man was supposed to be. In like a kid, out like a man.

"Okay, fella," the hack escorting me said, "you ready to go?"

"Yeah," I said, smiling, "le's go." I threw my hand up and down in one quick salute of good-byes and followed the hack down the long echoing hall. Then I saw a solid sight I'll never forget. There in the corners, by the steps, some with brooms in their hands, others on make-believe errands or mopping, but all waiting to say good-bye, were my people, my con buddies, my con brothers. As I walked toward the cell-hall gate that led to the outside, from either side of me and from their places in the corners and by the steps, their hands went up. My throat felt dry and my knees trembled in sudden longing for them and the familiar green bars and gray walls and blue hacks. But only for an instant. I moved through the long hall that led to the outside. At the front desk my property was returned to me —papers, books, music, and poetry I'd written; diplomas and old undelivered letters, many from Trina. I was handed some money—my accumulated savings from my 10-cents-a-day wages —and told to count it. The chaplain was there. "Well, good luck, Piri," he said, "and God bless you. You're going to make out fine."

"Thanks for everything, chaplain," I said, "you're a cool stud."

Then, for the first time, I noticed two men standing in a corner. Their look was Bronx warrants. The hack nodded to them and they came over. One frisked me and the other pulled out handcuffs. My hands went up from my elbows like it was natural, and the cold of the metal reminded me just how free I was. I shook hands with the chaplain from between cuffed hands and the *haras* helped me with my stuff. I held on to Trina's letters; nobody was gonna carry those. The last gate opened and I walked out between the *haras* and to their car about 400 yards from the prison walls. I felt like being dramatic and splitting, like they did in the movies, but my throat was dry.

I sat in the back of the car with one *hara*, and the car took off and Comstock's green bars and gray walls grew smaller. I tried for a pack of tailor-mades in my pockets. The *hara* pulled out a pack, and I took one. He lit it. I thanked him and started to read Trina's letters. They were all the same, meant the same: she wasn't there for me any longer. There were a couple of letters from her cousin. These said more: how Trina had gotten married, which I knew; that Trina had had a miscarriage; and that her second baby was born retarded. I shoved the letters into my pocket and just smoked and watched things go by, people, cars, trees, houses, mountains, roadside inns. At a diner the car pulled in. "Let's get something to eat," said the bigger of the *haras*. "Whatya say, kid, hungry?"

"No thanks," I mumbled. I was hungry, but I didn't want to go into that diner with handcuffs on.

Big *hara* looked at his partner and said, "We won't have no trouble if we take the cuffs off, will we?"

I smiled. "None at all," I said.

Off they came. We went in and sat down at a corner table. A broad gave us a menu, and big *hara* said, "You can eat anything at all, kid."

I thanked him and picked turkey, stuffing, mashed potatoes, cranberry sauce, pie, and milk. I ate good. Small *hara* bought me a couple of packs of tailor-mades and asked me if I wanted to go to the can.

"Yeah," I said.

"So, go ahead."

I got up and stood waiting for him to follow me.

He said, "Go ahead—you said no trouble, right?'

"Right," I said.

I sat and crapped for the first time in six years without having somebody pass by and dig me at my efforts. When I came out, the *haras* didn't seem to be looking at me, but I knew they were watching. Cool *haras*, but they were all right.

"Finished?"

"Yeah, finished."

"Le's go."

I reached into my pocket for my share of the bill and big *hara* said, "No, it's okay, kid. The state's still paying for you."

"Okay, I'll just leave a tip."

"Naw, that's included."

"I'd like to."

"Okay, go ahead, then."

And it felt great to leave half-a-man tip.

In the car I put out my hands, and big *hara* said, "Will it be necessary?"

"No," I said.

"Well, okay, then we won't put them on."

We talked small talk the rest of the way. The *haras* wanted to know how things had been in Comstock, how long I had pulled, and how it had been.

"Hell, man," big *hara* said at one point, "it was something rough, eh?"

"*Sí*, but it was my war, man."

We pulled into New York in the late afternoon and the *haras* first took me to the precinct of the area where the stick-up had occurred, where I was fingerprinted and allowed to telephone my aunt. Then we went downtown to the main office for full-length mug shot and more routine. Downtown I looked at all the familiar sights and went through the routine like it wasn't me. I felt good, and I even smiled for my mug shot. "Get serious," said big *hara*. I got serious. I should have known better. Getting mugged is serious stuff.

When we finished, it was about dinnertime. We went to a bar-restaurant and had some chow. After dinner I made another solo trip to the john. This *juanito* was next to a back exit; I couldn't help seeing that as I went inside. I thought how easy it would be to slip out the back way and cut out. I didn't know what I was gonna do. I thought about those two warrants. Suppose I got more time? I remembered that Bronx County had wanted Manhattan to give me and my boys a suspended sentence on attempted robbery in the first degree and turn us over to them so they could cool us for good on first-degree armed robbery. And the Bronx was handing out wild bits of time, like seventeen and a half to thirty-five years. If they had wanted us that bad, maybe even after six years they still had a yen. I didn't know what had happened to Danny and Billy. Maybe the Bronx had them doing some big time.

I stepped out of the john, which was partly hidden from the

haras, who appeared to be chewing food and the fat. I felt panicky, like I wanted to run. I started to move toward the back exit and stopped cold. *If I start running now,* I thought, *I gotta keep running.* The chaplain had promised to plead for me; my buddies had assured me I'd get a break; my aunt had said she'd prayed; and the *haras* had said I'd probably be released on my own parole, that I'd probably appear in court tomorrow morning and walk out. The odds were in my favor. *Run,* said my heart. *Don't be a jerk,* said my mind. My feet turned slowly back toward the *haras* and I walked back to the table.

"Finished, kid?" the big *hara* asked, smiling.

"A-huh."

He kept looking at me. The *haras* got up, and as we left I noticed that a big wall mirror showed the back exit clearly. I wouldn't have made it across the street. Instead I would have gotten time handed to me for attempting to escape, if I hadn't gotten wasted first. I was lost in thought as we headed toward the Bronx County Tombs, where I was to be checked in for the night—or longer. Big *hara* looked at me and said, "Kid, which section would you like to pass through?"

"Well, I thought since we're going up to the Bronx, we gotta pass through Harlem. Look, how about passing through Spanish Harlem—Lexington Avenue or Park Avenue, near 102nd, 103rd, 104th streets, all the way up to 117th Street and up till we hit the Bronx Tombs?"

"Okay, we go that way."

"Thanks a lot, you guys are okay."

"Forget it, kid, you've acted real nice."

The ride through the *Barrio* was stone-great. It was like all the bright bulbs in the stores, windows, and lampposts were screaming just for me. I heard all the noises I'd missed for so long—screaming broads, crying kids, hustlers, dogs yapping, and cats making holes in mountains of garbage. The stoops on 104th Street were full of people.

Big *hara* drove slowly to make my kick last, and I felt almost a great love for this understanding fuzz. My Harlem had a somewhat different face. Big brick housing projects were all over the place, big, alien intruders. They had been mutilating my turf while I was gone, but the heart was still there. New faces and old hearts.

"How does it look?" big *hara* asked. "Change any?"

"Yeah, a little, but my people are still here."

Harlem fell back, and in a few minutes the car stopped in front of a tall gray building, the Bronx Tombs. I was going to be buried again. I had just come to life for a short while, and now I'd have to start again in the middle of a cell, 6 by 9 by 10, or something like that. Big *hara* put the cuffs on me in the car, just in case a big wheel was present when they brought me in. He was almost embarrassed to put them on. I smiled at him in the dark and said, "I dig, man." The clack-clack of our shoes on the pavement made the same beat as my guts. We walked up the short steps and stood in front of a barred door with a small window. A hack opened the window and said, "Yeah?"

It reminded me so of a speakeasy scene in the flicks that I almost said, "Joe sent us."

"What you got?" said the hack in the window.

"Warrant, parolee from Comstock State Prison," said big *hara*.

The big door opened and we went inside. My handcuffs were removed, my stuff was checked, and I was frisked. "Take it easy, kid," said big *hara*. "We'll see you in court tomorrow, and you'll probably be home for supper."

I nodded my head in hopeful agreement. A blue-clothed hack said, "Okay, fella, this way," and he led me to my new pad. I had been free about twelve hours.

I studied my new home. It was three parts concrete, one part steel bars—yellow bars, or were they buff? I chuckled. Green, yellow, buff—they still were bars underneath. I looked up and around and I saw that I wasn't alone. There was an emaciated-looking kid, about twenty years old, sitting on the toilet. The cell had double bunks, an arrangement in which, upstate, weak cats would lose their behinds in a minute. The thin kid smiled hello. I played it *cara palo* and just motioned with my finger toward the bunks. The kid said, "One on thees top."

I dug his bad English and answered him in Spanish, "Up or down?"

"You're Spanish?" he asked in Spanish.

"Yeah, I'm a spic. Which bunk?"

"I haf thees one," he said, pointing to the bottom one. "I'm wounded," he added in Spanish. "Four bullets hit me. I shot a policeman."

I dug his chest and belly, all red and mad-looking. His stomach had a scar like mine. I felt I was looking at myself six years ago. I spread my blankets out, took my shirt off, and stretched out on the bunk. I lit a tailor-made and smoked away the bad feeling of being in a cell again. When the kid lay down, I gave him a cigarette and he told me his story. He had been thrown out of a bar after a brawl, had gone home for a piece and had come back gunning for the bartender. Some guy yelled to him to drop his gun. "I thought he was a friend of the bartender," he said. "He had a gun and started to shoot. I shot him four or five times and he did the same to me. I didn't know he was a detective. What do you think is going to happen to me?"

I leaned over the top bunk and flicked the tailor-made into the toilet. "*Chico*, did the *policía* die?" I said.

"No, he's alive."

Jesus, I thought, *this kid shot a cop and got shot; I shot a cop and got shot. What's happened to me is going to happen to him. He's going to do time, maybe a lot.* "I don't know, *Chico*," I said. "I'll talk to you about it tomorrow, eh? Don't worry. Is it your first bust?"

"Yes, yes, it is."

"*Bueno*. You'll probably get a break, don't worry about it. *Buenas noches*."

"*Buenas noches*."

The next morning I was taken to the courthouse and jammed into a crowded bullpen. After half an hour I was called into the courtroom. I stepped through the door and into a paneled world of man-made justice, with its row upon row of spectator-filled benches and its black-robed judge shuffling men's histories on white papers. I looked around for familiar faces, expecting none. I found two: big *hara* and little *hara.* They took their places behind me, and big *hara* said in a low whisper, "Good luck." The district attorney said something to the judge. Another guy read off the charges against me. The judge said something and the district attorney said that my crimes had been many and serious and people had been hurt. The judge mentioned that I had been incarcerated for six years. The D.A. said that until investigation and probation reports and so on had been made no disposition could be made; he asked that I be held in $5,000 bail on each count.

My God, it would cost me $10,000 to make it out them front doors, I thought. *Man, what about releasing me on my own—what's that word?—oh yeah, recognizance. I ain't going nowhere* . . . I heard the court clerk, or somebody, say, "November 28." That was two weeks away. A hack tapped me on my shoulder and I walked back from that big room of panels, big benches, big desk, big judge, and man-made justice into the bullpen, mentally kicking myself for not having taken the chance of cutting out in the restaurant.

I went back to my cell and spent the two weeks watching card games and listening to jokes and arguments. I kept thinking about God and *Tía,* and me and time. The night before my hearing, I decided to make a prayer. It had to be on my knees, 'cause if I was gonna cop a plea to God, I couldn't play it cheap. So I waited until the thin kid was asleep, then I quietly climbed down from my top bunk and bent my knees, feeling like for the first time in my life I was really going to get together with the Big Man.

I knelt at the foot of the bed and told God what was in my heart. I made like he was there in the flesh with me. I talked to him plain, like always; no big words, no big almighties, no big deals. I talked to Him like I had wanted to talk to my old man so many years ago. I talked like a little kid and I told Him of my wants and lacks, of my hopes and disappointments. I asked the Big Man to overlook my blanks and to make a cool way for me and that everything I ever learned or knew would be better if He and I could be buddies. I began to feel better inside, like God had become Pops and Moms to me. I felt like I was someone that belonged to somebody who cared. I felt like I could even cry if I wanted to, something I hadn't been able to do for years. "God," I concluded, "maybe I won't be an angel, but I do know I'll try not to be a blank. So in Your name, and in *Cristo*'s name. I ask this. Amen."

A small voice added another amen to mine. I looked up and saw the thin kid, his elbows bent, his head resting on his hand. I peered through the semidarkness to see his face, wondering if he was sounding me. But his face was like mine, looking for help from God. There we were, he lying down, head on bended elbows, and I still on my knees. No one spoke for a long while. Then the kid whispered, "I believe in *Dios* also. Maybe you don't believe it, but I used to go to church, and I had the hand of God on me. I felt always like you and I feel now, warm, quiet, and peaceful, like there's no suffering in our hearts."

"What's it called, *Chico*, this what we feel?" I asked softly.

"It's Grace by the Power of the Holy Spirit," the kid said.

I didn't ask any more. There, in the semidarkness, I had found a new sense of awareness. I was a down stud, and despite all my Bible lessons and trips into the world of the Big Man, it would take a lot of time to fully dig God; but at least I knew He was there. And, like the Bible lessons said, first would come faith, and then would come understanding. "Good night, *Chico*," I said. "I'm thinking that God is always with us—it's just us that aren't with Him."

I fell asleep thinking that I heard the kid crying softly. *Cry, kid*, I thought, *bigger ones done it. I hear even Christ cried.*

34. HEY, BARRIO— I'M HOME

The big day came at last, November 28, the day I would find out what was shaking. Once again I made it to the courtroom. My aunt and her pastor were there, their heads bowed in prayer.

My name was called and I rose, and the judge's voice came down from behind the big desk in that big paneled room.

"Have you been promised anything for accepting a plea of robbery in the second degree?" he asked.

"No, sir," I replied.

"Have you anything to say before sentence is passed?"

My Legal Aid court-appointed lawyer said something about six years in prison and rehabilitation. Then the district attorney, who's supposed to sink your lemon for you, opened his mouth and he talked better for me than my lawyer, saying he was willing to go along with leniency, a suspended sentence and probation. This shook me up inside, but my face still stood *cara palo*.

The judge said, "Can you keep your nose clean?"

"Yes, sir, I can."

"Okay, I'm going to let you go on probation for three years. Do right. You can go now."

Just like that, it was over. I was free. I turned and walked out through the swinging doors, my aunt and her pastor right behind me. We had to stop at the probation officer's desk, where I was given a card and told to report every week. The P.O. asked me if I had a job. I said no; he said get one fast. If I needed help I could get it, but if I messed up I'd be in trouble and back again. He told me I would have to report to him and to my parole officer, and if I screwed up on one I'd automatically screw up on the other. He warned me to stay away from my "old associates" and not to fuck anybody who wasn't my wife and said I could go.

I walked to the last door, the one that led to the street. One push and I was out. I stood there blinking at the bright sun. "I'm out! I'm out!" I said. Inside, the dizziness of being free was like a night that changed into day; all the shadows became daylight sharp. My first urge was to break out running as fast as I could, but I held myself down; I played cool and collected.

"You can thank God for all He's done," my aunt's pastor said.

"Yeah, Reverend," I said. But the thought of God was like having an obligation, and I didn't want any obligations, not after six years of obligations. I wanted to feel the street, and smell it and hold it between the fingers of my heart. The roar of a nearby elevated train drowned out all thoughts of God. I smelled the street and the people and the cold November air that meant freedom. I was gonna stay free, whether I made it to another country or whether I made it the right way. My head spun from the thought of having to go back to jail.

The next morning I went downtown with my aunt to make my first report to my parole officer. There were a lot of ex-cons in the office making their initial reports. A few of us knew one another. But each of us acted as though the other was a stranger, for one of the bad scenes of parole violation is associating with ex-cons or known criminals.

My P.O. didn't waste any time. He looked at his watch and told me, "You're thirty minutes late."

I nodded in agreement.

"It's a good way to start off, eh?" He was pretty insistent, but I wasn't gonna get mad, no matter what. I made my face stay the same, relaxed and soft. "You got a job?" he finally asked me.

"No sir, not yet."

"Get one, fast."

"Yes sir."

He looked at my records, and after a long while he crossed his eyes at me and said, "If you do right, you're gonna stay out, otherwise you go back so fast it's gonna make your head spin."

I nodded.

"We're here to help you, and if you got any kind of problem we'll be glad to help you solve it."

I thanked him and he told me to report every Thursday. I stood up and he smiled for the first time, and I figured that all that crap he had blown on me was just to see if I would blow my top.

We left and took the Lexington Avenue subway back to Spanish Harlem. The rumbling and noise of the train made me nervous. I still wasn't used to city noise. The noise in prison is different; it's the sound of people who have a single frustration in common. But in the city, in Spanish Harlem, there is more of a choice of noise. I watched the walls of the tunnel whip by as the train lurched like a drunk along the rails. Finally, we pulled into the 110th Street station.

"Let's get off, *Tía*," I said.

"But it's only 110th Street, *hijo*. We go one more stop."

But I didn't wait. I jumped through the closing doors, and waved her on, shouting, "I'll see you at home." My God! it felt good to be able to leave when I wanted to. How many times at Comstock had I wanted to jump through the closing doors of my cell before they locked on me? And now I had jumped through some closing doors. It was such a little thing, but what a great feeling it produced. I ran up the subway steps to the street. The air felt great, and I ran over to my aunt's house and bounced up the stairs thinking about the job I hadda get for myself, my parole officer, and my probation officer.

The next day a rabbi and his brother-in-law gave me a job in their dress-and-shirt company as an all-around handyman and clean-up man. For $40 a week I ran errands, hung up dresses, put pins and tags on them, and delivered them.

I worked steadily and reported steadily and visited my aunt's church from time to time. I saw Pops and my brothers and sister on Long Island, but I lived with my aunt in stone-cool Harlem. It was great to be back in the street. A lot of my boys were either hollowed-out junkies or in prison, but a few of them were still making the scene, and after a few weeks I was making it with them. In the back of my mind, I was a little worried, but after all, I told myself, I had spent a lifetime in that fucking jail and I owed myself some ballin'.

The first rule I broke was the one about not fucking broads who weren't your wife. I shacked up with one of the homeliest broads I ever had seen, but she looked great after my long fast. Having broken one rule, I found it easier to break another, and soon I was drinking again. Then I started smoking pot. This went on for some weeks; then, one morning, after a wild, all-night pot party, I crept into *Tia*'s apartment and dug myself in the mirror. What I saw shook me up. My eyes were red from smoke and my face was strained from the effort of trying to be cool. I saw myself as I had been six years ago, hustling, whoring, and hating, heading toward the same long years and the hard bit. I didn't want to go that route; I didn't want to go dig that past scene again.

I pulled away from the mirror and sat on the edge of my bed. My head was still full of pot, and I felt scared. I couldn't stop trembling inside. I felt as though I had found a hole in my face and out of it were pouring all the different masks that my *cara-palo* face had fought so hard to keep hidden. I thought, *I ain't goin' back to what I was*. Then I asked myself,

You remember all that crap you went through? What you want to do, go on for the rest of your life with your ass hangin'? Man, don't forget, you only get what you take. You can make a couple of yards a week and be cool about it. Just by the by, hustle a piece of junk and you're in. You don't use no more, so keep on not using and you're in like a mother. You can make cool bread now; why knock yourself out working? You ain't gonna live forever.

The thoughts pressed on my brain. I grabbed my face with both hands and squeezed hard, pushing it all out of shape; I pulled my lips out and my face down. The reefer kick was still on, and I could feel the smallness of the room and the neatness of its humble furniture and the smell of its credit, which $1.50 a week paid off. I pushed my way to the window, pulled the light cord and hid from myself in the friendly darkness. Easing the noise from the old-time window shade, I pushed up the window and squeezed my hand through the iron gate my aunt had put in to keep the crooks out. I breathed in the air; it was the same air that I had breathed as a kid. The garbage-filled backyards were the same. Man, everything was the same; only I had changed. I wasn't the grubby-faced Puerto Rican kid any more; I was a grubby-faced Puerto Rican man. I am an *hombre* that wants to be better. Man! I don't want to be nuttin'. I want to be somebody. I want to laugh clean. I want to smile for real, not because I have to . . .

I peered through the darkness. My lips wanted to form words; I wanted to tell somebody I wanted to be somebody. I heard the squeaking of old bed springs, the scrounging of alley cats in overturned garbage cans. I saw the stars up there in God's pad and the gray-white outline of clothes swinging on the black morning breeze, and I leaned hard against the gate that kept crooks out and me in and looked at my dark, long fingers wrapped tightly around the cold black metal. I felt like I was back at Comstock, looking out, hoping, dreaming, wanting. I felt like I wasn't real, that I was like a shadow on a dingy hallway wall next to scribbled graffiti: "Joe loves Lucy," "Baby was laid underneath these stairs, 1947," "The super is a rotten motherfucker," "Piri is a Coolie," "Wait for me, Trina"—*Trina didn't wait . . .*

I felt a wave of loneliness smack over me, almost like getting high. "Fuck it, fuck it," I said. The four-letter words sounded strange, dirty, like I shouldn't have been saying them. I said, "Motherfucker," and it sounded different, too. It didn't sound like long ago. It sounded not like a challenge thrown at the world but like a cry of helplessness. I pressed my eyes hard into the curve of my elbow. *I don't want to keep on being shit in a cesspool, squishing out through long pipes to hell knows where: I wanna be nice, all the way, for real . . .*

I remembered my aunt's church around the corner. *If God is right, so what if He's white?* I thought, *God, I wanna get out of this hole. Help me out. I promise if You help me climb out, I ain't gonna push the cover back on that cesspool. Let me out and I'll push my arm back down there and help some other guy get a break.*

The rest of my first year out drained away fast. I fought to keep from being swallowed up again by Harlem's hustles and rackets; I started to visit *Tía*'s church on 118th Street; I got a raise from the rabbi and encouragement from my probation officers. But there was something missing and I knew what it was: Trina. I couldn't get her out of my mind. I couldn't walk through familiar streets without thinking, *There's where we used to go*, or *There's where we used to eat.* I tried to push her away from my mind but I knew I'd have to see her again. Her husband had turned out no good; I heard from here and there what a hard life he was giving her. I wondered if she had changed.

One night I met her cousin Ava on the street. She was married now and had two children. We talked about old times and she invited me up to her mother's house. "We're having a little get-together and all the family will be there," she said.

"All?" I asked.

"Yeah, all," she repeated.

"When?"

"Tonight. It's about seven o'clock now—say about nine."

"Great. I may just drop on by."

"May?"

"Yeah," I replieed, "*may*," but I knew I'd be there.

I went home thinking all the way. I tried to lay out the scene I'd pass through at nine o'clock that night.

I'd walk up the stairs at number 129 cool, oh so cool, wearing my best vines. Ava would answer the door.

"Hi, Piri."

I'd smile. "Hi."

"Come on in."

I'd step in and dig the scene. Ava's brothers would be on the sofa, her mother would be in the easy chair and Georgie, Trina's husband, would be sitting on the other chair. Trina would be standing by the window looking outside, her face in profile, sad-looking but bravely beautiful.

I'd walk into the parlor and there would be a breather silence, like if God walked in on a bunch of sinners. Ava and her brothers would look at each other knowingly and expectantly. Ava's mom would sit still and quiet, and Georgie, that dirty rat, would turn pale and start shaking all over, smiling like a scared punk. I'd ignore him and look into Trina's eyes, and she'd whisper, "I've waited so long, Johnny Gringo, my Piri, I've waited so long."

I'd look, oh, so cool, so bad, so brave, and hold out my arms and say, "Come on, Marine Tiger, we're going home, baby. And bring your kid; it's my kid now."

Trina would melt into my arms and I'd bruise her lips and I'd crush her tight and we'd be like one Puerto Rican instead of two, and we'd turn and walk away toward the door. And Ava would shout, "Look out, Piri, he's gonna jump you!" and I'd feel the knife bite deep into my shoulder muscle, the pain going deep, and I'd hear screams from Trina's throat.

I'd lurch forward and with a great effort straighten up and

face Georgie. His face would turn gray and splotchy with fear; he'd stand there paralyzed. I'd reach my arm behind me and grab the handle of the knife that is sticking in my back and, with a suave pull, squish it out of my back.

"*Don't kill me, please,*" Georgie would beg.

I'd look at him with contempt, fling the bloody knife away and start walking slowly toward him. Georgie would back away trap himself in a corner. I'd measure his face and crash my fist into it. He'd fight back weakly and I'd hit him with one fist and then another until he sagged slowly to the floor.

I'd feel blood in my mouth—the knife has punctured my lung; I may be dying—and I'd lean on Trina. She'd kiss me, and we'd walk out the door and . . .

"Hey, Piri, wanna go to a flick tonight?"

"No, I'm sorry, I got some place to go tonight."

"Oh, okay."

Back in reality, I walked down the cold street and ran up the long, dingy steps to my aunt's apartment. Twenty minutes later I was in the bath, getting ready for I didn't know what.

At nine o'clock I stood in front of the apartment in number 129 and knocked and waited. The door opened. It was Ava's mom. "Come in, *hijo*, come in," she said, hugging me.

I stepped into the apartment. There was no one on the couch, no one in the parlor. I saw a stranger sitting at the kitchen table. *Georgie,* I thought. Ava was just coming out of the john. She hugged me and I looked past her into the bedroom, where Trina was standing at the door looking at me. Georgie smiled and I was introduced to him. He smiled and offered me a drink.

"No, thank you," I said, and as a chair was offered to me, I added, "Mind if I sit in the parlor?" I sat on the chair that I imagined Georgie would have been sitting in and I looked at Trina. There was nothing to say, nothing to do. I just sat there and made small talk. *Trina, say something,* I thought, *anything.*

But Trina didn't say anything, and after what seemed like

many days, I heard myself saying, "Well, it's been nice visiting you all. I'm sorry, but I gotta go now, I, uh, got an appointment."

"Oh, I'm sorry you have to go, *hijo*," said Ava's mom.

"We'll see you again, won't we?" Ava asked.

"Yeah, sure," I said. I looked at Trina. She smiled something at me, and I walked out the door and down the stairs and out into the cold street, thinking, *What a blank that was. I should have known, nothing is run the same, nothing stays the same. You can't make yesterday come back today.*

35. I SWEARS TO GOD AND THE VIRGIN

I felt like walking and my walking got me to stop outside my old building at number 109. I wondered why I always looked at her like an old *novia.* I looked around and the street was swinging. I stepped into number 109's dark hallway and made my way up the dirty marble steps, careful that I wouldn't step into long-ago memories of sudden dog piles of dogs' mess or slip on anybody's piss water. The mood was the same. I was gulping tired air by the time I reached the fifth floor and stopped to rest—and then I heard the hushed noise up on the roof landing. I looked up into a pair of eyes hollowed out like death, like a want, like a stone junkie. It was a junkie. It was no stranger.

"Hi, *panín,*" I greeted. The eyes blinked, straining for some kinda recognition, and then knowing set in, and his voice curled down from his height:

"Damn, Piri! Is that you? *Coño,* ain't this a bitch? I'm fuckin' glad to see ya. What a blip, man; come on up. I thought you was the man. Them cats work on Sundays, too, Come on up, baby."

His voice didn't sound like Carlito's. It didn't sound like nothing at all.

"How ya been, Carlito? What's *nuevo?*

I looked up at him and dug the sad answer.

"*Nada* new, 'side's being strung out."

He had a hand and the fist was tightly closed. It didn't have to open for me to know what was in it. "Schmack?" my face told him. His hand opened up and the five-cent bag was trembling there, with its li'l bit of "push back my troubles."

"I was jus' gonna shoot up, man, an I heard you coming. I thought maybe you was the man. Them cats work on Sundays too."

I nodded: "Strung out, Carlito?"

"Twelve *bolsas*. It's a bitch man, like at five cents a bag an' a bean for works, that's some bread."

I made mental figures and my junkie *panín* needed seventy-two dollars a day to keep from coming apart—to just stay normal. Something I was doing for nothing. I eased by and moved up to sit on the steps above him.

"You don't mind if I cook breakfast," Carlito laughed to himself. "Heh-heh, cook my breakfast." He pulled out a medicine bottle full of water, a bottle top made of metal. He pulled apart the five-cent bag and shook it into the bottle top, carefully, so-o-o-o carefully, brushing the paper to make sure he missed none of his 'breakfast.' I said nothing, I just watched as I had watched times I couldn't count, other guys, and other "me's."

Carlito pulled the paper match from its cover and it was almost an apologetic tear; he laid the book of matches down slowly and deliberately, almost like savoring the coming moment when the smack would bite deep into his tracked-up arm and slam into his heart with all the fury of despair. The match was lit, and Carlito placed it under the bottle top.

"Oh, awh, haaaaa, this it, ahuh, gooood, right, bang." He blew the match out like a businessman after lighting up a dollar cigar. I thought, *Don't this bring me back a long time, don't*

I feel a yen for that kick? Don't I feel a something like him, like my eyes want to follow that fuckin' needle's thirst and trace the push and current of the tecata *through the highways and byways of my man's coughing veins. Like I feel way down deep somewhere the urge to put my arm down beside his in a humble-pie attitude and take my place among my boys who got beat not by the bop, but by . . .*

"Want a jolt, Piri? I don't mind sharing with you. I can try for an *ángulo* soon as we get off. You're from the old boys and I don't really mind; I mean I won't do this for nobody, cause it ain't like the old days, when everybody shared the stuff with each other. Naw, not like that at all. You gotta be real tight with a stud. You don't share with everybody for nuttin'. If a guy does in with you or a couple of guys and you make up the five-cent bag, okay, then you share, but you don't give up the stuff for nuttin', not to just anybody. So don't worry Piri, I can hustle for us later. Say, man, how bad is your habit?" he asked.

I looked at Carlito and at the needle and at his arm, with his pants belt wrapped tightly around his suffering veins popped out at attention.

"I'm clean, Carlito, I'm not using." My voice dropped to a whisper. "I'm not using." And oh, God, I found my mind, thinking, *Wonder what it would be like again? Wonder what it would be like again? Wonder what it would be like again? Wonder . . .*

"I'm clean," I heard myself saying. My eyes watched the needle, pushed on to an eye dropper, poised—almost, I swear, licking its chops as it got nearer to Carlito's veins—and I watched and remembered as he toyed with his love and the drug came back out again, into the eye dropper, and it brought back some blood.

"I'm glad you're clean, Piri," I heard Carlito's voice soft and tender and harsh. His eyes closed and the needle still in his arm like it didn't want to come out, like a lover who has loved and cannot find the way to withdraw. Carlito's fingers pulled out the needle and a juicy glob of dark, dark blood oozed out, a quick finger smeared the blood away, and more oozed out. Carlito opened a medicine bottle and poured a little water over the oozing hole where the lovers laid, and the blood stopped oozing. He pushed the needle into the water and sucked up plain old water and the works was washed, and the water was squirted out over the faintly blood-smeared arm and then was taken apart, ever so carefully. The works is a junkie's best friend after his smack.

I watched as the nod started to set in strong, and Carlito talked and I sat and listened.

"I'm glad you're clean; yeah, I mean it, man, I can be clean, too. In fact"—and I dig his low voice, muffled and full of hot-ashed talk of how he's gonna kick—"I'm gonna kick after I go in, yeah, baby, no more smack for me. Jesus, man, I got shame, I got self-respect, like anybody, like any fuckin' body else, and I can be clean too. Shit! I gotta quit, look at me." And I dug as he pointed to his face. It was lemon color—like jaundice.

"This junk gives all kinds of shit, I'm putrid like a mother-fucker. I'm rottening; dig." And he pulls his shirt up and shows me his lower back and in between the crack of his behind are sores, healing and unhealed.

"I gotta give this up, and I swears to God and the Virgin, next time I quits for good, man. Man, I've been to Lexington and all them other places. I'm gonna kick this time for good. I can get clean."

Thoughts walked into each other through my mind—*Everything happened yesterday. Trina was yesterday. Brew was yesterday, Johnny Gringo was yesterday. I was a kid yesterday and my whole world was yesterday. I ain't got nothing but today and a whole lot of tomorrows.*

I don't think my boy saw me go past him. I couldn't stand seeing my man, I couldn't stand hearing him talk about what he was gonna do. His voice faded behind me.

"I got dignity, man. I got self-respect and ahhh . . ." I reached the second landing and heard him call, "Hey Piri, you making it?" I looked up through the stair well and I saw his little head with the big eyes.

"Yeah," I yelled back, and walked out into the street, past hurrying people and an unseen jukebox beating out a sad-assed bolero.

GLOSSARY

a la canona: the hard way
abuelo: grandfather
adiós: good-bye
Ave *María*: Hail Mary
antipatía: antipathy, hostility
amigo: friend
ángulo: angle
así y así: so forth and so on
bacalao: salt cod
benedición: blessing
benditos: blessed
blancos, los: the whites
bodega: grocery store
bolo: dollar
bolsa: bag, package; deck of drugs
bomba: "bomb" (make it without paying)
botica: drugstore
bread: money
buena suerte: good luck
buenas noches: good evening
bueno: good
cabeza: head
cabrón: one who consents to the adultery of his wife
cara: face
cara palo: deadpan
caramba: dammit
carcel: jailhouse
chevere: great, swinging
chico: boy
chinga: intercourse
chota: "rat," "squealer" (informer)
Cómo estás?: How are you?
coño: damn
contrato: contract
coquís: crickets
corazón: heart
Cristo: Christ
cuchifritos: dish made of pigs' ears, tongue, blood sausage, green bananas, etc.
culo: ass, rear-end
cura: shot of heroin
de nada: you're welcome
deb: girl member of teen gang
despiertape: wake up
dinero: money
Dios mío: my God
El Viejo: The Old One
embalao: strung out on drugs, really hooked
está ciego: he is blind
Estados Unidos, los: the United States
frío: cold
fundillo: ass, behind
fuzz: cop or detective
guiso: an angle; having something good going for you
hara, la: the policeman
hombre: man
hijo: son
hijo de puta: whoreson, bastard
importante: important
isla verde: green island
jab: to ambush someone
jalumbo: jumbo
labia: yak
lágrimas: tears

lechón: pig
lluvia: rain
loco: crazy
malo: bad, evil; ill
mañana: tomorrow
mano: hand
maricón: homosexual, faggot
mi negrito: my little black one
mira, vieja: look, old woman
monga, la: the grippe
morenito: little dark one
moreno: dark brown, almost black
moto: motorcycle
moyeto: Negro, black man
muchacha: girl
mucho: much
mundo: world
muy bien, gracias: very well, thank you
nada: nothing
no comprendo: I don't understand
no quiero morir: I don't want to die
no se apure: don't worry
no te apures, hijo: don't worry, son
nombre, un: a name
novio, novia: sweetheart
nunca más: never more
odio: hatred
padre: father; priest
pajarito: little bird
panín: buddy, partner
panita: close friend, buddy
papipas: pig feet
pato: faggot, homosexual
pendejo: coward; one pubic hair from male
pensamiento: thought, idea
peso: dollar
pistola; *pistolita*: pistol, handgun; small pistol
plata: money (silver)
policía, la: the police
por Dios: for God's sake
por favor: please
Por qué?: Why?
prueba: test
puta: whore
puto: male whore
Qué es?: What is it?
Qué eso?: What is that?
Qué está pasando?: What is happening?
Qué te pasa?: What's the matter with you?
Quién es?: Who is it?
sangre: blood
sarito: made-up word expressing disgust
señora: woman
serio: serious
sí, para siempre: yes, forever
silla, la: "the chair" (electric chair)
smack, schmack: drugs
stud: any hip male
suave: smooth; easy
tapita: bottle cap
tecata: heroin, drug
Tía: Aunt
tocino: bacon; salt pork
tregeño, tregeña: dark-skinned
Tu madre se ha muerto: Your mother has died
turf: home street
un poco tiempo: a short time, a little while
V*en acá.*: Come along.
vendedor: dope peddler; seller
vente: "blow"; leave; come
waste: to beat up badly
yerba: "tea" (marijuana)

ABOUT THE AUTHOR

PIRI THOMAS was born on September 30, 1928, in New York City, the eldest of seven children. He grew up during the depression of the 1930's in Spanish Harlem, experiencing discrimination as a dark-skinned Puerto Rican. Poverty in the ghetto led him into drugs, youth gangs, and a series of criminal activities. He served six years in prison for armed robbery and while in prison, Mr. Thomas began his life of rehabilitation. He became a street worker in Spanish Harlem working with street gangs. Subsequently, he went to Puerto Rico, where he became assistant to Dr. Efren Ramirez, Director of the Hospital of Psychiatry in Rio Piedras, Puerto Rico. Mr. Thomas, an ex-addict, developed a program of rehabilitation of addicts using the ex-addict. He has lectured at colleges in the New York City area, as well as at the University of Chicago, the University of Wisconsin, Dartmouth, Bard College, Virginia State Teachers College, Northeastern University, University of Illinois and many others. His work in Spanish Harlem was the subject of the film *Petey and Johnny*, in which he both appeared and provided the narration. He is the author of many books including *Savior, Savior, Hold my Hand*, and *Seven Long Times*.